Who Should Sing "Ol' Man River"?

Who Should Sing "Ol' Man River"?

The Lives of an American Song

Todd Decker

OXFORD
UNIVERSITY PRESS

OXFORD
UNIVERSITY PRESS

Oxford University Press is a department of the
University of Oxford. It furthers the University's objective
of excellence in research, scholarship, and education
by publishing worldwide.

Oxford   New York

Auckland   Cape Town   Dar es Salaam   Hong Kong   Karachi
Kuala Lumpur   Madrid   Melbourne   Mexico City   Nairobi
New Delhi   Shanghai   Taipei   Toronto

With offices in

Argentina   Austria   Brazil   Chile   Czech Republic   France   Greece
Guatemala   Hungary   Italy   Japan   Poland   Portugal   Singapore
South Korea   Switzerland   Thailand   Turkey   Ukraine   Vietnam

Oxford is a registered trade mark of Oxford University Press
in the UK and certain other countries.

Published in the United States of America by
Oxford University Press
198 Madison Avenue, New York, NY 10016

Publication of this book was supported in part by the John Daverio Endowment
of the American Musicological Society, funded in part by the National Endowment
for the Humanities and the Andrew W. Mellon Foundation.

Library of Congress Cataloging-in-Publication Data
Decker, Todd R., author.
Who should sing Ol' man river? : the lives of an American song / Todd Decker.
pages   cm
Includes bibliographical references, discography, and index.
ISBN 978-0-19-938918-6 (alk. paper)
1. Kern, Jerome, 1885–1945. Show boat. Ol' man river.
2. Music and race—United States—History—20th century.   I. Title.
ML410.K385D44   2014
782.1'4—dc23   2014001405

1 3 5 7 9 8 6 4 2

Printed in the United States of America
on acid-free paper

for Jamie
the original O- M-- B---

CONTENTS

ABOUT THE COMPANION WEBSITE

www.oup.com/us/olmanriver

Oxford University Press has created a password-protected website to accompany *Who Should Sing "Ol' Man River"?* The site features sound examples of many of the recorded versions of "Ol' Man River" discussed in this book.

Full versions of most all the recordings mentioned in the book can be heard via Spotify. Links to specific tracks on this web-based listening service are provided on the companion website as well, where they are listed with full discographical information in the order considered in the book. A Spotify profile for this book—user name: whoshouldsingomr—contains playlists arranged by chapter.

Most of the film, television, and video versions analyzed in this book, as well as many of the recordings not available on Spotify, can be found on YouTube and other such sites. I recommend searching by performer name and the words "man river."

USAGE

The lyrics to "Ol' Man River" are quoted throughout the text as written by Oscar Hammerstein II, except where performers made changes. The first word of the title appears variously in print as "ol'," "old," and "ole" across the tune's history. Throughout the book, "old" and "ole" have been corrected to Hammerstein's "ol'" without comment.

THE AUTHOR IS DEEPLY GRATEFUL TO THE ESTATES OF OSCAR HAMMERSTEIN II AND JEROME KERN FOR PERMISSION TO REPRODUCE THE MUSIC AND LYRICS FOR THE SONG "OL' MAN RIVER." SPECIAL THANKS ARE EXTENDED TO ALICE HAMMERSTEIN MATHIAS, DAUGHTER OF OSCAR HAMMERSTEIN II, FOR HER SUPPORT.

Ol' Man Riv-er, dat   Ol' Man Riv-er, He mus' know sump-in', But

don't say nuth-in' He jes' keeps rol-lin', He keeps on rol-lin' a-

long._____   He don'   plant   ta - ters,   He

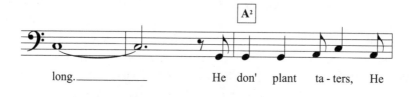

don' plant cot-ton, An' dem dat plants 'em is soon for-got-ten, But

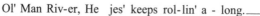

Ol' Man Riv-er, He jes' keeps rol-lin' a - long._____

B

You an' me we sweat an' strain, Bod - y all ach - in' an'

racked wid pain. "Tote dat barge!" "Lif' dat bale!"

A³

Git a lit-tle drunk an' you land in jail. Ah gits wear-y an'

sick of try-in', Ah'm tired of liv-in' an skeered of dy-in', But

Ol' Man Riv-er, He jes' keeps rol-lin' a - long._____

Who Should Sing "Ol' Man River"?

1

❧

Some Questions for "Ol' Man River"

In 1920, while riding a train along the Mississippi River on a journey to visit his father in Mexico, Langston Hughes wrote a poem titled "The Negro Speaks of Rivers." Hughes's ten-line poem—his earliest mature work, widely anthologized and familiar to generations of high school students—connects four rivers to the African American experience.

> I've known rivers:
> I've known rivers ancient as the world and older than the
>   flow of human blood in human veins.
>
> My soul has grown deep like the rivers.
>
> I bathed in the Euphrates when dawns were young.
> I built my hut near the Congo and it lulled me to sleep.
> I looked upon the Nile and raised the pyramids above it.
> I heard the singing of the Mississippi when Abe Lincoln
>   went down to New Orleans, and I've seen its muddy
>   bosom turn all golden in the sunset.
>
> I've known rivers:
> Ancient, dusky rivers.
>
> My soul has grown deep like the rivers.

How different is Hughes's poetic vision from the lyrics to "Ol' Man River," a Broadway show tune written just six years later by Oscar Hammerstein II to fit a melody composed by Jerome Kern?

Most readers of this book probably know Hammerstein's lyric—at least a line or two. The song's title, the repeated phrase "just keeps rollin' along," and the lines "tote that barge, lift that bale" entered the American language shortly after the song was first performed in late 1927. Until the 1970s, "Ol' Man River" was, practically speaking, an American folk song, a tune most everyone could be expected to know from repeated performance by all sorts of singers and players. Listeners who came of age after the emergence of disco and hip-hop, by which time "Ol' Man River" had slipped out of the pop music mainstream, might not know the song all that well or at all. Before reading the words to "Ol' Man River" as Hammerstein wrote them, consider poet Charles Bernstein's observation about the appearance of this song lyric on the page: "The dialect spelling looks strained if not condescending. . . . In performance, however, much of this strangeness, though by no means all, disappears."[1] This book is about "Ol' Man River" in performance, about how singers and other musicians performed "Ol' Man River," transforming it again and again into the song they wanted or needed it to be. Still, at this early point in the story, the words as set down by Hammerstein in late 1926 deserve some contemplation. The chorus provides enough to chew on.

> Ol' Man River,
> Dat Ol' Man River,
> He mus' know sumpin'
> But don't say nuthin',
> He jes' keeps rollin',
> He keeps on rollin' along.
>
> He don' plant taters,
> He don' plant cotton,
> An' dem dat plants 'em
> Is soon forgotten,
> But Ol' Man River,
> He jes' keeps rollin' along.
>
> You an' me, we sweat an' strain,
> Body all achin' an' racked wid pain—
> "Tote dat barge!"
> "Lif' dat bale!"
> Git a little drunk
> An' you land in jail . . .
>
> Ah gits weary
> An' sick of tryin';

Ah'm tired of livin'
An' skeered of dyin',
But Ol' Man River,
He jes' keeps rollin' along.

Consider the similarities and differences between Hammerstein's lyric and Hughes's poem.

"The Negro Speaks of Rivers" paints the history of black Americans in a series of tableaux, framing specific scenes along specific rivers. The Mississippi, by association with the Euphrates, Congo, and Nile, becomes an old river in the "new" world. Hammerstein doesn't name the Mississippi in the chorus to "Ol' Man River." His "Ol' Man River" could—perhaps—be read as any river or all rivers; his speaker as any or all oppressed persons: although the reference to cotton locates the action for anyone with a bit of historical geographical knowledge or anyone familiar with *Show Boat*, the Broadway musical for which "Ol' Man River" was written. Any ambiguity about the river referred to in the chorus is settled by the first line of the song's verse, where Hammerstein names "Ol' Man River" in no uncertain terms: "Dere's an ol' man called de Mississippi." Like Hughes, Hammerstein explicitly connects his river lyric to the black American experience along the Mississippi.

Hughes uses proper English; Hammerstein employs the black dialect of American popular song, slathering the most stereotypical pop culture blackness—should we say blackface?—all over the lyric. But as Bernstein noted, how this dialect is sung and heard is another matter.

Hughes's intent is straightforward. The allusive realm of the poem links the experience of black Americans backward in time and space across the Atlantic, in effect defining African Americans as a people distinguished from European Americans—white Americans go unnamed in Hughes's poem, except for Abraham Lincoln. What Hughes's speaker "knows" proves less important than the source of his knowledge: experience earned on the banks of four iconic rivers. Hughes makes it plain that black Americans—like whites—have a history that predates their arrival on America's shores. Hammerstein, in the spelled-out realm of popular song, gives a bit more information about what his singer knows and also hints at what the river knows or, at least, what the river won't say. The singer of "Ol' Man River" is stubbornly separated from the masculine river, which tacitly mocks the labor and mortality of those who toil on its banks. (Lincoln played a part in making the Mississippi male in the American imagination when he called it the "Father of Waters" in an 1863 letter written to be read as a public address and reprinted widely after the Union victory at Vicksburg. Lincoln's usage dates to the early nineteenth century. The Algonquin word from which Mississippi is derived is more properly translated—without apparent gender implications—as "big river.")[2] Lines like "He mus' know sumpin' / But don't say nuthin'" have caused many singers to distance themselves from Hammerstein's river. One singer—Sam Butera in a 1960s Las Vegas lounge act captured on disc—mockingly commented that for all his knowing something and saying nothing, "Ol' Man River" must, in fact, be "stupid." But Hughes's speaker is also separated from the rivers of which he speaks. Nature is silent in both poems. Only in Hammerstein's lyric does the speaker—more crucially, the singer—voice a complaint about the situation. It's hard to read Hughes's poem as a protest: in certain performances, Hammerstein's has been turned into just that.

Of course, one difference between "The Negro Speaks of Rivers" and "Ol' Man River" is the race of these poems' respective authors. Langston Hughes was a celebrated African American writer, a defining black voice of the twentieth century. The title of his poem speaks in transparent terms: Hughes—a Negro—speaks of rivers through the medium of poetry. This precocious poem announces the birth of a self-consciously black literary voice. Oscar Hammerstein II was a Jewish American lyricist and Broadway bookwriter. Born into American theatrical royalty, situated for his entire life at the center of the Broadway musical theater—in other words, a powerful and wealthy culture maker at the heart of popular culture—Hammerstein carries no natural authority to speak for African Americans. And as Hammerstein freely admitted in 1956, when he wrote the words to "Ol' Man River" he had never seen the actual Mississippi River.[3] But lyricists—especially when writing for the musical stage, where they are also dramatists—make no claims to authority or authenticity. Their demanding task involves writing for voices other than their own, articulating the emotions and ideas of a range of characters, often while serving the established personas of specific performers. Hammerstein, in concert with Kern, chose to write about rivers from a black perspective in a historically innovative way. It's difficult to imagine any other major Broadway lyricist electing to do this. In his effort to sympathetically imagine the life of a black laborer in the medium of a Broadway show tune, Hammerstein stands alone.

Hughes's motivation for writing "The Negro Speaks of Rivers" can be transparently understood as part of a writer's personal development. He surely never expected to make much money from his poem and, when he penned it at age seventeen, had little expectation of it even being published. It did see print in the NAACP magazine *The Crisis* in 1921 and reappeared in Hughes's 1926 collection *The Weary Blues*. Hammerstein's eminently commercial reasons for writing "Ol' Man River" were less personal than

Hughes's, a difference which further distances these two river lyrics from the 1920s from each other.

The idea for "Ol' Man River" began with Jerome Kern, who recalled in a letter how "Paul Robeson's speaking voice," encountered by Kern in a short-lived play called *Black Boy*, served as "that thing called inspiration" for the melody of "Ol' Man River."[4] Paul Robeson was a bright new star on the New York scene in 1926. He had filled theaters with eager white listeners for concerts of Negro spirituals beginning in 1925; a year before that he had thrilled white theatergoers in plays heavy with the frisson of race— meaning blackness—like *The Emperor Jones* and *All God's Chillun Got Wings*. Kern brought Hammerstein onto the project and "Ol' Man River" was among the first tunes the pair wrote for their musical adaptation of the still-very-new-but-already-bestselling novel *Show Boat* by Edna Ferber. Nothing in Ferber's novel precipitates the lyrical sentiments or musical and racial—again meaning black—grandeur of "Ol' Man River." The song's evocation of the black American experience is all Kern and Hammerstein's doing.

Hammerstein and Kern planned for Robeson to play the stevedore Joe: a minor character in the plot; a major character in *Show Boat*'s score. Robeson didn't sign on to *Show Boat* for its initial 1927 Broadway production but "Ol' Man River" succeeded just as well as sung by Jules Bledsoe, another black baritone familiar to New York audiences. Eventually, Robeson played Joe and sang "Ol' Man River" in *Show Boat*—in London in 1928, on Broadway in 1932, on the silver screen in 1936, in Los Angeles in 1940— just as Kern and Hammerstein had hoped. Closely tied to the specific characters and setting of *Show Boat*, "Ol' Man River" was written for Robeson and designed to evoke the Negro spirituals he was singing to wide acclaim in New York in the mid-1920s.

But this book is not about Hammerstein or Kern's motives for writing "Ol' Man River" or about *Show Boat*. (For that story, see my book *Show Boat: Performing Race in an American Musical*.) Instead, *Who Should Sing "Ol' Man River"?* is about what performers—black and white, male and female, singers and musicians, from pop to jazz to rock to soul to doo-wop to opera— did with and to this famous song. For unlike poems such as Hughes's "The Negro Speaks of Rivers," which remains a vessel of its author's voice and the expression of a particular place and time, popular songs like "Ol' Man River" are the property of anyone who chooses to sing them, remaining a part of popular culture for as long as singers and musicians still perform them and audiences still listen.

This book is about the performers who decided *they* should sing "Ol' Man River."

Performers wield tremendous power in American popular music, and by extension in American popular culture and memory. Performers have the power to remake any song in their own image. Copyright law grants tacit permission to record any song that has been recorded once. The owners of the song must be paid their cut, of course, but they have no say in how a song is performed or arranged. (The situation is more restrictive for the use of songs in movies.) Listeners decide if performer's choices work. "Ol' Man River" is one song many performers have felt compelled to record. This book considers, compares, and contrasts almost two hundred recorded and filmed versions of Hammerstein and Kern's tune, listening for how "Ol' Man River"—a song that, like Hughes's poem, wears blackness on its face—has been performed across the twentieth century and into the present.

But this book reaches beyond recordings. Made-for-television versions of "Ol' Man River" prove abundant in the 1950s and 1960s. And beyond these usually live performances for studio audiences and viewers in television land, entertainment industry newspapers like *Variety* and *Billboard* (which focuses on the music business) are filled with descriptions of performances of "Ol' Man River" that did not get recorded, filmed, or taped. The most evocative of these—often gleaned from vaudeville and nightclub reviews—also make the story told here. Some lost ways with the song, especially as sung by women, are accessible only in the echoing words of professional listeners whose job it was to describe performers' efforts in as few lines as possible.

The combination of recorded and reported performances yields a history that is spatial as well as sonic. Several venerable venues reappear again and again in the history of "Ol' Man River" and the pages of this book: Carnegie Hall, America's premiere concert venue for classical music and a hallowed hall for jazz, where serious and jazz-oriented "Ol' Man Rivers" were sung and played; Lewisohn Stadium, an outdoor amphitheater on the campus of the City College of New York (demolished in 1973) where Paul Robeson and Frank Sinatra both sang the song; the Apollo Theater, a legendary stage where performers sought the approval of the black audiences of Harlem; the Copacabana, an equally legendary midtown nightclub where performers, black and white, faced chichi white audiences; and the White House, where "Ol' Man River" has been performed for at least three presidents, sung and/or played by Sinatra (for Richard Nixon), Marvin Hamlisch (for Ronald Reagan), and Aretha Franklin (for Bill Clinton). "Ol' Man River" has been sung on the radio (again and again), on television (see Chapter 9), on vaudeville (by black and white, male and female), and even in church. (Black newspapers of the 1930s and 1940s regularly reported on special musical events in major black churches where "Ol' Man River" was a welcome selection;

such notices in the black press appear as late as 1966.)[5] The ubiquity of this song—especially in the middle decades of the last century—is hard to overstate.

Indeed, "Ol' Man River" is a candidate for popular song of the century. Its ascent to worldwide hit status was rapid. Already in 1928 there were complaints that Venetian gondoliers were singing it too much.[6] In 1932 it was an early favorite choice of theme song by the sponsors of the *Amos 'n' Andy Show*.[7] In 1933, still a scant five years old, "Ol' Man River" topped a list of the ten most popular songs of the previous decade.[8] In news stories announcing the coming boycott of the American Society of Composers, Authors and Publishers (ASCAP) in 1941—when songs handled by ASCAP disappeared from the air waves—"Ol' Man River" topped the sad list of tunes that would be lost to the listening public.[9] Some black voices celebrated this news: silencing "Ol' Man River"—or at the least toning down the racial language central to Hammerstein's lyric—forms a central theme in the history of the song.[10] And the popularity of "Ol' Man River" didn't lessen after World War II. It made a 1952 list of the "Top 25 Standard Sheet Music Sellers" and a 1953 list of the fourteen "All Time Song Hits—1894–1952" compiled for the *Encyclopedia of American History*.[11] It was the only Broadway show tune from a still-viable show on the latter list, which included chestnuts like "Stars and Stripes Forever" and "When Irish Eyes Are Smiling." Indeed, the only other show tune on the list was "Easter Parade," an Irving Berlin song from the 1933 revue *As Thousands Cheer* but better remembered from the 1948 film *Easter Parade*. Berlin had two other songs on the list—"God Bless America" and "White Christmas." For a long time, "Ol' Man River" was as familiar to the general public as Berlin's two songs remain to this day. At the end of the 1950s, "Ol' Man River" placed in the top five "most typical American songs" selected by New York radio listeners for inclusion on a record album presented to visiting Soviet premier Nikita Khrushchev.[12] Other top five songs, like "Star Dust" and "When the Saints Go Marching In," might have been new to Khrushchev but he probably knew "Ol' Man River." Russian audiences were familiar with the song thanks to Robeson.

Unlike most jazz standards and songs in the so-called Great American Songbook, "Ol' Man River" found a place in the history of rock and roll. As Chapters 8, 9, and 10 detail, the song's high season dates to the late 1950s and lasts until the end of the 1960s. No other song of similar provenance can make such a claim: it's the only Broadway show tune to be consistently covered by rhythm and blues, rock and roll, and soul singers.

Only the 1970s advent of the singer-songwriter and album rock pushed "Ol' Man River" out of the mainstream. It exited the repertory of jazz standards around the same time, failing to make the 1975 *Real Book* of essential jazz tunes. But beyond the transition year of 1970, "Ol' Man River" continued to be sung and played in styles and manners dating back to the song's phenomenal run from the late 1920s through the 1960s. And occasionally in these quiet decades for the song, a performer found something new to say with Kern's tune and Hammerstein's lyric.

Reviewing a radio performance of "Ol' Man River" in May 1929—the song was not even a year and a half old—the *New York Times* commented that the audience for popular music in America was "rapidly becoming expert in appraising renditions of 'Ol' Man River.'"[13] This book sets before the reader nearly eight decades of "renditions," a fantastic archive of musical performance: the rich and varied life of an altogether unique American song.

To begin, then, with this book's title, a question that draws attention to performers: *who, indeed, should sing "Ol' Man River"*?

Kern and Hammerstein, of course, knew the answer. Anecdotes passed on at the time by critic Alexander Woollcott pictured Kern "with the lovely melody of 'Old Man River' already in his head, [standing] hat in hand on a doorstep in Harlem. He wanted Paul Robeson to sing that song."[14] This knock on Robeson's door by a famous white songwriter who traveled all the way uptown to beseech a black man to sing a song written just for him—and remember, that black man initially declined the honor—provides a nice point of origin for the waves of cross racial tension that vibrate around "Ol' Man River" all along its history. Since the song's writers answer to who should sing this song is clear, let's begin with a short consideration of how Robeson sang "Ol' Man River" (⊙ Sound Example 1.1).

With no formal vocal training and no desire to sound like an opera singer—he never wanted a career in "classical" music—Robeson took a no frills approach to "Ol' Man River." He sang it like any other song in his spiritual and folk song-centered repertory. Robeson articulated Hammerstein's lyric clearly and delivered Kern's tune without much added drama. The melody of "Ol' Man River"—stretching across more than an octave and a half—was tailored to Robeson's voice: he had the requisite wide range and could sing softly down low and loudly up high. Robeson's untutored but not unsophisticated approach allowed the content of the songs he sang to do most of the work. He seldom added much of an interpretive gloss: excess angst was contrary to his temperament and even with light comic numbers he never mugged or hammed it up. The clarity of his diction was a marvel to many listeners: one pleasure his singing offered was the direct transfer of words into song.

Robeson's keynote was dignity—a powerful force in the advance of African American equality—and Kern and Hammerstein lodged Robeson's historically innovative brand of dignity deep within "Ol' Man River," demonstrating their skill at writing special material for individual talents. Robeson's persona was centered on the resource of his voice: an instrument the uniqueness and power of which every critic commented on and to which listeners still respond today. Robeson's default position of restraint and clarity, balance and control—a rather "classical" aesthetic in its emphasis on refinement—facilitated his acceptance by white audiences, for whom he was a nonthreatening figure of great power expressing in both the spirituals he sang and in "Ol' Man River" the fraught historical situation of African Americans. An important chapter in the history of the song—and this book—tells the tale of how Robeson broke open this strong but passive pose and turned "Ol' Man River" into a radical demand for change.

Robeson's way could—from a narrow perspective—be taken as a benchmark for how "Ol' Man River" *should* be sung. And some, perhaps many, listeners—and readers of this book—might feel this way. In teaching the history of American popular music to undergraduates at an elite university, I sometimes encounter students who hear a recording of Robeson singing "Ol' Man River" and immediately adopt the rather inflexible position that Robeson's way is the "right" or "only" way. This reaction highlights not only Robeson's genuine and enduring star power but also Hammerstein and Kern's ability to write a song that fit Robeson like a glove.

But "Ol' Man River" is an irresistible song and all sorts of singers have sung it in their own ways. Robeson's way has been but one way. "Ol' Man River" has flowed down many other channels in its eighty-plus years as part of America's, indeed, the world's, musical life. Many, mostly American, mostly male, singers have sung "Ol' Man River." Few, if any, could have hoped to match Robeson on his own terms. Instead, the singers profiled here did what American singers do—they made the song their own, recasting this song for Robeson for their own voices. Jazz players also took up the song, as did commercial arrangers and pop instrumentalists. Musicians of many kinds explored the musical resources of Kern's tune from within their respective musical realms, all of which are equally reliant on popular songs like "Ol' Man River." In short, a remarkably broad swath of the makers of America's popular music have, in effect, answered the question "who should sing "Ol' Man River?" with the positive reply "I should. This song has something in it that I can say. This tune suits my sound and style. These words can be, should be, my words." This book considers the results of this vast popular music experiment, where the text and melody of a Broadway show tune function as a kind of scientific control.

Recast as a historical question, the query *who should sing "Ol' Man River"*? becomes *who has sung "Ol' Man River"*? Which singers working in which styles thought the song was right for them, something their audiences wanted to hear, something that would sell, that would make sense in the pop music marketplace? As shown in the pages that follow—and in the chronological list at the back of this book—the range of performers who recorded this song composed for Paul Robeson has been incredibly, almost unbelievably broad. Many famous pop singers pop up: Al Jolson, Bing Crosby, Frank Sinatra, Judy Garland, Martha Raye, Sammy Davis Jr., Tony Bennett, Rosemary Clooney, and Dean Martin. Among jazz players: Bix Biederbecke, Cootie Williams, Benny Carter, Coleman Hawkins, Ray Brown, Duke Ellington, Oscar Peterson, André Previn, Dave Brubeck, Jimmy Smith, Count Basie, Earl Hines, Albert Ayler, Jo Jones, and Keith Jarrett. Among opera and classical singers: Lawrence Tibbett, George London, Robert Merrill, Simon Estes, Samuel Ramey, Thomas Quastoff, and Denyce Graves. Dig deeper in the "Ol' Man River" discography and a less predictable array of talents turns up: names like Ruth Brown, Sam Cooke, Lou Rawls, Mae Barnes, Bo Diddley, Bobby Rydell, Ray Charles, Aretha Franklin, the Ravens, the Flamingos, the Temptations, Cher, Screamin' Jay Hawkins, Abner Jay, Jeff Beck and Rod Stewart, Ivory Joe Hunter, and the Lumpen—a Black Panthers-affiliated doo-wop group. (The Lumpens' parody version "Ol' Pig Nixon" is considered in Chapter 10.) Another list includes performers who performed but did not record "Ol' Man River." Among their number are Harry Richman (white nightclub performer in the 1930s), Billy Eckstine (black jazz and pop singer in the 1950s, who "excited ecstatic feminine screams" with his "swing accompaniment" to the song), Nelson Eddy (white baritone, famous for his films with Jeanette MacDonald, on the radio in the 1930s, in nightclubs in the 1960s), Paula Laurence (a white Broadway comedienne, who sang it in "ridiculous French translation" in nightclubs in the 1940s), Herb Jeffries (a mixed-race singer who shifted his public identity between black and white and sang the tune slow then with "a little rhythm bounce in a second chorus" in 1950s nightclubs), Frankie Avalon (white rock and roll "teen idol" who sang it in nightclubs in the early 1960s), and many, many unknowns with minor careers like Sadie Cohen ("Voice is deep contralto, spectacular in handling of 'Ol' Man River'" said *Variety* in 1943 of her nightclub and army camp appearances), Cy Reeves ("bean pole comic" who ended his 1952 variety act with a "zany version of 'Ol' Man River'"), and Rollin Smith (known to British vaudeville as the "Colored Street Singer," Smith accompanied himself on the accordion).[15]

This welter of names—an unlikely mix for even the most eclectic of music histories or fans—hints at the breadth of musical styles in play in this story of one song. Brought within the same frame, this unusual group forms an extended family of singers and musicians, all alike in their desire to shape the contours and cadences of "Ol' Man River" to their own voices, all American musical kin by virtue of having rung changes on the same song.

And here, aesthetics enters the story. For each performance or recording offers a set of answers to the most basic question confronting anyone who thinks they should sing this song: *how should "Ol' Man River" be sung?*

"Ol' Man River" was presented to the public for the first time in a startling and quite serious context. At *Show Boat's* tryout opening night in Washington, D.C., on November 15, 1927, Jules Bledsoe, an African American baritone who aspired to sing opera, stepped to the footlights at the end of act one, scene one, and sang "Ol' Man River," verse and chorus. (Bledsoe's 1931 recording of the song captures a singer straining for effect (⊙ Sound Example 1.2). As Will Friedwald suggests, Bledsoe "tries much too hard to make the song as dramatic as possible," quite unlike Robeson's always restrained approach.)[16] After a planned break for applause, an encore verse (slightly altered from before) and chorus followed with Bledsoe backed up by a chorus of sixteen African American men singing in four-part harmony, rising at the close to a thundering *fortissimo*, followed by a blackout ending the show's first scene. Audiences—overwhelmingly white, as always is the case for Broadway shows—responded with tumultuous applause, a reaction repeated over and over across *Show Boat* history. One black commentator of the time noted that Bledsoe's performance "*more than pleased* the patrons of the Ziegfeld Theatre," where *Show Boat* ran on Broadway for seventeen months (emphasis added).[17] The outsized reaction elicited by this song endures. Getting to the heart of white audiences' applause for a song that often exceeds the simple pleasures of popular music is central to the story told here. Analyzing versions meant to *more than please* black audiences also forms part of the tale.

But however presented in its original theatrical context, "Ol' Man River" was immediately taken up by dance bands as a stand-alone popular song hit suitable for dance arrangements. Upward of a dozen dance bands recorded strict time fox-trot arrangements in 1928 alone. And the practice continued, with multiple up-tempo "Ol' Man Rivers" appearing every decade until the 1970s. It remained a dance or fast jazz jam tune for forty years— Dizzy Gillespie and company recorded a bebop version retitled "Ol' Man Rebop" in 1946—and as late as 2001, Rosemary Clooney was singing it fast in tribute to Bing Crosby, who almost always treated "Ol' Man River" as a rhythm tune.

Another enduring answer to the question *how should "Ol' Man River" be sung?* begins with the refusal to take the song seriously. The practice of changing the lyrics—in music history terms, creating a parody version of the original text while keeping the tune intact—has provided a potent means of critique for many singers, male and female, black and white. Musical choices, available to singers and instrumentalists alike, have also allowed for performances that can only be heard as satire. In these versions, the racial stereotypes invoked by Kern and Hammerstein are turned against themselves, often in transformative ways. In some instances, the performance of "Ol' Man River" as a parody becomes a wide-ranging protest against the entire Jim Crow America that produced the song and within which the song finds its historical footing.

Every performed version of "Ol' Man River" negotiates the color line that divided black from white and white from black in the years of legal racial segregation. It shouldn't come as a surprise, then, that the height of the civil rights movement—from the late 1950s to the close of the 1960s—saw the greatest proliferation of performed and recorded versions in the song's history. "Ol' Man River" was sung, played, and heard often in the years when de jure segregation was being dismantled. This period—which I call the song's high season—is explored at length in the final three chapters. After 1970, new versions of "Ol' Man River," so abundant in the previous decade, become scarce and retrospective. Put in this context, the performance history of "Ol' Man River" traces out some of the limits of the sayable in popular music, particularly around issues of black and white in the middle decades of the twentieth century. However a singer might tinker with the words as Hammerstein wrote them, "Ol' Man River" is—at its core—about the experience of being black in a segregated America.

The undeniable blackness of "Ol' Man River" is lodged in Hammerstein's lyrics, a text so controversial that one fundamental question in the history of the song is *what are the lyrics of "Ol' Man River"?* Key to the song's staying power has been the practice of changing the original words. Just like the show from which it hails, there is no definitive text for "Ol' Man River"—instead, the song text offers the performer an array of choices. As a prelude to this book's consideration of the many individualized approaches performers have brought to "Ol' Man River," a brief analysis of the text as set down by Hammerstein for *Show Boat*'s initial Broadway run proves helpful.

To a surprising extent, the verse to "Ol' Man River" has been sung almost as often as the chorus, a rarity among popular standards, suggestive of how singers have consistently approached this song as a soliloquy or sketch, an opportunity to be dramatic or play a part. The drama built into the lyric involves a whole set of racial questions, from the representation of a black laborer's experience and inner thoughts to interracial conflict in a context of unequal wealth and power to the relationship between blacks and the American landscape. In this respect, Hammerstein bit off more than

"Ol' Man River" was conceived as a solo for a black baritone backed up by a chorus of black men—all costumed as manual laborers along the Mississippi River. Pictured here are Paul Robeson and chorus in the 1936 film version of *Show Boat*. (Photofest)

Hughes did in his poem about the black experience and rivers. There are two verses to "Ol' Man River," providing popular singers who sing the verse a range of materials from which to tailor the song for their own purposes.

In context in *Show Boat*, Joe prefaces his solo chorus with these lines.

> Dere's an ol' man called de Mississippi;
> Dat's de ol' man dat I'd like to be!
> What does he care if de world's got troubles?
> What does he care if de land ain't free?

Joe introduces the song as a drama with two actors: himself (the singer, the "I" of the lyric) and the Mississippi (the "ol' man"). The singer and the silent, personified river share the stage from the start. Developing this opposition between the verse lyric's initial antagonists became important for many singers. For example, Robeson would come to sing "Dat's de ol' man I *don't* like to be."

The other verse of "Ol' Man River" is heard twice in *Show Boat*: first at curtain's rise, sung by the men of the black chorus; then as part of the written-out encore for Joe's solo (when Joe is joined by the black male chorus).

Show Boat began with perhaps the most controversial opening line of any major musical in Broadway history: these words sung to the same tune as Joe's verse given above.

> Niggers all work on de Mississippi,
> Niggers all work while de white folks play.
> Pullin' dem boats from de dawn to sunset,
> Gittin' no rest till de Judgment Day!

Black performers in the original cast had trouble with Hammerstein's use of the word *nigger* from the start. Some simply didn't sing during those two beats, leaving a hole in the music and leading the white stage manager to curse loudly, according to black newspapers (which followed the controversy closely).[18] More than a few early solo recordings of "Ol' Man River"— including one by Robeson—use Hammerstein's original first word. Soon the n-word was changed to "darkies" (only slightly less offensive but a much more common usage in popular song lyrics), then after World War II to "colored folks" (a change sanctioned by Hammerstein in 1946 and the words most often heard in productions of *Show Boat* for the last half century). Most white pop singers after the war sang "Here we all work." Al Jolson—who recorded the n-word in 1928—sang the even less specific "Lotsa folks work" twenty years later. These shifts did not happen by themselves.

As early as 1935, African American activists took aim at "Ol' Man River" in a more general attack on the public use of derogatory terms for black Americans. In the *Baltimore Afro-American*, an important black newspaper, the AFRO Juniors announced a campaign to change the channel when songs like "Old Folks at Home," "Old Black Joe," "That's Why Darkies Were Born," and "Ol' Man River" were sung on the radio. Acknowledging that many black performers sang these songs, the group insisted that, at the very least, "offending words should be changed to meet modern standards."[19] When black performers did make changes, they were lauded in the black press. For example, in 1942 the *Afro-American* featured an article about Wanzie Davis, a black corporal in the US Army, who made a point of singing "people all work" in his rendition of "Ol' Man River," a song Davis described as "one of my favorites." The paper noted how Davis' revision frustrated "old line white citizens" who relish epithets such as "d - - - y" and "n - - - - r" and praised by name the white public relations officer who offered "no objection... to [Davis's] revision of the song."[20] The history of "Ol' Man River" is made of many such stories, which together reveal how this song survived. Hammerstein's original use of a strong racial epithet put the song's racial questions front and center, ensuring that "Ol' Man River" would play a public role in midcentury campaigns by civil rights advocates to seize control of the language used to refer to African Americans.

Still, changes to the verse lyric that remove all mention of color, that elide the issue of race are, by definition, at odds with the most basic intentions of the song. The verse argues strongly that blacks alone have the moral standing to sing this song. For Hammerstein not only pegged the singer as black, he also gave the singer the opportunity to contrast his own heavy labor with "white folks" at play. Revisions to "white folks" would seem a necessity for white singers: Leonard Warren sang "rich folks"; Gordon MacRae sang "big boss." (Sinatra, a white singer with a singular relationship to "Ol' Man River," virtually always sang "white folks.") Black singers also changed the words on this line. Entertainer Sammy Davis Jr. usually sang "big boss." (Davis was captured singing "white folks" on one occasion: a television appearance in 1969, an important year for race relations in the United States and for "Ol' Man River" in American popular music—see Chapter 9.) Black vocal groups such as the Flamingos and the Temptations, singing for the youth-oriented pop marketplace of the 1960s, pressed on the class dimension by singing "rich boys." The most absurd of rewritings dates to a 1957 choral version by bandleader Fred Waring's all-white choral ensemble, who sang "Here we all work while the other folks play," begging the question of who "we" and "the other folks" are. (The apparent absurdities of Waring's revision turn out to be changes made to finesse a radically public, racially integrated performance of the song—see Chapter 5.) Singers opting for euphemisms reveal their own grappling with the racial questions in the text—for white singers, a more obvious identification with the "white folks" at play. The categories of black and white are essential to Hammerstein's song. "Ol' Man River" is always about both black and white.

After singing the "niggers all work" quatrain, Joe and the men of the black chorus continue with a verse lyric that graphically depicts the nature and context of their labors.

> Don' look up
> An' don' look down.
> You don' dast make'
> De white boss frown.
> Bend your knees
> An' bow your head
> An' pull dat rope
> Until yo' dead.

Here, a new character enters the drama: the "white boss" himself, variously altered by white singers to the racially unspecific "big boss," "boss man," and "rich boss." The dramaturgical possibilities latent in these eight lines and their admittance of a third character into the drama have been richly explored by many performers. Two commands from this section of the verse—"Bend your knees / An' bow your head"—have been interpreted as if spoken by the "white boss" himself in more than a few versions, letting the black protagonist impersonate his white oppressor. Of course, white singers are put in the position of playing a black character imitating a white character. In the 1960s, these lines were acted out in a performance tradition that transformed "Ol' Man River" into activist street theater.

Hammerstein provided yet a fourth set of ideas in the verses for "Ol' Man River," drawing directly on the Negro spirituals informing Kern's tune. In a final quatrain, the singer longs for escape from the Mississippi: not to freedom in the North—"Ol' Man River" expresses the postbellum predicament of black Americans: it's not about slavery—but to heaven.

> Let me go 'way from de Mississippi,
> Let me go 'way from de white man boss;
> Show me dat stream called de river Jordan,
> Dat's de ol' stream dat I long to cross.

Hammerstein draws close to the imagery of the spiritual "Deep River" here, with its references to crossing the Jordan River. (Note, yet again, the need for white singers to change the reference to the ubiquitous "white man boss" who stalks through every section of Hammerstein's verse. Here, Waring's version uses the poetically awkward "mean mean boss.")

The varied dramatic and thematic resources in the verse lyrics of "Ol' Man River" have remained a crucial part of the performance tradition of the song. Even instrumentalists have explored the verse, often with haunting sensitivity, hinting that those who play "Ol' Man River" are often interpreting the words as well as playing the tune, assuming their listeners are doing so as well.

The chorus of "Ol' Man River" is built like most popular songs of the 1920s: thirty-two bars divided into four eight-bar phrases arranged in the most common AABA pattern. In formal terms, "Ol' Man River" is utterly conventional, one among thousands of songs produced by the sheet-music-centered popular music industry of the time. But "Ol' Man River" is not a Tin Pan Alley product written for the lowest common denominator: the parlor singer or pianist. Kern and Hammerstein wrote with Robeson's voice in mind, adapting the standard forms of popular music to feature his singular gifts, in the process creating a chorus at once familiar in its shape and extraordinary in its effect. Kern's melody is discussed in Chapter 2: here, Hammerstein's contribution gets close examination, for the chorus lyric proves just as varied in its ideas, just as complex in its dramatic possibilities as the verse.

The opposition between singer and the "ol' man" dominates the first A phrase, with the "ol man's" silence hanging heavy over the scene, leaving the singer alone in a silent landscape.

> Ol' Man River,
> Dat Ol' Man River,
> He mus' know sumpin'
> But don't say nuthin',
> He jes' keeps rollin',
> He keeps on rollin' along.

The second A phrase locates the singer in the context of rural labor by way of nouns and verbs that are unusually concrete for a popular song about the American South—the number of which was already legion before "Ol' Man River" appeared.

> He don' plant taters,
> He don' plant cotton,
> An' dem dat plants 'em
> Is soon forgotten,
> But Ol' Man River,
> He jes' keeps rollin' along.

Hammerstein emphasizes hard work rather than lazy leisure at a cabin in the cotton so common to Tin Pan Alley's imaginary South. For a lyricist sometimes accused of opting for saccharine platitudes, there's precious little sentiment in the second A phrase of "Ol' Man River." The work is named—planting—as are the commodities produced—potatoes and cotton. These are not Jeffersonian yeoman farmers claiming the promise of the American continent but black folks laboring for someone else, the "white man boss" named by Hammerstein in the verse.

Several elements of continuity between the first and second A phrases warrant comment. Hammerstein repeats the title phrase—common in popular songwriting—but he also repeats the verb phrase "jes' keeps rollin' along," which gives the lyric a second, content-rich internal refrain. Indeed, with the immediate success of "Ol' Man River" in popular music the phrase "keeps on rollin' along" entered the lexicon of idiomatic phrases in American English. Hundreds of casual uses of "rollin' along" appear in newspapers, particularly in the 1930s and 1940s. Sportswriters used it for horses and men alike (for example, baseball pitching legend Satchell Paige), reporters on the transportation beat used it for trains and trucks, business journalists used it for companies, and any established public figures still wielding power into their old age could expect to have it used about them as well.[21] Winston Churchill even quoted Hammerstein in his speech to the British Parliament on August 20, 1940, delivered at the height of the Battle of Britain. Speaking metaphorically of the lend-lease program and the inevitability of the United States entering the fight against Nazi Germany, Churchill made use of "Ol' Man River": "Like the Mississippi, [the Anglo-American alliance] just keeps rolling along. Let it roll. Let it roll on full flood, inexorable, irresistible, benignant, to broader lands and better days." Churchill's assistant John Colville noted in his diary: "I drove back with him in the car and he sang 'Ol' Man River' (out of tune) the whole way back to Downing Street."[22]

Hammerstein's dual refrain in all the song's A phrases has been an open invitation to parody. Chapter 4 considers several remakes of Hammerstein's text, many of which indulge in filling in the following blanks: "Ol' Man _____ / He jes' keeps _____ along." Some quick examples of changes to the final verb: Cab Calloway sang "strollin' along;" Martha Raye had the "River" "truckin' on down;" and Sam Butera repeated the line five times over, so that "Ol' Man River" could go "rollin'," "swingin'," "movin'," "groovin'," and finally "rollin' along."

The B phrase—also known as the bridge or the release—takes a more personal turn, away from the "ol' man" and toward the most fraught phrases in the chorus, naming not only the singer but his audience, putting quotation marks around the words of the boss, and encouraging explicitly dramatic interpretations. As in the verse, but here with encouragement from the lyricist—himself a theater director—the black persona inside the lyric is invited to imitate his white oppressor.

> You an' me, we sweat an' strain,
> Body all achin' an' racked wid pain—
> "Tote dat barge!"
> "Lif' dat bale!"
> Git a little drunk
> An' you land in jail . . .

The "tote" and "lift" lines—with their imperative verbs and imperious exclamation points—have proven especially irresistible: performers have done more to those two lines than any other pair in the chorus. The references to drunkenness and incarceration—a perhaps surprising nod on Hammerstein's part toward pernicious stereotypes from the passed age of the coon song—have been called onto the carpet by many singers. Riffing on the theme of alcohol, Putney Dandridge sang "drink a little corn" (1936), Roy Milton sang "get a little stinko" (1950), and Ray Charles sang "take a drink of Scotch" (1963). Della Reese and Cilla Black, among the relatively small number of women to record the song, both sang "Let's get drunk and spend the night in jail" (1960s). Articulating other reasons why blacks might "land in jail," Robeson sang "Show a little grit" (1949) and Aretha Franklin inserted "Get uppity" (1994). Blues and cabaret singer Mae Barnes rewrote the final lines of the bridge in 1958, removing the episode at the jail and continuing the shrill demands of the white boss with the substitute lines, "'Where's that mop?' / 'Get that pail!'" White singers also made changes. Teen-idol-turned-lounge-act Bobby Rydell sang "get a little outta hand and you land in jail" to the tony crowd at the Copacabana in 1961. One surely unintended genius of Hammerstein's chorus lyric has been its invocation of a negative racial stereotype in these two lines only, which forced creative remaking of a part that has had the capacity to recontextualize the whole. Such remakings point toward the importance of details in the performance history of "Ol' Man River." This song rewards close listening.

On the final A phrase—when Kern's melody rises to its climactic height— the lyric turns inward. Hammerstein raises existential questions that are less specific to black or working-class experience than the previous phrases. If any part of the lyric tempts the listener to hear "Ol' Man River" as an exploration of some sort of universal human condition, it is these lines.

> Ah gits weary
> An' sick of tryin';
> Ah'm tired of livin'
> An' skeered of dyin',
> But Ol' Man River,
> He jes' keeps rollin' along.

The most celebrated example of a performer changing the lyrics of "Ol' Man River" remains Robeson's revision of the above first four lines to the more assertive,

> But I keeps laughin'
> Instead a cryin'
> I must keep fightin'

Until I'm dying.
But Ol' Man River,
He jes' keeps rollin' along.

Eliminating a moment in the chorus where the singer admits weakness, Robeson strove to purge the text of self-pity, removing existential despair and putting in its place the declared intent to act, to fight to the end. Kern's rising melody assisted this transformation of despair into resolve. The new lyric not only makes sense for a reading of American history that emphasizes black agency—the opposite of noble suffering—it also fits the melody better for later ears wanting to hear echoes of "We Shall Overcome" in "Ol' Man River" as an anthem for the American century. Almost no other singers embraced Robeson's changes but there were alternate ways to finesse the fear of death in Hammerstein's lyric into something more life-affirming.

The question of what lyrics to sing proves key across the history of "Ol' Man River." The most interesting performances frequently feature performers changing the text so as to take control of the song, to wrestle its contradictory positions to their advantage, to make the song work for new purposes, sometimes with the goal of giving the lie to the whole damn thing—in effect, letting shrewd performers (and their listeners) have their cake and eat it, too. Its attraction as a song with serious content open to this sort of intervention cannot be discounted in any account of the survival of "Ol' Man River" as an extraordinarily fungible piece of pop culture currency.

A final note about the lyrics: many singers have altered Hammerstein's use of improper grammar throughout the lyric. Sam Cooke and Lou Rawls both preferred to sing "something" and "nothing" in place of "somethin'" and "nothin'." Many singers—black and white—have been loath to sing "An' dem dat plants 'em / Is soon forgotten," finding more felicitous turns of phrase and using a plural form of the verb *to be*. When Hammerstein wrote the lyric, pervasive touches of ignorance—a caricatured "black" dialect at the center of popular song lingo—further marked the singing subject in "Ol' Man River" as an untutored African American. Later singers have not wanted to abandon the song but the urge to sing "you and I, we sweat and strain" rather than "you and me, we sweat and strain" has been great. (The opposite reaction—emphasizing the dialect—also shows up: Robeson sometimes sang "ribber"; Sinatra relished the word "dast.")

The line "You an' me, we sweat an' strain" raises a question every performance of "Ol' Man River" outside the context of *Show Boat* must answer: *Who are "you and me" in the world of "Ol' Man River"?* In this bridge lyric, upon which the entire conceit of the song is hung, the singer invites the listener into a common worldview: performer and audience form a "we." As New York City mayor Fiorello LaGuardia noted of "Ol' Man River" on the occasion of Kern's death, "Ah, that is music! That will live. And it is ours."[23] *Whose* is it—exactly? Here, again, the black singing subject embedded in most every line of "Ol' Man River" raises a challenge for non-black performers. This, of course, has not prevented many whites from singing this song. Often, the means of getting past these lines have been ready to hand: slipping the lyric past the listener by casting the tune as an up-tempo dance number, embellishing the melody with sonic beauty that paints so broad a canvas the voice of protest in the lyrics is lost, or using the song to display artistry, whether that be an exhibition of improvisatory flights or a more mundane display of breath control. Still, the challenge of who the "we" in the lyric refers to remains. How these lines should be sung, who they address, what they capture about the American experience of race will be returned to again and again in this book. Throughout the song, but in the bridge lyric most intensely, Hammerstein, likely without knowing it, laid down a challenge that endured for decades and continues to haunt any performance of "Ol' Man River."

The question in this book's title contains an ethical dimension. Jewish lyricist Ted Koehler declared "I Got a Right to Sing the Blues" (with the help of Harold Arlen's music). *Who has the "right" to sing "Ol' Man River"?* Hammerstein's lyric seeks to express the African American experience— specifically, that of laborers along the Mississippi River, by inference in the American South. Who has the right to sing such words? Who should articulate the pain and resignation of Hammerstein's lyric? Whose voice should be permitted to soar on the wings of Kern's tune? Who should take matters into their own hands and rewrite the lyric or recast the tune?

Many white performers have endeavored to sing "Ol' Man River" in a serious manner. Frank Sinatra sang it this way for a half century, almost always singing "white folks" as if he weren't himself white. (Sinatra's historic role helping Italian Americans move into the unmarked category of "white" surely plays a part in his history with the song.) Performances of "Ol' Man River" by white singers were applauded by white audiences into at least the late 1960s. And white opera singers kept singing it into the 1990s. The historical context for this performance tradition demands close consideration. Why white singers wanted to put on this song written for Paul Robeson and what singing it allowed them to articulate forms a compelling tale of racial performance across the middle decades of the twentieth century (see Chapter 6). But almost no white singers sing it any more. When did this change happen?

In 1992, at the height of the era of political correctness, white American operatic bass Sherrill Milnes was prevented from singing "Ol' Man River" in Washington, D.C., on an annual Fourth of July concert featuring the National Symphony and telecast live on PBS from the steps of the Capitol. Milnes, who told the story in his 1998 autobiography *American Aria*, had programmed "Ol' Man River" along with Rodgers and Hammerstein's "It's a Grand Night for Singing," a setting of the Gettysburg Address, "America the Beautiful," and other patriotic songs. Of "Ol' Man River," Milnes wrote,

> Even with the original words, which some consider politically incorrect, it is still a classic. Ordinarily most singers now slightly alter the words to take out the most potentially offensive sounding phrases without losing any of the original flavor. For me the beauty of the words and the music transcend any racial overtones, and the singing of the piece can reflect the character of Joe in the original show even with some changes.
>
> I had rehearsed all the music with Mstislav Rostropovich, then the music director of the National Symphony, and all was ready. The audience of a half million to three quarters of a million people was gathering outside on the National Mall in front of the Capitol building. It was going to be a thrilling concert. Then thirty minutes before the beginning, I received word that "Ol' Man River" could not be sung, because the lyrics were "politically incorrect." I argued with them about the words, the classic nature of the piece, the beauty of the music, and its huge fame and familiarity, but to no avail. Someone from Congress had decided that it was too controversial. We were not allowed to perform it![24]

Milnes's defense of "Ol' Man River" uses ostensibly reasonable arguments— the song's "a classic," albeit with some "potentially offensive sounding phrases" easily altered "without losing any of the original flavor." And, without calling attention to his own whiteness, Milnes argues that from his perspective it's possible to "transcend [the song's] racial overtones" while still faithfully reflecting the character of Joe. This position is aesthetically and historically naïve, an expression of nostalgia on Milnes's part for earlier decades when white singers could and did sing anything they wished without being questioned by other whites. (Blacks, as will be shown, did challenge white singers who took up "Ol' Man River." The case of operatic baritone Robert Merrill is covered in Chapter 6.) By the waning years of the twentieth century, the free pass for a white baritone to metaphorically play the part of Joe in a concert context loaded with symbolic national meaning was no longer available.

As the episode on the Capitol steps suggests, by the 1990s the season for "Ol' Man River" was largely past. This book traces out several other passages through which "Ol' Man River" traveled, drawing out historical continuities and disjunctions that demonstrate how the meaning of "you and me" in Hammerstein's lyric changed with the times. In the process, the facile claim that "Ol' Man River" is "a classic" will be challenged on every turn. A song such as this can never be a "classic": it's too wrapped up in history to achieve any supposed universal expression—if, indeed, any piece of music can make such a claim. (I don't believe any can.)

Hammerstein's lyric inserts "Ol' Man River" into the concrete realities of American racial history. For this reason, a crucial question in this chapter of queries returns to the ethical word "should" introduced at the start and prominent in this book's title: *should anyone sing "Ol' Man River"?*

In an interview with black critic and historian Henry Louis Gates Jr. published in 1997, African American writer Albert Murray referenced "Ol' Man River" spontaneously in a discussion of representations of blackness in mainstream (white) popular culture.

> It's like the reaction to *Porgy and Bess*. Man, you put a bunch of brown-skinned people onstage, with footlights and curtains, and they make anything work. White people have no resistance to Negro performers: they charm the pants off anything. Black people make you listen up. They're singing "Old Man River"— "Tote that barge, lift that bale"? What the fuck is that? Everybody responded like "This is great." That type of fantastic charm means that black performers can redeem almost any type of pop fare.[25]

Murray dismisses the song while praising black performers' ability to sell it. He is far from alone among black (as well as white) intellectuals in thinking "Ol' Man River" would best be consigned to oblivion. This view of the song and other songs like it dates back at least to the early 1940s, when Mrs. Velma G. Williams, "one of the three colored members" of the Washington, D.C., school board, put "Ol' Man River" on a list of songs to be eliminated from the curriculum.[26] Songs by Stephen Foster (such as "Old Folks at Home"), James A. Bland (a black composer who wrote "Carry Me Back to Ole Virginny"), and George Gershwin made the list as well. Similar "South" songs show up clustered around "Ol' Man River" for much of its history, as subsequent chapters show.

An interesting tacit gloss on Murray's comments comes from the good-sized group of extremely well-known black performers with long careers who never recorded the song, among them Thomas "Fats" Waller, Charlie Parker, Lester Young, Billie Holiday, Ella Fitzgerald, Harry Belafonte, Sarah Vaughan, and Marian Anderson. (Louis Armstrong performed but did not record the song. His relation to "Ol' Man River" is equivocal at best.)

Still, a deeper look at what black performers who took up "Ol' Man River" did with it—did *to* it—yields a more subtle analysis of the place of black performers in American popular culture than allowed for by Murray. The black jazz and popular music performers who decided they should sing or play "Ol' Man River" consistently addressed the song with intelligence and subtlety: their sense for its combustible contents is always clear.

How whites embodied the song's expression of a serious black character serves as a crucial parallel narrative, yielding surprising glimpses of the promise of America working itself out. Among these moments is a 1964 recitation of "Ol' Man River" by actor Henry Fonda on network television, a performance that embodied Hammerstein's goal of ennobling the struggles of working people in the supposedly trivial medium of the popular song.

The arguments these performers made by way of performance will fill the pages of this book, the underlying subject of which is the power of performers to make this song their own.

Who Should Sing "Ol' Man River"? unfolds along thematic and somewhat chronological lines. After considering how Paul Robeson used "Ol' Man River" on recordings and in concert during the roughly three decades when he sang it (from 1928 to 1960), I consider four approaches to the tune that were widely operative from its appearance in 1927 to about 1970 and, in some cases, linger into the present. Separate chapters explore how "Ol' Man River" was treated as a dance and rhythm tune, put to work as a parody, dressed up for easy listening pleasure, and taken on by white male singers who assumed the role of Joe in a metaphorical manner. Frank Sinatra's way with "Ol' Man River" gets its own chapter. The final three chapters attend (mostly) to the song's unlikely high season. Between 1958 and 1969, more recordings of the song and a greater variety of interpretations were released into the marketplace than during any other period, placing "Ol' Man River" in a musical mainstream experiencing profound, ongoing change and a nation living through a revolution in race relations. Many, many singers and musicians reached for "Ol' Man River" in these times. Chapter 8 lays out the song's high season on records; Chapter 9 analyzes its appearances on television. Chapter 10—extending the story into the 1990s—listens closely to key recorded or filmed versions by African American artists who reinterpreted the song using the expressive resources of gospel, soul, and black pop—musical styles that arrived on the scene decades after "Ol' Man River" had earned its place as a song everyone knew. These transformations— some deeply personal—bring to the fore the rich possibilities latent in Hammerstein's lyrics and Kern's tune, resonances these black performers were eager to explore.

I have no desire to pontificate on who should or should not sing "Ol' Man River." I offer no final answer to the question on the title page. As a historian, I begin with the question *who should sing "Ol' Man River"?* because, in its rhetorical flexibility, this query captures the aesthetic and ethical dilemmas running through this song's unique history. Presenting the story of "Ol' Man River" and its many performers is my goal. I hope that reading these pages will lead the reader to the recordings themselves. In the age of digital music and YouTube, with the history of popular music laid out before our impatient, wandering fingertips, the performance history of "Ol' Man River" is effortless to access, easy to listen to, simple to compare. Hearing the voices of those who thought they should sing "Ol' Man River" will yield its own set of answers to the questions posed in this first chapter. In those that follow, I offer a listener's companion to this remarkable history of performance and a hopefully useful guide to listening anew to this inexhaustible song which—the phrase can hardly be resisted; I'll only use it once—went "rollin' along" for decades and still echoes today.

2

ᐠᐁᐟ

Robeson's Revisions

Paul Robeson's revision of the words to "Ol' Man River" is a familiar story and a good one. Succinctly put, Robeson changed select lines to eliminate negative stereotypes and inject a message of resistance and perseverance. Most biographies of Robeson mention these revisions, some on the way to generally condemning "Ol' Man River." Books on Robeson have—understandably—not put Hammerstein and Kern's song at the center: this chapter on Robeson does just that. Focusing narrowly on Robeson's relation to this one song across his years in the spotlight illuminates both the career of this important American and the shifting creative dynamics rippling through any performer's career. Robeson sang "Ol' Man River" innumerable times, in many different contexts and in several different ways. His more than three decades singing the song reward close study. Specific contexts shaped his power to revise the words, and his gradual alteration of the lyrics occurred in response to specific events. Robeson's audiences demanded he sing "Ol' Man River." Their reactions to his changes, along with those of the black and white press, the singer's vociferous, at times violent enemies, and even Hammerstein, tell a parallel story of Robeson's reception in his time and after. And at the level of musical choices, changing the lyrics changed the way Robeson sang "Ol' Man River." His history with the song, captured on many recordings, tells a rich story of a performer fitting a song to his own purposes.

Much has been made of Robeson's resistance to Hammerstein's opening line and his supposed refusal to sing the word *niggers*. But in 1930 Robeson recorded "Ol' Man River" as originally written—controversial opening word and all (⊚ Sound Example 2.1). Around this time Robeson began including "Ol' Man River" in his concerts. Did he sing "Niggers all work" in those contexts as well? Programs from the period that reprint song lyrics suggest he did. The 1930 recording—which has not generally been reissued—seems to fly in the face of historical memory of Robeson and "Ol' Man River." Understanding the larger context for this and other recordings proves a necessary part of telling the whole story of Robeson and the song Hammerstein and Kern wrote for him.

In the 1936 film *Show Boat*, Robeson sang "Darkies all work." A recording of this film version sounded "the only jarring note" at a 1943 launch of a Liberty ship named for Frederick Douglass, an event of tremendous pride for the black community of Baltimore. Robeson was supposed to attend but couldn't make it. The engineer who played the "disliked" disc was named and raced—"Martin Zeck, white"—by a black newspaper reporting on the event.[1] Black listeners listened closely: Robeson knew this. The dialogue between the black audience and "Ol' Man River," which runs throughout this book, begins with the black reaction to Robeson. His out-sized presence often served as a primary filter through which the song itself was heard.

In 1929, the African American poet Countee Cullen wrote an article about Negro spirituals and popular music for *Radio Times*. "Ol' Man River," a hit song often sung on the radio, inevitably came up. Cullen wrote, "I am sure there are some people who believe that Jerome Kern's melody 'Ol' Man River' is a spiritual."[2] Robeson certainly knew that "Ol' Man River" was not a spiritual, and yet for all practical purposes he treated it as one. Robeson seamlessly integrated this Broadway show tune into his concerts of Negro spirituals and folk songs, recognizing the power Hammerstein and Kern's song had with his audiences. Even if he didn't care to sing "Ol' Man River," Robeson's audiences, accustomed to shouting out requests for encores, would always ask for it. Robeson's revisions were spurred, in part, by the non-negotiable contract with his public that, whenever and wherever he appeared, even at non-musical events, he would sing "Ol' Man River." For example, as reported on the cover of *Billboard* during World War II: while laid over at an air base in Newfoundland during a USO tour per-forming for soldiers in Europe, Robeson "walked up to a mike in the ter-minal waiting room and gave out with three numbers, including 'Ol' Man River,' for the base personnel, the GIs and others waiting for plane trans-portation.... And how the guys loved it."[3] If he *had* to sing *this* song, as political activism began to overshadow his performing career Robeson had to arrive at a strategy that allowed him to bring "Ol' Man River" into align-ment with his priorities as a public figure. In an effort to turn the song to-ward his own ends, Robeson made substantive changes to the lyrics at key moments in his career as an activist representing black Americans, persons of African descent in any country, and at the broadest level, working people all around the world. These changes illuminate the delicate relationship between Kern's tune and Hammerstein's words as negotiated by a singer determined to turn "Ol' Man River" into a tool for his own use.

One aspect of "Ol' Man River" that Robeson did not change was the melody. Indeed, a primary reason for the song's outsized impact was the subtle artistry of Kern's tune. Before delving into Robeson's history with "Ol' Man River," it's important to get a better sense for just how perfectly the tune fit the man who inspired it.

Unlike Broadway show tunes, folk songs and spirituals aren't designed to show off the vocal range, power, or control of the singer. Take, for example, the spiritual "Deep River," performed and recorded by Robeson many times. Expressing a longing to cross the Jordan River, a metaphor for going to heaven, "Deep River" has a similar majesty to "Ol' Man River" and Hammerstein's verse lyric even mentions the Jordan. In the widely known version of "Deep River" published by Harry T. Burleigh in 1917, this traditional melody follows the form of a popular song.[4] Like "Ol' Man River," the melody is organized into an AABA pattern. The A phrases of "Deep River" are sober, stately, and rather wide in range: an octave and a fourth (⊛ Sound Example 2.2). The B phrase has a more urgent message and a more active melody: "Oh don't you want to go to that gospel feast." The highest note of the song comes here, expanding the melody's overall range to an octave and a sixth, the same range as "Ol' Man River" (⊛ Sound Example 2.3). All three A phrases in "Deep River" are identical. There is no musical development across the tune and, as noted, the song's melodic peak comes in the bridge. As with most such folk music, repeating the same melody and the same words supports an open-ended musical experience. "Deep River" unfolds without any real change in the flow of the melody or the emotions, except for the insistent bridge. But, of course, the song can't end at the bridge. Closure only comes with a return to the A melody, which does not welcome overly dramatic or loud delivery. Most performances of "Deep River" end on a quiet, contemplative note—fitting for a song carrying a message of confident assurance in the promise of a heavenly reward.

Here's where "Ol' Man River" differs from "Deep River" and all other folk music or spirituals. "Ol' Man River" was also built along an AABA pattern but Kern shaped the melody of each A phrase differently, slowly expanding the range of the song to peak at the end of the thirty-two bars. The song practically—indeed, physically—demands a big finish. (A more precise description of the song's form would be $A^1A^2BA^3$. Throughout the book, I will refer to the four phrases of the chorus in this manner. Music for the chorus melody, with the phrases labeled, is provided at the front of this book.)

Kern's first A phrase sounds the most like a folk song or spiritual. Its narrow range and repeated use of the same rhythmic idea set up the chorus as a straightforward, even naïve sort of tune. The complicated melodic trajectory to follow is not suggested to the listener. For the second A phrase—beginning at "He don' plant taters"—Kern expands the range, rising to an expressive stepwise descent on the word *forgotten*. The preceding word *soon* marks a new high point in the song's range and also pushes against the bass line in a novel manner, providing the first hint of a "blue" note. Skipping for the moment over the song's contrasting B phrase, on the third A phrase Kern expands the range yet again. Indeed, the melody rises to its highest notes at the very end of the song, on the final repetition of the title and the last "just keeps rollin'." Given the wide overall range of "Ol' Man River," singers are forced by nature to sing high and sing out at the close. Some have found the tune's climactic notes too challenging to attempt. Even Robeson punted on the high notes by dropping down an octave at the close of the final A phrase when the song was taken at a brisk tempo, as demonstrated by his first recording of the song in 1928 with the Paul Whiteman Orchestra (discussed later). Kern's three distinct A phrases would make little sense in any other order. Each builds on the last, carrying the singer and listener into new territory, taking the melodic ideas of the first A phrase into progressively higher realms. Hammerstein's lyric follows this logic as well, building rhetorically to its own parallel climax. In combination with the song's B phrase, which, like "Deep River" offers a sharp contrast, the larger shape of "Ol' Man River" forms a rising trajectory of emotion and thought. This design, when effectively delivered, practically commands applause, an aspect that puts "Ol' Man River" squarely in the Broadway show tune category. Unlike spirituals and folk songs, "Ol' Man River" demands an audience—it's a song to listen to, a song to be performed, a tune to be cheered.

When performing "Ol' Man River," Robeson, a self-styled singer of folk melodies, let Kern's melodic contour do most of the work. He allowed the natural dynamic variety built into a song that starts so low and ends so high carry the message. This approach yielded performances that, as Charles Bernstein has written, manage to be "so inspirational but at the same time unsentimental."[5] Later singers—especially white classically trained baritones—emphasized the high notes that mark each successive A phrase and also chewed the scenery a bit during the bridge. These versions slip over into sentiment. Robeson didn't take this approach. Indeed, he seems at times in his recordings and performances of "Ol' Man River" to be struggling against the relationship between Kern's high notes and Hammerstein's words. This tension becomes particularly acute as Robeson began to revise the lyrics.

Robeson's complicated relationship with "Ol' Man River" spanned almost the full length of the singer, actor, and activist's long career. Kern and Hammerstein wrote it for him and told him as much in late 1926. (Robeson had been a big name on the Broadway scene for barely two years.) After initially saying he would sing the song in *Show Boat*, Robeson withdrew from the production in January 1927 and resisted efforts to reengage him all the way to the show's opening in December of the same year. Robeson was, however, in New York when *Show Boat* opened on Broadway. He witnessed the success of the show and undoubtedly heard and saw Jules Bledsoe sing "Ol' Man River" on the stage of the Ziegfeld Theatre. Within months, Robeson was willing to be in *Show Boat* in London. There, he used the role of Joe and the song "Ol' Man River" to maximum advantage, emerging from the production as a beloved British icon. In the midst of this success, Robeson hated the part. His wife Eslanda wrote to a friend during the run-up to the London opening, "The part is [sic] *Show Boat* is a ridiculously easy one," adding he could "sing the song hit of the show, 'Old Man River,' and it wouldn't tax his voice as much as a rehearsal."[6] At the end of the ten-month run she wrote, "Paul is sick to death of *Show Boat* and will kick up his heels with glee when its [sic] over."[7]

A few years later, Robeson joined the cast of *Show Boat* on Broadway in the 1932 revival. Edna Ferber noted in her memoir of that production, "I witnessed a New York first-night audience, after Paul Robeson's singing of Ol' Man River, shout and cheer and behave generally as I've never seen an audience behave in any theatre in all my years of playgoing."[8] Despite this success and for no apparent reason, Robeson withdrew from the Broadway revival before it closed. Black newspapers openly questioned why. And in a theater economy collapsing under the Depression, Robeson passed up the chance to join *Show Boat*'s national touring company, an opportunity taken by most of the other principals. With Robeson again saying no to *Show Boat*, Bledsoe returned to the role of Joe for the tour.

Robeson could escape *Show Boat* but he couldn't avoid singing "Ol' Man River" on the concert stage. Robeson began his performing career as an actor but it was his recitals of Negro spirituals, accompanied by the accomplished African American pianist Lawrence Brown, which made him a true star of the 1920s. Robeson and Brown's first all-spirituals concert in April 1925 initiated a format that served Robeson to the end of his public career. Audiences cheered and wept, demanding encore after encore. Critics hailed the duo and regularly described what they offered as more than just a concert but an experience. Robeson was praised for expressing "all the plaintiveness of the colored race" with "a haunting tenderness, a wistful longing, an indescribable seeking for something just beyond, to be found in the voice of the Negro, and in no other voice."[9] The Robeson-Brown recital experience captured contemporary white fascination with black music and performers in a tremendously attractive package. In later years, Robeson would turn the format toward activism and his concerts would become sites of intense, even violent confrontation. With startling and enduring power, "Ol' Man River" distilled the Robeson recital experience into the form of a song. Kern and Hammerstein's initial plan for *Show Boat* had Robeson and Brown offer a short recital during act two as part of the show's story. Robeson rejected this plan but—once *Show Boat* had opened and he had played Joe—there was no way Robeson could avoid singing "Ol' Man River" at his recitals. It was the only Broadway show tune in his regular repertoire.

"Ol' Man River" first appears on Robeson and Brown's surviving printed programs in March 1931 as the last listed number for a Carnegie Hall concert.[10] Robeson had sung the song in Carnegie Hall a few months earlier as an encore "after repeated clamors from the enthusiastic audience," described by a black newspaper as "very largely Caucasian."[11] Including the number on the program eliminated the need for audience members to request it. Putting "Ol' Man River" last remained Robeson's practice wherever he sang in the run-up to the Broadway revival opening, whether the Royal Albert Hall, the London Palladium, Manhattan's Town Hall, or Yale University. If he sang concerts on successive nights, he programmed "Ol' Man River" both nights. During the run of *Show Boat*, Robeson sang "Ol' Man River" as the last of five songs on a program at Lewisohn Stadium, an outdoor venue in upper Manhattan where "Ol' Man River" would be heard on many occasions, sung by Robeson and others. "Ol' Man River" remained the last programmed number on his programs until about 1936, when the rhythm spiritual "Joshua Fit de Battle of Jericho" moved into that spot (where it had been before "Ol' Man River" entered Robeson's repertory). Perhaps Robeson determined that letting the audience request "Ol' Man River" gave the song greater impact. Perhaps he thought he could avoid it, unlikely given its strong personal connection to him on stage and screen. Robeson could not escape the song even if he wanted to and so he changed the words. The role of his audience in forcing him to make some creative changes to the lyrics should not be underestimated.

Jules Bledsoe was giving recitals, too—always singing "Ol' Man River" and always reminding audiences and the press that he was the first to sing it. Bledsoe and Robeson performed at Carnegie Hall within weeks of each other in 1931. Audience response and critical reaction suggest something of the contrasts between these two singers—a difference Bledsoe simply couldn't make up. Robeson's Carnegie Hall appearance, for a packed house, earned superlatives: "For outstanding personality, voice and diction, Robeson as a singer has no match since [the black Broadway star] Bert Williams, while in stage presence his experience as a star has given a distinction that is his own."[12] Bledsoe received less fulsome praise: "A good-sized audience responded warmly to Mr. Bledsoe's singing, remarkable, among other things, for its dramatic intelligence and its hushed tones."[13] In the matter of sheer star power, Bledsoe couldn't compete. And, to be fair, Bledsoe's ambitions were narrowly focused on a career as a classical singer—a tough road for a black singer at the time. Robeson, by contrast, wanted to use his multi-platform stardom to play a role in the drama of black American history, to play the stage of history and advance the cause of civil rights for black Americans and human rights for all working people. Both men put "Ol' Man River" to work in their efforts to meet these personal goals.

Robeson made six commercial recordings of "Ol' Man River" between 1928 and 1948. A handful of live performances between 1949 and 1960 were captured on tape and film. This body of recordings documents thirty years of Robeson singing the song. Robeson's studio recordings of "Ol' Man River," made under varied conditions, often out of his artistic control, show great diversity. On almost all these recordings, and in his appearance in the 1936 *Show Boat* film, Robeson worked under constraints. The live recordings, however, were in his control: they are expressively consistent and filled with intellectual conviction precisely applied to the song's varied themes. From the late 1940s onward, Robeson wielded "Ol' Man River" as a weapon in his fight against injustice and inequality. Only at this point, having wrestled with Hammerstein's text, did Robeson begin to sing "Ol' Man River" with an intensity of purpose that signals comfort with this song that had been written expressly for him to sing.

Robeson recorded two contrasting versions of "Ol' Man River" in 1928, the song's first year in the spotlight. His recording with the Paul Whiteman Orchestra put Robeson squarely in the middle of popular music stereotypes of blacks and the South; his recording with the cast and orchestra of the London *Show Boat* captured the power of Robeson's innovative concert persona. Close comparison of these two versions sets the stage for Robeson's later history with the song as well as the larger question of where "Ol' Man River" fits in the world of popular music.

The Whiteman version opens with a banjo plucking out the opening of Kern's chorus, followed by quick quotations of George Gershwin's *Rhapsody in Blue* (a Whiteman signature number) and the pseudo-spiritual "Goin' Home" (a popular song abstracted from Antonín Dvořák's *New World Symphony*). Kern drew on "Goin' Home" in the bridge of "Ol' Man River": perhaps Whiteman's arranger heard the connection.[14] These three opening elements position this "Ol' Man River" as slightly highbrow—this is not a dance record—and on the serious side of the metaphorical South of popular music. The awkward place of "Ol' Man River" in the capacious category of pop songs about the South proves a persistent theme across the song's history.

Robeson starts in on the chorus directly, singing at a relatively pushed tempo that prevents him from doing much more than presenting the tune. At the height of the tune's range—from "of dyin'" to the end—Robeson drops to the lower octave, altering the contour of the melody and the overall trajectory of the tune appreciably (⊕ Sound Example 2.4). Perhaps the tempo forced this choice, as the notes were clearly in Robeson's range. Almost every singer who recorded an up-tempo "Ol' Man River" in 1928 made exactly this adjustment. That Robeson does it here serves as one indication that he was not in control of this session.

After Robeson's opening chorus, the orchestra erupts into a very fast instrumental pass through the verse, avoiding thereby the question of that troublesome first word. Whiteman treats the verse as dance music and not a work song, directly contradicting the content of the lyrics. The arrangement sounds like a minstrel show breakdown or the dance on the levee during the wedding scene at the close of *Show Boat's* act one, where the black chorus (together with the bride Magnolia) does an energetic dance to entertain the white onlookers. Whiteman's arranger misses the point or, more charitably, shies away from any musical exploration of Hammerstein's contentious lyric, turning a statement of racialized labor performed "while the white folks play" into a stereotypical happy dance for black folks.

With a sudden shift in tempo and mood, a second male solo voice comes in singing the "don't look up" section of the verse in a relatively staid fashion. The dramatic potential of the text is not explored but the "white boss" does make his appearance. Soon enough the orchestra comes back in with the lively levee dance that, in turn, introduces a similarly lively instrumental chorus spotlighting a banjo on the tune. Shimmery vibraphone effects add some musical moonlight in the breaks—the empty measures at the end of each A phrase—perhaps painting a picture of free and easy music-making on the river (⊕ Sound Example 2.5). (In *Show Boat*, the black chorus hums "Ol' Man River" as a prelude to an atmospheric love scene played between the white principals on the top deck of the boat. The temptation to idealize the Mississippi landscape by way of picturesque arrangements of "Ol' Man River" is discussed in Chapter 5.)

Further quotes from "Goin' Home" lead into Robeson's second trip through the chorus, this time with a women's chorus providing background "oohs." From the bridge to the end of the record, Robeson and the women take turns on the melody. The women take the climax and close of the tune: an odd choice given Robeson's presence. His relatively minimal contribution to this version will disappoint listeners interested only in hearing Robeson sing. Whiteman clearly didn't see Robeson as central to the number in the same way Kern and Hammerstein did. (In *Show Boat*, Joe sings with a chorus but remains the central figure.) Instead, Whiteman's version situates "Ol' Man River" in a mythical musical South, where the banjo takes the tune and colored folks dance. Robeson is there but his star persona is given no power to realign conventional elements.

By contrast, Robeson's other 1928 version put him front and center. Made inside Drury Lane Theatre, where he was appearing in *Show Boat* to wide acclaim, this recording uses the orchestra, chorus, and conductor from the London production and documents Robeson's historic moment of connection with the British public. At a more comfortable tempo, Robeson sings in his restrained, even stolid style. The richness and power of his voice are on display without his trying too hard, an effect that remained central to his singing of this song. Crafted for his voice, all he need do is sing it. The troublesome verse lyric is avoided in favor of a second time through the chorus, this time with the men of the Drury Lane chorus. Robeson sings the added fills in the breaks designed by Kern and Hammerstein to effectively feature him (◉ Sound Example 2.6).

In 1932, Robeson joined other members of the Broadway revival cast of *Show Boat* under the baton of Victor Young to record a deluxe album of four 78s, the first in a long line of studio-cast versions of the score. Packaged by RCA Victor in a handsome album, critics praised the unity of the collection, "obviously recorded as a unit and with great care."[15] Using a full orchestra, Robeson gets a lush setting to deliver verse—the one beginning "Dere's an ol' man"—and chorus. With this full backing and a consistently histrionic arrangement, Robeson puts a little more explicit passion into the song. He gets close to emoting in a way he doesn't elsewhere, though there is still a distance in his singing (◉ Sound Example 2.7). This recording anticipates many later quasi-symphonic settings recorded by white male opera and operetta singers profiled in Chapter 6. The RCA Victor version declares that "Ol' Man River" is *important,* anointing the song as special rather than locating it among other South songs. Robeson generally didn't sing "Ol' Man River" this way—although his 1948 recording, again with the resource of a large studio orchestra, leans in this direction (albeit with the added element of revised lyrics). Robeson's 1932 "Ol' Man River" recording, like the Whiteman version from 1928, is best heard as an example of the singer fitting in to someone else's sense of how "Ol' Man River" should be sung and, along the way, collecting a paycheck.

Robeson smiles at the very end of the elaborately conceived, visually arresting "Ol' Man River" in the 1936 film of *Show Boat*. Singing as the character Joe, Robeson was playing a part. Still, the smile at this moment doesn't make much sense. This small gesture, which comes before the sound of Robeson's voice falls silent on the soundtrack—he was lip-syncing and chose not to do so with exactitude—marks the exceedingly narrow room Robeson had to define himself in Universal's lavish screen production of *Show Boat*.

Robeson's "Ol' Man River" in the 1936 film does, however, capture the element of his physical presence, a key part of his stardom. Director James Whale, working from an idea described in detail by Hammerstein in his screenplay, swings the camera in a full circle around Robeson's body during the verse: Robeson is initially treated as a sculpture. (It wasn't the first time. Robeson was captured in a life-size bronze nude titled "Negro Spiritual" by sculptor Antonio Salemme in the 1920s. With arms reaching heavenward, the sculpture might be imagined as the final pose from a performance of "Ol' Man River," except Robeson didn't sing the song that way. The bronze was lost during World War II.) Continuing with the shot, Whale pulled in for an extreme close-up with the start of the chorus. This part of the number is more about Robeson than the content of the song being sung. Later, Whale cuts away from Robeson to stylized, expressionistic images meant to illustrate the song. Prominent here are images of a shirtless Robeson, carrying a cotton bale on his back and, later, flexing his muscles as an expression of weariness after heavy labor. Over literal depictions of Joe drunk and in jail continue the pattern of Whale's simplistic interpretation of the lyrics, which reveals throughout a fascination more with Robeson's body than with the content of the song—although Whale, working again from ideas in Hammerstein's script, does keep the sequence focused on black labor. Hammerstein wanted the "white man boss" to be pictured as well, further evidence that the lyricist was always thinking about "Ol' Man River" as a scene of racialized, unequal power relations.

By the end of the 1930s, Robeson was fundamentally rethinking his career. A shift in his thinking had been on the way from before he made the *Show Boat* film. In 1935, when challenged by a black newspaper, Robeson defended playing Joe on the big screen: "To expect the colored artist to reject every role with which he is not idealogically [sic] in agreement is to expect the colored artist under our present scheme of things to give up his work entirely.... Under such an arrangement, I might as well give up my singing, my concert, work everything,... I shouldn't accept the role in *Show Boat*."[16] By 1938, his story changed, as reported by the same newspaper: "Paul Robeson feels that his portrayal of the roles of the ignorant 'colored boy' who had enough gold in his voice to compensate for all his other faults, has now reached the point of diminishing returns. And this is true so far as movies and musicals are concerned, but Paul Robeson's race is better off because he was the Emperor Jones, and because he sang 'Ol' Man River' in *Show Boat*."[17] The work he could accomplish by appearing on stage and screen for white audiences had been done: it was time to move on. But abandoning commercial musicals and films did not mean Robeson wanted to lose the mass audience such outlets provided. In 1939, a British journalist caught Robeson in a new venue, with a clear rationale for why he was there and what he could accomplish by singing and changing the words to familiar songs.

> A few months ago Paul Robeson decided to stop singing in "celebrity" concerts. That is why tens of thousands of cinema-goers have been able to hear Mr. Robeson sing "in person" in the vast London cinemas.... Nor did Mr. Robeson claim the privilege of a "celebrity" and sing only once during the evening. He sang as acrobatic turns have performed, as swing crooners have crooned—three performances daily. To the sixpennies, the shillings, and the one-and-sixpennies, he spoke through the microphone: "Now what would you like to hear?" or "What'll it be this time?" Then: "'Ol' Man River?' You shall have it." "'That's why darkies were born?' O.K.! But I've changed it because I don't think that's why darkies were born."[18]

Robeson knew his chosen audience—the popular crowd, the masses— wanted to hear familiar tunes. He wanted to sing what they wanted but he had an agenda as well. Changing the words was part of Robeson's strategy. Perhaps he had to make the changes simply to make singing certain songs bearable for himself.

Later in the 1939 interview, Robeson noted, "I am far more interested in appealing to the people by singing folk songs—even sentimental songs— which they like, than in 'showing off' with so-called 'classics.' I would rather sing at fifty concerts with the right audience than one with a tough audience who want me to give them Brahms." Robeson didn't want his singing to be mere "showing off." It had to have meaning for a mass, popular audience, which more and more became a politicized entity in his mind as activism consumed his public life. "Ol' Man River" fit the bill and he was willing to treat this show tune—the history of which he knew very well— as if it was simply a folk song or spiritual, tacitly inserting Hammerstein and Kern's song composed with a commercial intent into categories of "authentic" music about which Robeson cared deeply. Whatever later audiences might think of "Ol' Man River," Robeson thought of it as a song that could serve his needs, that reached the audience he wanted to reach, that let him turn his talents toward what mattered most.

The earliest evidence for when Robeson began to change the words to "Ol' Man River" dates to 1937—one year after the *Show Boat* film appeared in theaters. Robeson was singing in London at a political rally in Royal Albert Hall calling for "arms, food and justice for democratic Spain." Robeson's change to the well-known lyrics of "Ol' Man River" was news enough back in the States to warrant reporting in the *New York Times*: "[Robeson] altered the line 'I'm tired of livin' and feared of dyin' to 'I must keep on struggling until I'm dyin'."[19] Perhaps Robeson was still trying to find the right word: he would sing "I must keep fightin'" not "I must keep on struggling," which doesn't really fit the tune. Perhaps the reporter didn't catch the change correctly. (The *Afro-American* reported the change to "fightin'" in a short piece on the singer's 1938 visit to Madrid.)[20] The context—London's premiere concert hall turned to political purposes—suggests Robeson's future. About a decade later, all of Robeson's concerts would be political events of one sort or another, and "Ol' Man River," which he always had to sing, would become a directly political song.

Robeson apparently didn't sing his new lyrics on his return engagements at Manhattan's Lewisohn Stadium in 1940 and 1941: reviews don't mention a change to the lyrics. The 1940 concert was thematically programmed to highlight issues of race and democracy: William Grant Still's "And They Lynched Him from a Tree" was sung, as was the song "Ballad for Americans," which Robeson sang together with a large interracial choir.[21] Had he changed the lyrics to "Ol' Man River," it would have likely been reported.

But at his 1947 Lewisohn concert, Robeson did change the lyric and, once again, the *Times* noticed, this time getting the revision right: "His first encore was 'Ol' Man River.' As he came to the end he sang: 'I must keep fightin' until I'm dyin',' and a burst of spontaneous applause arose from the audience."[22] Three more encores followed, including "The House I Live In," a song about racial and religious tolerance made famous during the war by Frank Sinatra. Robeson made some pointed changes to the lyric for "The House I Live In" as well, and the song remained part of his repertoire to the end of his career. Whenever these two songs are found together—which happens in the careers of Robeson, Sinatra, and the soul crossover singer Sam Cooke—the critique at the core of Hammerstein's lyric is being attended to. (Chapter 7 returns to the dual history of "Ol' Man River" and "The House I Live In.")

Robeson committed his revision of Hammerstein's lyrics to record for the first time in 1947 at one of his last commercial recording sessions. The sessions yielded a set of four 78s released by Columbia Records the following year as *A Robeson Recital of Popular Favorites*. (Tellingly, Robeson did not include "Ol' Man River" on his thematically conceived album *Songs of Free Men* from 1947.) Normand Lockwood's arrangement is earnest and powerful, scored for full orchestra but centered on Robeson's voice. Improved postwar technology makes for a remarkably clean recording: Robeson sounds closer than he ever would on record. This version gives the listener solid evidence for how Robeson was altering "Ol' Man River" at this point. Further changes to the lyrics were coming but here—before the watershed year of 1949—Robeson was making only three changes to Hammerstein's words.

At the outset of the verse, Robeson increases the distance between himself and the "Ol' Man," Hammerstein's stand-in for the American landscape.

> There's an old man called the Mississippi.
> That's the old man I **don't like** to be.

The original text has the singer longing to be disinterested like the river: Robeson rejects this desire at the outset, refusing both the river as a model for himself and the river's attitude toward those who suffer.

At the final A phrase, Robeson waxed his much reported change: "But I keeps laughin' / Instead of cryin' / I must keep fightin' / Until I'm dyin'." He emphasizes the word "fightin'" in an unusual manner, inflecting the melody in a way that pushes that word to the front. Robeson rounds out the chorus with a small but significant change: "but Ol' Man River" is altered to "**and** Ol' Man River he just keeps rollin' along" (⊕ Sound Example 2.8). This change of conjunction demonstrates how closely Robeson was examining the text and anticipates a contraction he would add in his final round of revisions. The new lyric excises Hammerstein's existential dread—weariness with life, fear of death—and puts heroic resolve in its place. Robeson had tried for decades to fight the dominant images of blacks across the cultural landscape. Those efforts, in his view, had largely failed. Here, with a song his audience loved and demanded, Robeson could articulate in no uncertain terms his resistance to noble suffering as the keynote of black identity. In the process, he turned the listener toward the words at a point in the song where most singers luxuriate in high notes that thrill the ear without necessarily penetrating the understanding. Robeson, still resisting the structures that defined black identity, makes a principled stand in the midst of a lyrical melody.

These changes were in place as early as 1946, when the *Baltimore Afro-American* printed Robeson's complete revised text in their review of a Robeson recital in Chicago's Orchestra Hall. The paper recommended the new version for use by all singers in its national black readership. The *Afro-American* defined the connection between Robeson as artist and activist—"There's no separation of art and politics where Mr. Robeson is concerned"—and also noted the transformation Robeson had effected on his signature song: "So it looks as if 'Ol' Man River' had better wake up and get on the side of the people."[23]

In 1949, Robeson's career and life reached a turning point. In April, he made comments at a conference in Paris that exploded into controversy in the US press. Robeson said that given the state of race relations at home, he could never imagine American blacks going to war against the Soviet Union. At the height of the Red Scare, his words provoked swift condemnation from powerful figures in the white political establishment, leading eventually to a call to testify before the House Un-American Activities Committee in 1956. After making his remarks at the Paris conference, Robeson sang "Ol' Man River," as well as a Russian army song. His changes to Hammerstein's lyrics went unnoticed in the American press.[24]

After leaving Paris, Robeson gave concerts in Scandinavia and the United Kingdom before heading east for engagements in Poland, Czechoslovakia, and, finally, the Soviet Union. In June, just before returning home, Robeson sang a concert in Moscow's Tchaikovsky Hall. He had sung "Ol' Man River" in the hall on a previous visit in late 1936. On that occasion, Chatwood Hall, an African American writer who moved to Russia to "find a country where there was no jim-crow," described the Russian audience's "whole-hearted response" to Robeson's "serious" "'Ol' Man River'" as of a piece with other songs on the program which "record the suffering of a race from oppression and exploitation."[25] Hall noted no changes to the lyrics in 1936, suggesting that singing in support of the Spanish cause in 1937 was the specific impetus for Robeson's earliest moves to alter Hammerstein's text. At his 1949 concert, Robeson sang his fully revised version of "Ol' Man River" and pointedly drew attention to the fact that he was changing the lyric. His prefatory words on the concert platform made the *New York Times*, which reported Robeson "said in the old words of the song, man was tired of living and afraid to die. But the new words, he told the audience, are 'We must fight to death for peace and freedom.'"[26]

Oscar Hammerstein released a statement just days later. One black newspaper described the reply as "a tongue-lashing."[27]

> I see by the papers that Paul Robeson believes that the words of "Ol' Man River" should be changed. As the author of these words, I should like it known that I have no intention of changing them or permitting anyone else to change them. I further suggest that Paul write his own songs and leave mine alone.[28]

Oscar Hammerstein knew Paul Robeson. He had dealt with him professionally in the 1920s and the 1930s. Robeson had not been particularly cooperative. For example, Hammerstein personally met with Robeson in 1935 to ask him to be flexible on the shooting schedule for the *Show Boat* film, for which Hammerstein was hurriedly writing the screenplay because Robeson refused to cancel a London concert engagement. Robeson wouldn't budge.[29] Hammerstein and Robeson had shared public political commitments in the recent past: both men signed on in 1945 as board members for Pete Seeger's People's Songs, an effort to invigorate the singing of folk and protest songs, and in 1946 both men lent their names as sponsors to the American Crusade to End Lynching.[30] Hammerstein's suggestion that "Paul write his own songs"—use of the singer's first name is telling—has a sharply personal ring to it. After all, Hammerstein wrote "Ol' Man River" specifically *for* "Paul." Surely Hammerstein had a particularly personal reaction any time Robeson used "Ol' Man River" for his own purposes.

Robeson's 1949 Tchaikovsky Hall concert was recorded. In addition to his earlier changes, he made other small but significant revisions not captured on any earlier recording. He altered the climactic "he jes' keeps rollin' along" to the slightly fussy "**he'll** just keep rollin' along" (⊚ Sound Example 2.9). Coming after his assertion of a willingness to fight until he's "dyin'," the qualification of that contraction makes sense. Once again, as with the change to "I don't like to be," Robeson puts room between himself and the lyric's themes of complacent nature and resigned suffering. But does it work when "he'll just keep rollin'" is sung at the top of his range, where Robeson's glorious voice shines at its brightest? Who is listening to the lyrics at this point? Can a hard-to-hear contraction impact how the listener hears Kern's soaring tune? Perhaps Robeson made this change more for himself as part of a detailed effort to eliminate every bit of Hammerstein's lyric that rankled in the singing.

Another change, at a less musically effulgent point in the song, also first caught on recording in the Tchaikovsky Hall concert, has endured as a powerful symbol of resistance to Hammerstein's suggestion that blacks are drunkards. Robeson didn't eliminate the notion that black Americans might "land in jail." Instead, he changed the action precipitating incarceration.

> "Tote dat barge!"
> "Lif' dat bale!"
> **You show a little grit.**
> And you land in jail.

"Show a little grit" is a brilliant change. It fits the tune at a spot where the melody can't overwhelm the words. Indeed, in Moscow, Robeson spit out the word, almost speaking it (◉ Sound Example 2.10). (As Chapter 6 details, white male singers taking a dramatic approach to the song shifted briefly to a spoken-shouted voice on the bridge—however, they used it for the boss man's cries of "tote" and "lift.") The jagged melodic contour of the bridge serves the new text well and the word *grit* comes off as at once unexpected and resonant. Robeson's change to a small part effectively remakes the whole, becoming the key to a rich new way with the song. And as a lead in to Robeson's version of the final A phrase, the new bridge rebalances the song around a lyrical high point—"I must keep fightin'"—rather than the melodic peak of the final phrase. "Show a little grit" locks in place a process of revision only the most inattentive listener wouldn't get. And by this point in his career, Robeson didn't have inattentive listeners—whether for or against him. The governor of Trinidad, grudgingly attending a Robeson concert in 1949, noted the changes to "Ol' Man River," adding "If I had not had my ears pricked for communistic sentiments, I should not have noticed this."[31] Challenging his audiences with a song they all knew, in the words of social movements scholar Shana L. Redmond, "at Robeson's hands, old man river had been transformed from a weak, pitiable Black man to a righteous iconoclast and global freedom fighter."[32]

With his recording, film, and theater careers largely over, Robeson's public appearances, at which he virtually always sang "Ol' Man River," became political events. Some were actual political rallies (like the one that sparked his initial changes to the lyrics in 1937). Just weeks after his Paris remarks and Moscow concert, Robeson sang "Ol' Man River" in Newark, New Jersey, at a political rally in July 1949, where he was quoted as saying, "I am a radical and I am going to stay a radical."[33] The next month, a Robeson concert at Peekskill in upstate New York gained national attention for a violent confrontation between attendees, mostly blacks and Jews, and a mob of white, anti-Robeson protestors.

By the end of 1949, the State Department was seeking to take away Robeson's passport—he filed a countering lawsuit—and in March 1950, NBC canceled Robeson's scheduled appearance on *Today with Mrs. Roosevelt.* He was effectively banned from the national media and, in August, his passport was revoked. It was withheld until 1958 when a Supreme Court ruling invalidated State Department regulations denying passports due to supposed disloyalty. In the words of Coretta Scott King at a Carnegie Hall tribute on the singer's seventy-fifth birthday, Robeson was "buried alive" for "having tapped the same wells of black militancy" as her husband Martin Luther King Jr.[34]

Paul Robeson performs in Peekskill, New York, in 1949 while surrounded by union members protecting him from violent, racist protestors, who would turn their fury on the departing audience members. "Ol' Man River" was on the short program that afternoon. (Author's collection)

"Ol' Man River" in its revised form remained a Robeson staple throughout the 1950s, sung by Robeson in several symbolic instances where he used technology to defy the State Department's attempt to limit the reach of his voice. At the Peace Arch rally in 1952, Robeson sent his voice across the US-Canada border in an open-air concert in a park where symbolic passage between the two nations was open and free. The concert, repeated annually for a three more years, defied Canada's unprecedented refusal to let Robeson cross the border without a passport—a courtesy granted all US citizens. One Canadian official noted, "I would be reluctant to see Robeson, the singer, refused entry into Canada but it is going to be difficult to separate him from Robeson, the political propagandist."[35] Indeed, by this point in his journey there was no difference: Robeson had become what biographer Jordan Goodman calls "pure Robeson, art and politics uncompromisingly combined."[36] In a short speech to the Peace Arch crowd, Robeson said, "You have known me through many years. I am the same Paul—fighting a little harder because the times call for harder struggles." The International Union of Mine, Mill, and Smelter Workers, sponsor of the event, produced a commemorative recording of the 1952 Peace Arch concert; with a specially designed label picturing Robeson singing behind jail bars marked with the stars of the US flag: his powerful voice, assisted by his equally powerful hands, bends the jail bars back to reveal his face. The close of the record captures the enthusiastic response of the crowd to the musical moment they had all been waiting for: Robeson's "Ol' Man River" (☉ Sound Example 2.11). Another concert recording, also from 1952, captures Robeson singing with great forcefulness. Only now, with control of the small elements of the text that he didn't like, does Robeson really let it loose (☉ Sound Example 2.12). And Robeson reached across the seas as well. He sang a concert for an audience of five thousand in Wales by way of a transatlantic telephone hookup in 1957, and he sent a recorded greeting—a speech and three songs—to a conference of African and Asian nations in Bandung, Indonesia, in 1955. For the Bandung recording, Robeson sang "Ol' Man River" after offering the spiritual "No More Auction Block" and the "Hymn for Nations," a lyric exalting brotherhood and peace between nations set to the tune of Beethoven's "Ode to Joy." Recounting Robeson's use of the song at the Peace Arch concerts and on the Bandung recording, Redmond claims that "Ol' Man River" was "by 1955, received as an anthem of the disenfranchised and oppressed."[37] For some listeners, those devoted to Robeson and the causes to which he sacrificed his career, this was undoubtedly so. In the midst of very public struggles, "Ol' Man River" became a tool expressing Robeson's refusal to be silenced, forged by him from a song he initially refused to sing. But Robeson's "Ol' Man River" as anthem never penetrated the mainstream of popular music and culture, as attested by multiple examples in the chapters that follow.

After the return of his passport, Robeson returned to major concert halls—concerts at Carnegie Hall and Royal Albert Hall in 1958 were captured on tape—and departed on a world tour. While visiting workers at the building site of the Sydney Opera House in 1960, Robeson sang "Ol' Man River" without accompaniment. His impromptu performance was captured on film (often posted on YouTube: search "Robeson Sydney Opera House"). This may be Robeson's final recorded "Ol' Man River" (☉ Sound Example 2.13). At the word *fighting*, Robeson shakes his fist, still calling attention to one of his most significant revisions to Hammerstein's text. Shortly after his journey to Austrialia, Robeson's health failed and his public life came to an end.

Not everyone appreciated how Robeson was using "Ol' Man River" in these years. The *New Yorker* labeled him "Old Man Marx." A sympathetic 1955 opinion piece in a British paper felt that Robeson's changes unbalanced his art.

Mr. Robeson was once a very great singer—some would even say a great artist; on Saturday the once-great artist, singing carelessly, lazily and unmusically, was concerned only with demonstrating that by altering the words you can make any piece of vocal music serve your political ends, and in so doing win the bargain-priced applause of the already converted.[38]

Other voices embraced the changes. The British Peace Committee reportedly cheered his "peace" version of "Ol' Man River" at an outdoor rally in London in 1950.[39] A black woman quoted in the *Daily Worker*, the newspaper of the Communist Party USA, had her own view: "I think of Paul Robeson as Old Man Freedom himself."[40]

The New York City Labor Chorus, drawing on members of over twenty local unions and District Councils, recorded "Ol' Man River" with all the Robeson revisions in place in the 1990s on their CD *Workers Rise!: Labor in the Spotlight* (⊙ Sound Example 2.14). As the group's website notes, the Labor Chorus stands "ready to perform on picket lines, at union conventions, union rallies and shop steward meetings, as well as at community events, churches, colleges, and schools. Our repertoire represents the great legacy of U.S. labor music. The repertoire includes songs of labor struggles, protest, and social significance." Robeson's changes to Hammerstein's lyric secured the place of "Ol' Man River" in this body of labor songs wielded by the NYC Labor Chorus as "a powerful cultural tool in the arsenal of workers." Robeson would surely have added his voice to their numbers.

But Robeson's changes to the lyrics of "Ol' Man River" were not taken up by later solo singers. They are—to a surprising extent—unique to Robeson's way with the song. Many later black male baritones and basses sang "Ol' Man River"—some built their careers on the song—but none captured on record adopted Robeson's confrontational position toward Hammerstein's lyric. Other singers and musicians would transform "Ol' Man River" into a song of protest but not in so direct a manner and not with such prominence. And, as shown here, there are plenty of Robeson recordings from before the 1940s that capture him singing the lyric without alteration. This less confrontational approach served any black bass taking up the role of Joe in *Show Boat*. "Ol' Man River" was written to be sung by a black male character of innovative seriousness for a Broadway musical comedy. Robeson's dignified concert persona is written into the show by way of "Ol' Man River." Indeed, the resilience of *Show Boat* on the musical stage owes much to "Ol' Man River." Robeson's embodiment of dignified, noble black suffering—even if Robeson himself eventually actively discarded this pose—has retained its power with white audiences into the twenty-first century.

For example, black singer Lawrence Beamen sang "Ol' Man River" on the 2009 season of the television reality show *America's Got Talent*. A native of Mississippi, in his pre-performance profile Beamen says, "Each time I open my mouth to sing I think of the South." Condensing "Ol' Man River" for the purposes of his minute or so on television, Beamen begins with the last line of the verse, singing "What does he care if the land is free," a change to the lyric that makes little sense. Beamen slides to a very low note—establishing his credentials as a bass—before shifting easily into the chorus, which adds some subtle backbeats, giving the performance a contemporary feel. After the first A phrase, Beamen skips ahead to the bridge, singing with more energy and dropping to an audience-pleasing low note on "jail"—a trick Robeson and Sinatra, among others, used. At the final A phrase, Beamen again skips forward in the song, leaving out "I gits weary" and going right to the climactic "but Ol' Man River, he just keeps rolling along." Now, his performance is about breath control—a long final note—and high notes. A touch of contemporary and gospel vocal styling updates what is essentially a Robeson-style performance emphasizing dignity and vocal control. The audience and two of the judges—Sharon Osborne and David Hasselhoff—rise to their feet. Beamen ends in tears—not something Robeson would have ever done. Osborne goes to the stage to hand Beamen a Kleenex and tells him, "You are one class act." Hasselhoff comments, "What you brought to this show is class, grace, and talent and we have a lot to learn from people like you." The still-seated judge, Piers Morgan, says "I'm not quite sure how much this audience likes you." The crowd responds by rising to their feet with yet another roar. Here, again, is that outsized reaction Ferber wrote about back in the 1930s. Robeson continued to get that reaction until he revised and repurposed "Ol' Man River." When he did that, the inevitably smaller audiences longing for a radical voice of protest kept on cheering but the mass audience and the powers that control access to the masses turned away.

Robeson's way with "Ol' Man River" modeled several possible approaches to finding success with this most famous song. A quasi-spiritual, quasi-folk song that has the contours of a show tune, when sung by a black male singer "Ol' Man River" serves as an apt showpiece for the bass voice, an aspect of the tune that attracted rhythm and blues, doo-wop, soul, and gospel singers to the song (as later chapters will show). With a big vocal finish built into the melody, "Ol' Man River" lets the voice loose in a manner that is not operatic—but might sound sort of operatic or "classical" to inexperienced listeners. This kind of "big" singing is, perhaps, genuinely American, and Robeson provides the historical template for those who came after, offering the pleasures of a loud, triumphant, popular music voice that has the patina of art without the distance of European-derived high culture.

It also works, of course, when trained black opera singers perform it. African American mezzo soprano Denyce Graves recorded a powerful and controlled "Ol' Man River" on her 2004 CD *Kaleidoscope*. With only piano accompaniment—recalling Robeson's concert recordings—Graves sings the verse, beginning with "colored folks work." With the clearest of diction— again, recalling Robeson—Graves cuts to the heart of the song, lending her exceedingly rich voice to a song associated with deep male voices (⊕ Sound Example 2.15). Graves's recording is a rarity. None of the other great black female opera singers of the last eight decades recorded "Ol' Man River." And while Graves evokes Robeson, she also makes one long to hear Marian Anderson sing "Ol' Man River." The pathbreaking contralto who triumphed on the international concert stage and became a symbol of the fight for racial integration in the 1930s sang many of the spirituals Robeson was known for. But Anderson did not cross the line into popular songs. Graves's twenty-first century recording gives a hint of how Anderson, famous for singing spirituals, might have approached "Ol' Man River."

For some listeners—those who stay with Robeson beyond 1949—"Ol' Man River" affords the pleasures of unabashedly liberal sentiments articulated within the conventions of popular culture. Hammerstein wrote another song to be enjoyed in this fashion: "You've Got to Be Carefully Taught" from the 1949 Broadway musical *South Pacific*. With an appropriately obsessive, vocally ungrateful melody by Richard Rodgers, Hammerstein put a nervous disquisition on learned prejudice in the mouth of Lt. Joe Cable, a white man from a wealthy WASP family, a scion of Philadelphia's Main Line who has fallen in love, in spite of himself, with a native island girl. "Ol' Man River" carries a complementary message of racial protest but, unlike "You've Got to Be Carefully Taught," remains a song that listeners take pleasure in hearing. Cable, a white character with whom the Broadway audience is expected to identify, struggles with having fallen in love across the color line. Cable eventually rejects the girl he loves, and, at story's end, dies offstage on the battlefield. The dramatic stakes for Cable's song are high, even if the musical pleasures of "You've Got to Be Carefully Taught" are few. By contrast, Joe—a black character with no role in the plot and lacking even a last name—stands like a statue and sings a beautiful song about racial injustice as a fact of his life, a feature of the landscape. In the end, "Ol' Man River" sung in this way, inspired by Robeson's voice and persona, makes few demands on the listener besides witnessing noble suffering or applauding a man who declares in song that he will not be moved.

In the twenty-first century, German bass-baritone Thomas Quasthoff included "Ol' Man River" in his repertoire before his retirement from performing in 2012. Although he has never recorded it, Quasthoff can be heard and seen singing "Ol' Man River" on the Berlin Philharmonic's 2008 Silvesterkonzert, broadcast live on German television and often up on YouTube. Bootleg concert recordings circulate on the Internet as well. Concert reviews provide clues to Quastoff's attitude toward "Ol' Man River." Before singing the song as an encore for a concert of cantatas by Johann Sebastian Bach to texts meditating on death, Quastoff, in the words of one reviewer, noted "a similarity in sentiment between them [the Bach cantatas] and 'Ol' Man River': the 'tired of livin'" part if not 'scared of dyin'."[41]

As captured live, Quastoff departs from most traditions around the singing of "Ol' Man River" by non-black performers from the world of classical music. He freely alters the melody with some original bluesy touches (Quasthoff's known for singing jazz); he draws attention to the lyric's black dialect on the words "taters" and "skeered" in a way American singers would avoid as stereotype; he sings "tote" and "lift" without undue emphasis, and, on one bootleg recording, Quastoff shouts out the word "achin'" on the line "body all achin' an' wracked with pain." This last choice, drawing the listener to the question of the singer's body, carries particular power in Quasthoff's case.

Quasthoff was born in 1959. His mother took Thalidomide, a cure for morning sickness that, before being pulled from the shelves in 1962, created a cohort of so-called Thalidomide babies. The drug left Quasthoff with a shortened stature and malformed upper limbs. As one reviewer noted, projecting mightily onto Quasthoff's appearance, "Born with severe physical deformities, he seems to know all there is to know about sorrow and alienation (as in Schubert's 'Winterreise'), and resignation and hope (as in Brahms's 'Four Serious Songs') and courage and overcoming. In a word, he has soul."[42] This reading of the voice through the singer's body essentializes Quasthoff's "struggles" and jars against the singer's public persona as a positive, energetic individual who succeeded by cultivating and believing in his talent—in the words of his publicity, he's an "artist with physical disability" and not a "handicapped person who can sing." Still, Quasthoff's personal circumstances—visible on his body like blackness was on Robeson's— allow him to deliver "Ol' Man River" (for some audiences) as a metaphorical meditation on noble suffering and personal triumph in the face of unchangeable circumstances.

Quasthoff will likely disagree with what follows: perhaps his version of Randy Newman's 1977 pop hit "Short People" better reflects the singer's attitude toward how his art, his body, and his moment in history relate.

Quasthoff likely sings "Ol' Man River" simply because it's a famous bass-baritone showpiece and he is a famous bass-baritone. Still, for the purposes of this book, reflection on Quasthoff's embodiment of "Ol' Man River" allows the contemporary listener to imagine, perhaps, how some white audiences understood Robeson in the 1920s. Quasthoff and Robeson, both endowed with extraordinary voices that could not be denied a hearing, were similarly marked in physical terms by something the majority audience in their historical moments—white; able-bodied—generally understood as an impediment to be overcome. Each man's ability to do so—Robeson to transcend the limitations and stereotypes put on black performers in the age of Jim Crow; Quasthoff to forge a career as a classical singer in an audiovisual era centered on singers with conventionally beautiful bodies as well as voices—marked both as more than just gifted singers but also as exemplars of the human spirit, embodiments of overcoming that audiences have attended to with a hush and embraced with cheers. Hammerstein and Kern's unusual song served both men in their respective historical moments, demonstrating the prismatic potential of "Ol' Man River" to refract all sorts of meanings across its long history.

3

⌀

Ol' Man Rhythm

B lame it on Bing Crosby—or better still, Paul Whiteman, the much-maligned, white "King of Jazz" in the 1920s. Whiteman's dance band, with Crosby on the vocal, recorded an up-tempo "Ol' Man River" on January 11, 1928, just weeks after *Show Boat* opened. This successful record—Whiteman's outfit was a top band of the moment—helped launch Crosby's long career and serves as a point of origin for decades of fast recordings of "Ol' Man River."

The speed or tempo at which "Ol' Man River" has been played and sung is the central consideration in this chapter—specifically versions of the song that are, relatively speaking, fast. One way to quantify the tempo, or speed, of a recorded "Ol' Man River" is beats per minute or bpm. The words "ol' man" as set throughout the chorus provide a reference point for the quarter-note beat underlying Kern's tune as published. Whiteman's version with Robeson, discussed in the previous chapter, varies in tempo and uses a lot of rubato (stretching of the tempo) but Robeson's two vocal choruses can be clocked at about 120 and 130 bpm, respectively. Crosby's version remains in strict time throughout and moves at an appreciably faster bpm of 190. The Crosby disc is for dancing: it was one of many in that first year of the tune's popularity. From the start, "Ol' Man River"—conceived as a ballad—was also treated as a rhythm tune. (Popular songs can generally be sorted into two broad categories: ballads and rhythm tunes. Depending on performers' choices, "Ol' Man River" fits in either category.)

"Ol' Man River's" long history as a rhythm tune reveals much about the musical possibilities latent in Kern's melody. As a result, this chapter deals mostly with musical issues—what musicians did with and to "Ol' Man River," how they changed the tune, the harmony, and even the form. But—it should be no surprise—Hammerstein's lyric and the song's origins in *Show Boat* have a way of forcing their way into the story.

The Whiteman-Crosby version has all the stiffness of Twenties dance music, reminding the listener that "Ol' Man River" hails from the Jazz Age. The A phrases, in particular, have a snap that cries out for some jerky Charleston-esque dance moves (⊕ Sound Example 3.1). The narrative of *Show Boat* ends in the 1920s and most stage productions conclude with a stageful of flappers doing the Charleston—*never*, however, to the strains of an up-tempo "Ol' Man River," which remains sacrosanct in *Show Boat*. Whiteman's record puts the listener close to the historical moment when "Ol' Man River" entered popular culture, when a disc of an attractive new tune at a danceable tempo with a jazzy vocal made for a good party record. Jack Hylton and His Orchestra's version—also 1928 but hailing from London where Hylton was a popular favorite—runs just a hair behind White-man's at about 186 bpm. Hylton's first chorus supports the tune with the rhythm section playing four, even, heavy beats to the bar, a sign to listeners of the time that "Ol' Man River," in this guise, could be counted among blues songs (⊕ Sound Example 3.2). But Hylton's arrangement changes style a bit too much to be a solid dance record. With a more consistently danceable beat, Kenn Sisson and His Orchestra play in an unbuttoned, loose, "hot" style on their 1928 recording, again at that same tempo—right around 190 bpm (⊕ Sound Example 3.3). On all three of these discs, "Ol' Man River" is aligned to the current dance beat with little real concern for the song's origins in *Show Boat*. (Not all 1920s dance discs of "River" went quite this fast. Rare versions preserved in the Library of Congress clock in at 170 [Willard Robison and His Orchestra], 160 [Don Vorhees and His Orchestra], and 146 [Buddy Blue and His Texans].)

The Whiteman-Crosby version also serves as a point of origin for "Ol' Man River" as a jazz jam tune. The legendary cornetist Bix Beiderbecke recorded the song two or maybe three times in 1928. He's definitely on the Crosby version but the cornet solo on the recording by Lou Raderman and His Orchestra remains in dispute: the bandleader claimed Bix was there. In July, Beiderbecke recorded "Ol' Man River" yet again, this time in a small group setting *sans* arrangement. Jazz players all knew the tune by then: Bill Rank on trombone even solos on the verse. In his 1931 obituary for Beiderbecke, French jazz critic Hughes Panassié invoked this small-group "Ol' Man River" as an example of Beiderbecke's skill at leading others in hot improvisatory contexts. Whenever he plays the bridge, Beiderbecke generally sticks to Kern's notes, changing up their rhythmic placement rather than obscuring the tune with melodic invention (⊕ Sound Example 3.4). As Beiderbecke's versions from 1928 suggest, in its first year of life "Ol' Man

River" found a sure and varied place in jazz as a rhythm tune suitable for hot improvisation, a position it would maintain for four decades.

Bing Crosby had been with Whiteman just over a year when he recorded "Ol' Man River." He would record the song four times in the studio and perform it often, including during a medley of signature tunes at one of his last concerts in 1976. With the exception of a brief, mid-Forties foray into "Ol' Man River" as a serious ballad—the approach some listeners might expect from a singer famous for his silky baritone—Crosby stuck with his

Bing Crosby photographed for maximum effect around the time he first recorded "Ol' Man River." (Photofest)

initial rhythm tune approach from 1928 to the end of his life. From his first crack at the tune, Crosby knew how he wanted to change "Ol' Man River."

Every time Crosby sang "Ol' Man River" at a fast tempo he rewrote the melody of the bridge the same way, adding a blue note on the word "land" (⊚ Sound Example 3.5). This touch—which no singer stole, except for Rosemary Clooney (and her goal was to copy Crosby)—demonstrates how small musical changes can shape the overall tone of the song. Crosby's blue-note bridge injects a bit of hipness at exactly the spot where "Ol' Man River" gets serious about inequality. Crosby, of course, had no interest in being serious, no desire to use "Ol' Man River" to make any larger point. It was, for him, a song to sing fast and light and jazzy.

In the late 1920s, Crosby was on the cusp of changing how most all popular singers sang: the 1928 recordings of "Ol' Man River" show how far ahead he was. As Crosby biographer Gary Giddins notes, the singer's "Ol' Man River" "created a stir among musicians and fans, expanding Whiteman's following among young listeners. Cultural historian James T. Maher, in high school at the time, believed Bing's version spoke specifically to his generation."[1] The other singers who recorded "Ol' Man River" in 1928 have difficulty matching Crosby: they might sing it fast and light but jazzy proves tough. For example, the singer on Lou Raderman's recording speak-sings much of the time and finds no attractive ways to reshape the tune for the fast tempo (as Crosby does at several points along the way). Almost every 1928 band singer *except* for Crosby drops the octave at the highest notes that end the melody. Recall that even Robeson did this on his 1928 disc with Whiteman. Crosby doesn't drop the octave, nor does he try to sing the song's climactic phrase in full voice. Instead, he backs off vocally, lightens his delivery, and tosses off the end, subordinating the peak of the melody to the overall easy touch he takes with the whole song. Bill Challis, the first of many prominent jazz arrangers to take on "Ol' Man River," supposedly encouraged Crosby to sing the tune as written.[2] Crosby remembered, "I just barely made it and I think I busted my shoelaces or something trying to hit those high notes."[3] The Crosby-Whiteman disc outsold all others in 1928 and Crosby's approach to the vocal proved its effectiveness to the end of the twentieth century. Crosby solved the challenge of up-tempo "Ol' Man River" right out of the gate.

Some up-tempo vocals from 1928 tackle the verse: a part of the song Crosby never touched. Several recorded rhythm versions from that first year use the n-word: among them the white vocal harmony group, the Revelers; the black voice and piano duo, Layton and Johnstone; and the unknown quartet featured by Columbia Records on a disc that put the blackface performer Aunt Jemima—Queenie in *Show Boat* at the time—singing "Can't

Help Lovin' Dat Man" on the B side. But other early versions taking the rhythm tune approach changed that first word: white singer Willard Robison begins "Darkies all work on the Mississippi"; black singer and bandleader Noble Sissle sang "colored folks work."[4] These two contemporary recordings demonstrate that "colored folks" didn't follow "darkies" as a less offensive, second-round replacement for "niggers." Black singers like Sissle arrived in 1928 at the revision of the verse's first word that Hammerstein only endorsed as standard in 1946. (As late as 1938 the n-word was occasionally heard in nationwide radio broadcasts of "Ol' Man River," as evidenced by a black newspaper critic's strong objections to a performance by an unnamed white singer on the Lucky Strike *Hit Parade* radio show.[5] The resilience of "Ol' Man River"—still charting ten years after its debut—is worth noting.)

Arriving on the scene when the jerky Jazz Age was just about over, to survive as a rhythm tune suitable for dancing, Kern's melody had to quickly demonstrate its capacity to work under a new prevailing popular music beat called swing. With a successful transition to swing in the early 1930s, "Ol' Man River" began a series of transformations that would continue for four decades as each new generation of jazz and pop musicians sought to get their listeners to dance or tap their feet to the strains of a pseudo-spiritual, anthem-like show tune tricked out as a rhythm number. The consistent popularity of the song in its first decade practically speaking required it be usable as a dance tune. Indeed, in 1933 "Ol' Man River" topped the list of the ten most popular songs of the previous decade, as voted by 370 American orchestra (or dance band) leaders and musical authorities.[6] Some of this popularity sprang from *Show Boat*'s consistent presence on stage and also from serious singers treating the song seriously but there was nothing like the dance bands to keep a tune in the public ear.

Swing—played by bands made up of brass, reed, and rhythm sections—rolled onto the popular music scene with energy and style as the Great Depression took firm hold on the US economy. Innovations in popular dance, such as the lindy hop—known among white dancers as the jitterbug—responded to and egged on the relaxed but driving swing beat. Playing for dancers opened ample space for improvising soloists to show their inventiveness, allowing "Ol' Man River" to retain its dual identity as a danceable song and a jazz jam tune. By the mid 1930s, swing dominated popular music, social dancing, and youth culture, holding the field without real challenge to the end of World War II. "Ol' Man River" thrived in the age of swing, appearing in just about every major band's book. Richard Crawford and Jeffrey Magee's survey of the core repertory of jazz standards includes "Ol' Man River" among the most-recorded tunes on jazz records—functionally speaking, jazz usually meant dance on records—made between 1900 and 1942: a notable achievement for a song introduced in the late 1920s.[7] The three swing recordings described next map out the musical possibilities latent in the tune as discovered by swing players and arrangers. These sophisticated popular musicians uncovered new aspects of Kern's soaring melody.

Fletcher Henderson's band—under the direction of Henderson's brother Horace—recorded a swing "River" in 1933. Henderson, a black bandleader and arranger, was one of the architects of Thirties swing in his capacity as arranger for the white bandleader Benny Goodman. (Goodman's band played but never recorded "Ol' Man River.") By bumping up the tempo to about 240 bpm—some fifty points beyond the 1928 norm—Henderson had time to get through the song's chorus five times in a three-minute re-cording. The fourth pass features saxophone great Coleman Hawkins impro-vising on the A phrases, with the bridge given over to the trumpet section in a syncopated style. The strong contrast between Kern's A and B phrases was often emphasized on jazz instrumentals in this manner (⊙ Sound Example 3.6). (Hawkins would record a different solo take on "Ol' Man River" in 1944.) The bridge on Henderson's out chorus quotes "St. James Infirmary," a well-known, low-down tune with a lyric set in New Orleans. Arranger Hen-derson might have been thinking of the Mississippi as a connecting link between the songs. Cut away from *Show Boat* and the concert spiritual, "Ol' Man River" would frequently find a spot among "Southern" songs, especially for jazz musicians.

Luis Russell and His Orchestra, a black dance band, found a new rhyth-mic matrix for the tune in the mid-1930s.[8] Russell's version turned into a signature number for his band, which was billed for a time as the "Ol' Man River Orchestra." Audiences at Harlem's Apollo Theater surely heard the song there in 1934 and the venue would host many varied versions of "Ol' Man River" into the 1960s. On his 1934 recording, Russell lowers the bpm of the melody to the 160s but double-times the rhythm section, turning "Ol' Man River" into a genuine flagwaver, the fastest category of swing for dancers and improvisers (⊙ Sound Example 3.7). Many later versions in all sorts of styles would follow suit, creating the illusion of a fast tempo while giving the singer a bit more space to put over the lyric.

The Casa Loma Orchestra, a white band, also used the double-time ac-companiment approach in 1934. Their version, at about 144 bpm, opens with a staccato statement of the tune by the reeds which, in its faithfulness to Kern, reveals a perhaps surprising riff-based melody. (A riff is a concise musical idea repeated again and again in swing arrangements, often marked by a distinctive rhythm.) Every measure of Kern's three distinct A phrases uses the same rhythmic profile (except, of course, for the long, held notes on the second syllable of "along"). Casa Loma's arranger exploits this aspect of the tune to show off the band's ability to play in perfect synchronization. Using a clipped sound throughout, the Casa Loma "River" is lean and tight (⊚ Sound Example 3.8).

As I showed in my book on *Show Boat*, Kern culled the basic rhythm heard throughout the A phrases of "Ol' Man River" from a song called "De Old Clay Road," introduced on the Broadway stage by Jules Bledsoe in late 1926 in the show *Deep River*.[9] Kern and Hammerstein both saw *Deep River* and were just starting to write *Show Boat* at the time. Kern improved tremendously on "De Old Clay Road," transforming a kernel of composer Laurence Stallings's disorganized song into a tightly constructed masterpiece of melodic flow. At a slow tempo, Kern's tune ebbs and flows only to overflow in its final phrase, an aspect of the melody that vocalists have milked and audiences have relished. But the patterned rhythmic organization of the melody also contains riches for musicians less in love with long lines and more concerned with rhythmic drive. Passed along to a dance band arranger in the 1930s, this rhythmic idea became a riff ready for swing treatment. The Casa Loma recording draws out the rhythmic pattern underlying the tune and, in effect, transforms how "Ol' Man River" can be heard. It is, in fact, Jerome Kern's finest rhythm tune.

A generation older than more self-consciously jazzy songwriters like George Gershwin, Kern resisted dance band versions of his songs. Indeed, Kern hated dance arrangements so much that in 1924 he refused to release the songs from his show *Sitting Pretty* to be recorded by anyone. Predictably, the songs from *Sitting Pretty* never generated much in sheet music sales and were forgotten. Dance band discs were too important to song promotion. Composers effectively had to let arrangers and players have their way. Thankfully Kern learned this lesson *before Show Boat*.

The up-tempo swing approach to "Ol' Man River" ended up impacting vocalists, who now had to deliver the tune at a very fast clip. In facing this challenge, singers effectively rewrote Kern's melody, often doing so above a simplified version of Kern's harmonies or chord changes (or, in jazz parlance, changes). Henry "Red" Allen's vocal on the Henderson disc is in the Crosby mode: understated but jazzy. The tempo's so fast it's tough to do more than chant the lyric: indeed, Allen flattens out most of the melody to a single pitch and finds a different, less-blue note for the word "land" in the bridge (⊚ Sound Example 3.9). Luis Russell's singer Sonny Woods also alters the contours of the melody, similarly smoothing out Kern's long lines. This approach allows Woods to sing with a kind of wild and crazy flair. On the bridge, Woods hits the word "wracked" with a wailing, high blue note that's hard to take all that seriously, an early hint that some singers saw a fast "Ol'

Man River" as a chance to send up the song's stoic pose (⊙ Sound Example 3.10). The up-tempo, wild vocal approach would have a long life. Singing bandleader Cab Calloway would give a slightly crazy performance of the song in the 1960s on an episode of *The Ed Sullivan Show* featuring the Beatles (see Chapter 9). Other singing bandleaders of the 1930s, such as Putney Dandridge and Nat Gonnella, also ironed out the tune. It must have seemed a practical approach with the bpm so high.

Facilitating, at times necessitating, the choice to flatten out Kern's vocal line was the decision made by some arrangers to use the same chords for each of the song's three A phrases. This alteration to Kern's changes reduced the harmonic variety of the original and made it impossible to sing the tune as written. This strategy of making all three A phrases identical draws on Duke Ellington's 1930 "Old Man Blues." Ellington did not include a vocal and, beyond the suggestive title, the origin of the composition in Kern's "Ol' Man River" is only evident on the bridge, which quotes Kern's melody (which, in turn, quotes the spiritual "Goin' Home"). Apart from the tell-tale title, "Ol' Man Blues" carries a very Ellingtonian element of plausible deniability. Fletcher Henderson's "Wild Party" from 1934 similarly repurposed a simplified set of "Ol' Man River" changes, although without making reference to the tune. Trumpeter Dizzy Gillespie also used the simplified changes for his "Ol' Man Rebop," recorded in 1946 at one of the sessions that came to define bebop, a jazz style centered on virtuoso soloing and not intended for dancing. Gillespie probably wouldn't have reached for "Ol' Man River" in this way had it not been an up-tempo swing standard for the previous almost twenty years. Gillespie, Henderson, and Ellington each simplify the harmonic content of Kern's song by using the same chords for all three A phrases. None include a vocal on the chorus; none take up the challenge of the song's verse (as so many jazz players did). As such, these three versions nod toward "Ol' Man River" without truly taking it on.

The flag-waving swing "River" crested in 1941 with a version led by trumpeter Henry "Red" Allen—who, as noted, sings and plays on the Henderson version from eight years earlier. Allen's very hot "River" uses a boogie-woogie bass at a blistering 240 bpm. This disc earned a scathing review in *Billboard*, worth quoting at length.[10]

> Out-and-out sacrilege is committed on the first side of this disk [*sic*], the sort of
> musical mayhem that make violent mental cases of listeners who consider jazz
> one of the lower forms of life even in its milder ramifications. Classicists who
> figure that way are, of course, narrow-minded and prejudiced, for fine jazz can
> be just as much of an art form, if along far different lines, as symphonic music,
> but they do have a case when all-out distortion of one of America's great light

classics is committed such as here. Of all the songs in the book, why a musician like Allen (known to a handful of jazz followers, but unknown to the great mass of the public) elects to massacre a well-loved favorite like the Jerome Kern *Show Boat* standard is not only a mystery but a disgrace. Fast, hot, noisy, tuneless, offering only some out-of-the-world instrumental work—plus an unfortunate attempt by Allen to sing the lyric in a blatant, grating scat style—this is not merely bad but aggravating listening.

Absolutely nothing is offered to music machine operators or their patrons here.

As this reviewer's outsized response signals, some listeners couldn't handle "Ol' Man River" being treated this way; Kern almost certainly shared this view (and, of course, collected his royalties). But whatever such aggrieved listeners might have thought, Allen and others like him did offer something to the popular music marketplace and the listening and dancing public: nothing short of the reinvention of "one of America's great light classics" as a very fast swing tune.

But not all fast versions were manic attempts to whip up the crowd. A tradition of relaxed soloing to a driving beat also emerged, attracting all sorts of improvisers, from Les Paul (1940, electric guitar) to Chet Atkins (1954, guitar, with a country fiddle chorus by Dale Potter) to Art Van Damme (1954, accordion, with vibraphone solos by Charlie Calzaretta) to Henry Cuesta (clarinet virtuoso on *The Lawrence Welk Show* in the 1970s). On Les Paul's version, singer Jimmy Atkins "puts his heart into his voice"— says the radio announcer—for a vocal chorus. On Paul's solo chorus—he quotes "Sailing, sailing over the bounding main" while improvising on Kern's chords—the men of the Fred Waring chorus "ooh" their way through the tune behind him. This layered recording juxtaposes Paul's jazzy solo with the rhythmically square singing of Waring's all-white group (⊙ Sound Example 3.11). Ray Charles explores just this approach in his "Ol' Man River" of 1963, a stunning transformation of the song treated in the final chapter.

The proliferation of fast to very fast versions of "Ol' Man River" begs the question of what—if anything—remained of Hammerstein's complex lyrics. As noted, Whiteman's arrangement with Robeson quoted the faux spiritual "Goin' Home," and Henderson's linked "Ol' Man River" to New Orleans. Both Hylton and Sisson's versions quote Stephen Foster's "Old Folks at Home," the latter in a slightly creepy minor mode. All these references reinforce "Ol' Man River" as connected to popular music evocations of the American South. A more explicit linking to such songs comes in the Mills Blue Rhythm Band's 1937 medley "Camp Meeting Jamboree." Here, vocal choruses of "Old Folks at Home" and "Ol' Man River" segue smoothly one into the other—with yet another blue note for the word *land* in the bridge; they don't steal Crosby's (⏵ Sound Example 3.12). With the third song in the medley, "Raise a Ruckus Tonight," things start getting rowdy: the cry "let's smoke some tea," or marijuana, suggests this camp meeting's on the secular side. Indeed, the whole of "Camp Meeting Jamboree" sounds like a spoof, albeit performed by some seriously good players. The potential for a fast "Ol' Man River" to cross the line into satire of the Hammerstein-Kern original would be realized in a more concentrated manner in a 1938 recording by Cootie Williams and His Rug Cutters, which features a sub-stantive rewrite of the lyrics, including some "tea" smoking, and is consid-ered at length in Chapter 4.

Popular songs invoking "Ol' Man River" also provide clues to what, if anything, the song meant in its up-tempo jazz and pop music contexts be-fore World War II. Most of these miss the subtleties of Hammerstein's lyric entirely, suggesting that songwriters were responding to "Ol' Man River" in its popular music guise as a rhythm number rather than the song's original context in *Show Boat*. The 1930 tune "Where That Ol' Man River Flows" calls the South "a paradise," with the singer "ailing" from being away from home. The 1935 tune "The Voice of Old Man River" has the river "calling" the singer "home." The lyric goes on to imagine a South where banjo playing is the main occupation: "They just laugh and sing, and play and play / To make the time fly by. / And the song they sing is nothing but rhythm." Both these tunes tap into the most stereotypical depictions of happy blacks in the South: mention of watermelon or chicken eating lies just over the ho-rizon. Both songs miss Hammerstein's juxtaposition of black labor and white power. These unreflective takes on "Ol' Man River" suggest that the fast tempo approach has the power to undo the lyrics so completely that Hammerstein's critique of the happy cabin in the cotton tradition in pop-ular music is, to quote Hammerstein's lyric, "soon forgotten."

"Ol' Man River" was also treated to virtuoso arranging and often entered the books of especially virtuoso bands. Saxophone player and bandleader Benny Carter arranged a hot swing version for his band, captured on two radio hookups: in 1942 the band played at 176 bpm; in 1944, the heat was turned up as high as 200 bpm. At the close, Carter slips into half time, giv-ing this very fast "River" an expansive finish. One reviewer noted a "Harlem-ese groove, with plenty of zing" in the arrangement when played on a nightclub stand in Philadelphia.[11] Another commented that "Ol' Man River," placed as Carter's finale, was "grooved for attention."[12]

Taking a more symphonic approach, Stan Kenton's 1944 recording treat-ed the tune to a subtle arrangement running in the 160s bpm. Kenton's arranger Joe Rizzo plays around with the order of the chorus's four distinct phrases, mixes in motifs from the verse, and even contrapuntally combines the melodies of the A and B phrases (◉ Sound Example 3.13). At one unexpected moment the key of the song modulates up a step without warning in midphrase, keeping the listener on edge, frustrating any easy humming along. (Modulation involves changing the key or tonal center, of an arrangement in a noticeable manner, usually upward by a step as a means to build energy near the close.) Kenton delivers a characteristically slick confection, intended for close listening, that plays with the building blocks of Kern's song in compelling ways.

The abrupt modulating approach also shows up in more informal small combo settings. Django Reinhardt and his Quintet of the Hot Club of France's 1947 version, with a bpm in the 160s, features some slippery upward modulations midphrase in the first two A phrases, something the players must have agreed on in advance (◉ Sound Example 3.14). Stephane Grappelli, violinist with the Hot Club, kept the shift alive into the 1980s and 1990s. On these later versions, Grappelli precedes the fast chorus with a slow tempo chorus, and sometimes even a bluesy pass through the verse, suggesting an engagement with Hammerstein's lyrics. On a 1982 release, British guitarist Martin Taylor plays a snatch of the Confederate battle song "Dixie" before Grappelli leads the duo into a slow pass through verse and chorus of "Ol' Man River," followed by the modulating, up-tempo version (◉ Sound Example 3.15). (This was not the first time "Dixie" and "Ol' Man River" had been juxtaposed on records. Chapter 8 considers an American dance band—Lester Lanin and His Orchestra in a 1957 recording—who similarly led from one song to the other [◉ Sound Example 8.1]. Sharp contrasts of musical style and context, date of recording, and the national origins of the performers demands that these pairings of the same two tunes be heard differently.) On their 2010 disc *1910*, celebrating the centenary of Reinhardt's birth, the French guitar group Les Doigts de l'Homme included "Ol' Man River" with the slippery modulations in place as part of the tune's gypsy jazz inheritance.

(The practice of abruptly changing key in the middle of "Ol' Man River" dates back to 1928, when Victor Arden modulated between phrases on a performance captured on a piano roll [◉ Sound Example 3.16].)

As jazz diversified in the postwar decades, fast-flowing versions of "Ol' Man River" showed up in new settings. Kern and Hammerstein's ubiquitous song was played at a 1949 Jazz at the Philharmonic Concert in Carnegie Hall, where Robeson had sung it in 1931 and would sing it again in 1958. The mood in the hall for Jazz at the Philharmonic (often abbreviated JATP) was appreciably different from either of Robeson's concerts and

"Ol' Man River" was turned to markedly different ends by Hank Jones on piano, Buddy Rich on drums, and Ray Brown on bass. This interracial trio played "Ol' Man River" as a rhythm section feature during a concert with an all-star lineup: Ella Fitzgerald, Charlie Parker, Coleman Hawkins, and, as a surprise guest, a young Canadian pianist named Oscar Peterson, who was pulled out of the audience for his New York debut by producer and emcee Norman Granz. (Peterson would record a virtuoso "River" ten years later.) The trio's "Ol' Man River" begins with bassist Brown soloing on the tune, plucking Kern's melody very softly and filling the breaks himself. The identification of the tune with instruments in the bass register proves an enduring aspect of the song's place in jazz and instrumental music more generally. Brown's hushed playing effectively draws the audience into the reduced scale of the trio after the noisiness of the preceding group numbers. Next, Jones takes two, also mostly *sotto voce* solo choruses at the piano. Jones's second chorus features big, loud fills from Rich, one of which gets a big laugh from the crowd. At one point, Jones plays a snatch of Gershwin's "I Got Rhythm" (⊕ Sound Example 3.17). The final A phrase returns the tune to Brown, still playing very quietly. He ends the number all alone with a coda that quotes Kern's bridge melody. "Ol' Man River" well serves the celebratory, positive energy of the JATP concerts, with none of the players taking it too seriously. It's either a refusal to lend any credence to the song's noble suffering or, perhaps for these players and this crowd, just another jazz tune, the lyrics or original meanings of which doesn't matter much at all. Still, ending "Ol' Man River" on a drawn-out pianissimo is, in its way, subversive. There's no exultant shout at the end, no angst-ridden cry: Kern's notes serve Brown's purposes and Hammerstein's contribution seems completely elided.

Not all up-tempo instrumental versions disengage from the lyric. Legendary stride pianist Willie "The Lion" Smith played "Ol' Man River" live in Zurich in 1949 in response to an audience request. Smith turns in a rather serious version, beginning with the verse. His pianism is grand, full voiced, rhetorically nuanced, and rhythmically free. His playing tracks the unheard lyrics, a not uncommon practice among jazz musicians. For example, the bridge gets dissonant harmonies that respond to the content of Hammerstein's words (⊕ Sound Example 3.18). But after a half chorus, still in the slow tempo, Smith launches into a full-out stride version, fast and loud—as stride almost invariably was—and with virtuosity to spare. The tempo breaks on the final phrase, returning to the opening rhetorical style, here almost hymn-like, with a deceptive cadence drawing out the tune at the close. Smith thinks through the tune, even as he enjoys the pleasures of playing it fast. This approach marks many postwar up-tempo solo and small group jazz versions.

So-called Dixieland or trad jazz players also picked up "Ol' Man River." The defining, much-copied version is Eddie Condon's, best heard on his 1955 LP *Bixieland*, a tribute disc to the memory of Bix Beiderbecke. The track begins with a slow, melodic first chorus, a cornet solo by Wild Bill Davison that treats the tune as a sort of deliberate march. On the bridge, Davison hits a high blue note on "land" in jail—a melodic touch squarely in the Twenties tradition, another variant of the Crosby bridge. With a lick from the drums initiating the second chorus, the tempo picks up as a kind of second line response develops, bringing in clarinet Edmond Hall and trombone Cutty Cutshall (◉ Sound Example 3.19). The out chorus—first half piano solo by Gene Schroeder—ends with a stretch of collective improvisation in the full-on Dixieland style. Condon's two-tempo version suggests the musical progression of a New Orleans funeral procession: a slow march escorts the coffin to the cemetery; an up-tempo burst of exuberance leads the mourners back to town. Condon's slow-then-fast "Ol' Man River" is satisfying on several levels: the song's connection to the South and the actual Mississippi is made by way of jazz history (Dixieland in the postwar imagination is linked to jazz as played on riverboats); the seriousness of the original gets at least some acknowledgment (perhaps weakening the resistance of listeners who don't like the up-tempo approach); and the decision to treat "Ol' Man River" as a fast jazz jam feels motivated (in a way swing treatments generally don't). Copycat versions of Condon's approach continued for decades (see recordings by the Fairweather-Brown All Stars, the Dukes of Dixieland, and Al Hirt).

The format of an expressive, slow first part followed by an exuberant, fast second part might seem a perfect match for Louis Armstrong, who was widely active during these years, often played in a Dixieland style, and was, of course, for many the living embodiment of New Orleans. Armstrong, like all jazz players, knew "Ol' Man River" and he even complimented Kern in his 1936 book *Swing that Music*: "That big river has always made me a little sad and I think that is so with all the people who have lived down near the delta. Mr. Jerome Kern sure knew what he was doing when he wrote 'Ol' Man River,' for Miss Ferber's *Show Boat*. He must have been down there."[13] (Neither Kern, Hammerstein, nor Ferber had been.) Armstrong uses "Ol' Man River" as part of his description of the Mississippi itself, how the river's flow slows "like a dying old man" once it hits the delta. The connection is geographical rather than historical or cultural: the song, for him, is Kern's melody.

Armstrong never recorded "Ol' Man River" (unlike his New Orleans peer clarinettist Sidney Bechet, who recorded several versions in several styles). The only documented period when Armstrong performed the song was a 1959 European tour, where "Ol' Man River" served as a feature for bassist Mort Herbert. Armstrong and his group of All Stars performed "Ol' Man River" once when stateside that year, during a concert at an air force base in Biloxi, Mississippi. Perhaps, again, it was the Mississippi connection. At a performance in Scandinavia captured on tape, Armstrong sings the chorus and participates in a Dixieland group chorus. He leaves the text unchanged except in two places: on the second A phrase the river "just keeps oozing along" and, at the close of the chorus, Armstrong declares he will "soon be dying"—in place of "scared of dying." Armstrong paid attention to Hammerstein's words: his changes are subtle, perhaps just meant to help him get through a tune that never generated much interest for him.

The history of "Ol' Man River" on records includes several episodes that might best be called musical oxbow lakes. An oxbow lake occurs when a stretch of a slow-moving river meanders down a valley in a snake-like course only to be cut off over time from the river's main channel. Left behind is a lake beside a flowing river, a remnant of the river's former path through the landscape. By (hopefully not too tortured) analogy, on occasion a rhythmically innovative approach to "Ol' Man River" has cut a new interpretive course for the song—captured in similar recordings—only to fall from favor and out of musicians' practice. Left behind is recorded evidence for a way with the song that, unlike several rhythm tune approaches discussed earlier (gypsy and Dixieland jazz), did not survive as part of nostalgic recreations of the song's past.

One "Ol' Man River" oxbow lake dating on records to the late 1950s and early 1960s features drum solo or percussion-centered treatments. These recordings seem to be echoing each other more than interpreting the song itself, suggesting that, for a certain period, drummers latched on to "Ol' Man River" as an appropriate vehicle for long soloing. Drummer Jo Jones recorded two solos in the late 1950s: one as part of Mae Barnes's vocal version and a second six-minute-plus track without a vocal. (Jones returned to the tune on his 1976 LP *The Main Man*.) On the Barnes version, Jones plays the stems (or marks the rhythm of the tune) on the bridge (◉ Sound Example 3.20). Singer Tony Bennett shared the spotlight on "Ol' Man River" with Cuban percussionist Candido Camero on several occasions during the late 1950s and early 1960s. Bennett delivers the tune in yet another variation of the one-note approach, then steps aside while Candido goes to town for a long, long time. As with Jones's recordings, Candido's solo uses Kern's tune as a frame. The arrangement uses Bennett to build energy going into the drum solo by way of the abrupt upward modulation trick applied repeatedly to the catchphrase "he just keeps rollin'" (◉ Sound Example 3.21). One reviewer described the Bennett/Candido combination as "flipping [the] audience."[14] (The point of origin for Ol' Man Drum Solo dates at least to the early 1940s. In 1943, Oscar Bradley, drummer with Benny Carter's band, used a "fast" "Ol' Man River" as a similar frame for a solo.[15] In 1949, Buddy Rich turned in a "show-stopping drum solo" to the tune on the stage of the Paramount Theater in New York's Times Square.[16])

Bennett's version also spends some time on a one-chord vamp, repeating "rolling along" over and over. This practice, on records at least, dates to the mid-1950s, and can be heard on a 1957 "Ol' Man River" by the Sparks, a group of amateurs who won a movie studio contest that quickly led to a contract with Decca Records. The youthful group's "River" was described by *Billboard*'s rhythm and blues (R&B) reviewer as "a honking, stylized instrumental version of the great Jerome Kern standard. Arrangement varies considerably from the usual pattern, but deejays will likely get a hoot out of the fine horns."[17] The Sparks' noisy, crudely recorded disc crosses Kern's melody with the twelve-bar blues (◉ Sound Example 3.22). In what might be heard as yet another attack on the sacred work of a great American songwriter, this version aptly illustrates why the jazz and pop crowd hated rock and roll: scant respect is paid to *Show Boat*'s most famous song. But why did the Sparks chose to mess around with this old show tune in the first place? They don't seem to be critiquing "Ol' Man River," just playing with it, breaking it open, exploring how it might be crossed with the current definition of the blues. The Sparks probably didn't know the song's history as a bluesy tune in the 1920s and were equally unlikely to know the complicated jazz history "Ol' Man River" had already lived through. Their "honking, stylized" R&B version points toward the future. Many, many more such remakes were to come. And whatever their background or intention, the Sparks *knew* "Ol' Man River" and believed it was a tune their audience might know and like as well. For a group of young musicians, described by *Variety* as "an instrumental-vocal quintet in the rock 'n' roll groove," "Ol' Man River" was—in 1957—still part of popular music and popular culture.[18]

A cluster of Latin versions offers another example of an interpretive oxbow lake in the history of the song, again emerging in the 1950s. The approach begins, on record at least, with a 1955 disc by the Tito Rodriguez Orchestra, a dance disc for the mambo craze. The song likely received Latin-style treatment earlier. As Latin jazz scholar John Storm Roberts notes, "The most thoroughly ignored of all Latin-jazz phenomena were the mostly African-American bands that played a mix of mambo, bebop, funk, and

Latin jazz for black dancers." Roberts highlights in particular a "multi-ethnic" band run by Hugo Dickens that had a number called "Old Man River Mambo" in their book: a favorite in Harlem clubs, such arrangements are a likely source for the string of recorded Latin versions that survived.[19] The Tito Rodriguez Orchestra floats the tune at an easy 117 bpm over a battery of Latin percussion giving the track a complex rhythmic groove. Kern's tune welcomes the treatment, especially the bridge which reveals its disjunct or leap-heavy contour when heard in piano octaves. For later listeners, Rodriguez's Ol' Man Mambo hints at what Ol' Man Salsa might have sounded like if the Latin approach had survived beyond the 1960s (◉ Sound Example 3.23). For a good stretch of the recording, the Rodriguez band settles on a one-chord groove—similar to what the Sparks did two years later. Later Latin "Rivers" explored the tune in familiar ways. On his 1966 version, drummer Willie Bobo, born to Puerto Rican parents in New York's Spanish Harlem, plays the stems very clearly at the start of his solo (◉ Sound Example 3.24). Saxophonist Jimmy Castor's 1968 recording does what Casa Loma did in 1934: treats the tune as a riff by phrasing in a manner that brings out its persistent pattern. Castor does this above a thick Latin texture. The effect is substantially the same (compare ◉ Sound Examples 3.25 and 3.8). The—for the time—obligatory bongo solo, arrives about halfway through Castor's track, yielding, as on Tito Rodriguez version from a decade earlier, to a one-chord groove.

These drum-centered and Latin rhythm oxbow lakes in the history of "Ol' Man River" get so far from the song's original context as to verge on the abstract. They are responding to each other more than to the song, its lyrics, or its origins in *Show Boat*. Yet, they are firmly part of the history of "Ol' Man River," remnants of past players and dancers who turned Hammerstein and Kern's song to their own expressive purposes during a period when the song seemed to be everywhere.

Post-bebop jazz players who still wanted to play tunes recorded "Ol' Man River" quite often. Several swing combos and pianists kept the rhythm tune approach alive in a context where their audience was listening rather than dancing. Many such players also dealt with the content of the song, manifest in the many versions which include the verse. Only Oscar Peterson plays the verse fast, spotting it at the opening and the closing of his 1959 recording (◉ Sound Example 3.26). Given Peterson's penchant for very fast tempi, it's not surprising that his, at 153 bpm, is the fastest of this group. Trumpeter Kenny Dorham and tenor saxophonist Gene Ammons both offer the verse done slowly before launching into up-tempo extended improvisations on the chorus. Dorham's version, on a 1960 disc of all *Show Boat* tunes, starts out with the verse in a stark arrangement for two: Dorham with Jimmy Heath on tenor sax (◉ Sound Example 3.27). Will Friedwald aptly describes Dorham's recording as "boppish and swinging with just a hint of defiance—a perfect 'River' for the start of the sixties."[20] Ammons, recording in 1961 for his LP *Jug*, lines out the verse in a quasi-gospel style before sliding into a sophisticated but still honking version of the chorus (◉ Sound Example 3.28). Ammons takes the chorus at 111 bpm—a bit below 120 bpm, a benchmark of sorts for the rhythm approach—but his rhythm section lays a solid groove beneath his solo, which puts this version in the Ol' Man Rhythm category. By contrast, tenor sax player Ike Quebec's 113-bpm version, on his 1962 LP *It Might as Well Be Spring*, sounds more turbulent: Quebec's rhythm section double times to urgent effect (◉ Sound Example 3.29). The diversity heard within these four jazz instrumentals released in a four-year period suggests that "Ol' Man River" was definitely in the air at the turn of the decade and that jazz players tried, in small ways, to interact with the song as a whole, dealing with verse and chorus and inflecting something of the lyrics' meaning. There was never only one way to play this tune. This standard has always been open to varied treatment.

Swing bands, surviving and even resurgent in the late 1950s and 1960s, continued playing "Ol' Man River" at a quick tempo and in virtuoso arrangements. Count Basie had a version arranged by swing veteran Jimmy Mundy in his band's book from at least 1958. An unreleased studio recording from 1958, a track on Basie's 1958 studio LP *Not Now I'll Tell You When*, and several live recordings and films all hover just shy of 190 bpm. Mundy's grand, Hollywood-style arrangement is a roaring showpiece featuring drummer Sonny Payne, making it part of the drum-centered oxbow lake. In a 1961 performance captured on film at the Juan-les-Pins jazz festival, the entire band exits the stage in the middle of the number, allowing all attention to settle on Payne. Basie's solo chorus at the piano comes at about the midpoint of the arrangement, introduced by a crashing, concerto-like cadenza—one sign this whole arrangement has tongue firmly in cheek. While soloing, Basie sticks to the melody in octaves, exploring Kern's tune in his own spare style, offering a study in how the riff-like pattern of "Ol' Man River" can be swung with maximum subtlety. This strategy of soloing on the tune by playing Kern's notes largely as written, altering only their rhythmic placement, dates back to Beiderbecke. Basie makes only one change to the tune on his studio recording: at the end of the bridge, he doesn't play "land in jail" and instead inserts a signature ornamented note. For a listener who's humming along, that phrase gets no support from Basie (◉ Sound Example 3.30). On several live versions, Basie also alters the end of the tune, substituting Kern's climax with a joking "shave and a haircut—two bits" finish that even garners some audience laughter. Basie's version takes the humorous approach of the JATP trio and blows it up to noisy big band proportions, toying with the tune in a virtuoso style that can be enjoyed on many levels at once.

Maynard Ferguson's big band take on "Ol' Man River," from the same years as Basie's, takes the song a bit more seriously. A slow introduction—fragments of the verse setting off lengthy, free-form cadenzas by the baritone sax—sets up the scope of this version, which is meant for attentive listening. The chorus is played in two tempos: moderately fast for the full band's harmonized pass (embroidered by a sax solo); then drivingly fast for a pair of virtuoso solo choruses (Ferguson on trumpet, Jimmy Ford on alto sax) which generally depart from the tune. It's easy to forget what song is being played (never the case on Basie's version, except during the drum solo). Halfway through the final chorus, it all slows down for a contemplative rendering of the bridge. The deliberate pace continues with a very high trumpet solo for Ferguson on the final A phrase, climaxing with a very, very long cadenza on the penultimate syllable of the song: the "a" of "along," a note many singers linger over but none improvise upon (◉ Sound Example 3.31). Much of Ferguson's version amplifies the inherent drama of the song: this instrumental shows how musicians and arrangers can expand the space of "Ol' Man River" in ways singers cannot. Of course, the indulgent cadenzas framing the arrangement suggest this "River" is primarily a vehicle for virtuosity. As both Basie and Ferguson's versions suggest, "Ol' Man River" was still fitting raw material for such a purpose at the start of the 1960s.

Not every big band version from these years strives for the size and scale of Basie and Ferguson. Soul jazz organist Jimmy Smith turned in two versions of "Ol' Man River" in 1962: a radio-ready single 45 and a longer track—with a slow introduction using the song's verse—on the LP *Bashin'*. Hearing "Ol' Man River" in this crowd-pleasing jazz idiom, with a cool swinging beat and the hot sounds of the Hammond B3 organ, just makes you want to snap your fingers or even dance. Perhaps only Smith's supremely confident version manages to make "Ol' Man River" sexy—but not without some complex touches, such as clashing, overlapping lines in the horns at the bridge, which build up energy released by a smearing burst of sound from Smith at the organ (◉ Sound Example 3.32). Smith's funky version is recalled by the retro jazz of the City Champs' 2009 recording, evidence that the memory of a cool but soulful "River" persists as a reference point for later musicians.

Veteran pianist Earl Hines's inclusion of "Ol' Man River" on his 1968 LP *Earl Hines Plays Evergreens* suggested a false future for the song. After this recording, "Ol' Man River" generally disappears from the jazz discography.

Relatively few jazz musicians recorded Kern's riff-heavy tune after 1970 and those who did generally took up retrospective styles and approaches. (Keith Jarrett's "Ol' Man River" offers one exception. Captured during a 2002 concert—available on the 2006 DVD *Tokyo Solo*—Jarrett takes a tender, intellectual, gently rhythmic approach to the tune. Here, a post-1970 jazz player does find something new to do with the old song.) As noted, "Ol' Man River" didn't make the 1975 publication of *The Real Book*, a compendium of essential songs for professional players. More recently, jazz historian and critic Ted Gioia left "Ol' Man River" out of his 2012 book *The Jazz Standards*, suggesting that contemporary fans of the music need know nothing about Hammerstein and Kern's once ubiquitous jazz song.

Besides disappearing from jazz—at about the time jazz of any sort disappeared from the popular music charts—the vitality of "Ol' Man River" in the creative world of popular music also exhausted itself around 1970. The tune's capacity to assimilate new dance beats or inspire new approaches was finally spent, leaving the listener to only imagine what Ol' Man Disco and Ol' Man Hip-Hop might have sounded like. (For an exception to this post-1970 decline, see Ol' Man Reggae in Chapter 5.)

Jazz and pop vocal groups explored "Ol' Man River" as a rhythm tune from early on. Recording in Berlin in 1929, the Comedian Harmonists took the song at 134 bpm and did not sing the lyrics, a strategy that opened the way for rhythmic exploration not permitted by Hammerstein's words. Like Casa Loma, the Comedian Harmonists reveal the riff hidden in Kern's tune, especially in their treatment of the bridge, which would sound awkward if they were singing the words: they put extreme dynamic swells on the words in capitals—"You and ME / we sweat and STRAIN / body all ACHin' / an' wracked with PAIN" (◉ Sound Example 3.33). The Revelers' equally rhythmic version from 1928 clocks in at 114 bpm. The Revelers sing the lyrics— as noted earlier including the n-word—with ambiguous, perhaps parodic, perhaps offensive results that highlight the dramatic elements in the song (see Chapter 10).

Mel Tormé and the Mel-Tones, with the Boyd Raeburn Orchestra, turned in a sort of hyper vocal jazz version in 1946, with very close harmony, soloing at extreme registers, and constantly shifting, nervous vocal accompaniment textures. While this recording features progressive approaches to arranging and singing, it also references a South song many black listeners wished would go away. On his solo, Tormé interpolates the lyric "when it's sleepy time in the southland," riffing on Louis Armstrong's theme song "When It's Sleepy Time Down South," which, controversially, included the phrase "darkies singing soft and low" (◉ Sound Example 3.34). (Armstrong's

1951 recording of "Sleepy Time" included "darkies" and was attacked in the black press.) The Mel-Tones' "River" is simultaneously hip in form and backward-looking in content, and the group seems perfectly comfortable with the song's racial content. By contrast, the Pied Pipers, a similar white vocal group, express ambivalence about the lyrics in their version for the pop market, also waxed in 1946. On the bridge they sing "You and me / We wrack our brain / Trying to think of a new refrain / Tote what barge? / Lift what bale?" (◉ Sound Example 3.35). Ensemble vocal versions often point toward the sociological aspects of the song—in *Show Boat*, it's about black laborers as a group. The Pied Pipers' revision might be heard to implicitly ask why a group of white men and women are even singing this song.

But the most spectacular vocal jazz version belongs to the Skylarks, a white group recording on the brand new Verve record label. Made up of three men and two women, the Skylarks had appeared on television with pop singer Dinah Shore. At their initial appearance in a Los Angeles nightclub in 1955, a reviewer described their "professional polish both as a visual and a vocal act."[21] The group's 1957 LP *Ridin' on the Moon* is a forgotten masterpiece of jazz arranging and singing. The Skylarks' "Ol' Man River"—included on the album and released as a single for radio play—puts the singers on the tune and a swing band conducted by Buddy Bregman in the breaks above a Latin-style beat (here's another entry in the Latin "River" oxbow lake). The result scores very high on the hipness scale. Kern's angular bridge gets some spectacular chromatic remaking (◉ Sound Example 3.36). An extended ending leads to a one-note vamp on the line "ol' man river keeps on rolling along." Like the Sparks, and recording in the same year, the Skylarks felt the moment was right to start dismantling the song's form, turning "Ol' Man River" into a kind of cubist assemblage of familiar elements made delightfully strange.

"Ol' Man River" attended at the birth of rhythm and blues. Just after World War II, with major changes in popular music clicking into place, vocal groups began treating the song in a new rhythmic spirit. Kicking off this performance tradition in 1947 was the proto-doo-wop group the Ravens, who recorded one of the most influential versions of "Ol' Man River" ever made. The Ravens recorded for New York City–based National Records, a somewhat atypical upstart label of the postwar period. (Small labels would be instrumental in the emergence of rock and roll.) After two years of manufacturing discs for major record labels, the owners of National decided in 1944 to turn their pressing plant toward making their own products under their own label.[22] National's only black vocal group, the Ravens were signed by artists and repertoire (A&R)-man Herb Abramson, who would shortly go on to found Atlantic Records, an R&B label that would be central to the shift in popular music to come.[23] One advantage National enjoyed over smaller labels was reliable national distribution, which no doubt helped the Ravens' "River" become a national hit. Their disc reached #10 on *Billboard*'s "Most-Played Juke Box Race Records" chart in February 1948.

With a bpm in the mid 130s, the Ravens recast the old chestnut in a rhythm and blues matrix, renewing "Ol' Man River" for the postwar popular music transformations to come and creating what *Billboard* called a "click disc."[24] When rock and roll arrived, "Ol' Man River"—courtesy of the Ravens—was ready. The easy, riff-based groove the Ravens laid under the tune would be directly copied by many singers and arrangers over the next fifteen years, making its own interpretive stream that drew in black and white performers and audiences. It scored with black audiences right off the bat, as the reviewer for the *Pittsburgh Courier* pointed out:

> Featuring the lowest and most exciting bass voice in show business today, together with the highest and sweetest falsetto-tenor on records, the rhythmic and mellow harmonies of the Ravens have the greatest range and the most compelling new sound to be heard on discs today. "Ol' Man River," the way the Ravens do it, is not just another "standard." In an unforgettable driving style, they streamline the "Ol' Man" til he, and everyone who is within earshot, starts "jumpin'."[25]

The Ravens' gently rocking "Ol' Man River" begins with a double hit high in the piano followed by a disinterested unison vocal riff from the group— "do-do-do-DO, do-do-do-DO." This groove—a call and response between piano and backup voices—acts as the setting for a solo chorus by Jimmy Ricks, the young singer described by the *Courier* as "the lowest and most exciting bass voice in show business today" (⊙ Sound Example 3.37). The Ravens were unusual among black vocal groups at the time for having a bass, rather than tenor, as the lead soloist. Ricks set the pattern for doo-wop's adaptation of the black bass voice, historically linked to singers like Robeson, into a postwar guise that points toward the future. (Seventies sexy soul bass Barry White never recorded "Ol' Man River" but hearing Ricks helps us imagine if he had.) This is R&B singing recorded at the moment when black music was being rebranded as R&B. (*Billboard* abandoned the term "race records" in favor of "rhythm and blues" just over a year after the Ravens' "Ol' Man River" charted.) The Ravens also had racial uplift in mind. "You and I," they sing, correcting Hammerstein's grammar in a clipped style and continuing on the bridge with zero emotional investment in the text (⊙ Sound Example 3.38). The Ravens' Ol' Man R&B, like many swing versions from the generation before, refuses to take "Ol' Man River"

The Ravens, debonair initiators of "Ol' Man River" as a rhythm and blues tune. (Photofest)

seriously as an expression of existential angst, whether understood as black or universal. The well-known song is just an excuse to tap your foot and hear a great bass voice.

A decade after the Ravens' disc came out, their riff still worked. Singer Earl Grant's 1957 version adapts the arrangement for sax, organ, and rhythm, the coolness of the original sliding easily into a soul jazz groove (◉ Sound Example 3.39). Pianist and singer Hadda Brooks turned the groove in a jazz direction one year earlier (and revived it on her 1994 CD *Anytime Anyplace Anywhere*, which, like several other examples noted above, preserved the memory of a good time "Ol' Man River" for listeners who like their pop music retro). The white vocal group the Smart Set freely adapted the Ravens' double-hit riff for a close harmony version in 1958 (◉ Sound Example 3.40).

The double-hit piano chords sound in the low brass in black singer Jesse Belvin's soulful version from 1959 (◉ Sound Example 3.41). And the Cues recorded a close cover of the Ravens with added strings in 1960, pushing the song even further toward a black pop sound and demonstrating the remarkable continuity of doo-wop singing from just after World War II all the way to the start of the 1960s (◉ Sound Example 3.42). All these variations on the Ravens measure yet again the distance "Ol' Man River" had cleared between the song and the show. These adaptations begin with the Ravens' record rather than the song as Hammerstein and Kern wrote it.

Not all postwar pop vocals poached the Ravens' riffs. Several 1950s pressings used backup singers offering easy grooves behind charismatic soloists. Ruth Brown's version (recorded in 1954 with the Drifters; released as a B side in 1956 credited to Ruth Brown and Her Rhythmakers) uses male backup vocals—"do do, DO do DO do"—and a relaxed rhythm section at a steady, danceable 142 bpm (◉ Sound Example 3.43). The Tune Weavers put a version of "Ol' Man River" on the flip side of their 1957 hit "Happy, Happy Birthday Baby." Their backup voices sing "chug chug, rollin' along" in the healthy 160s bpm while the female solo sings the tune at half that tempo, an old trick dating at least to the Russell and Casa Loma recordings from 1934 (◉ Sound Example 3.44). In 1958, on the verge of a major crossover breakthrough, gospel-turned-soul singer Sam Cooke followed the Tune Weavers approach with a bit faster beat. With a vamp built on the phrase "rolling along," Cooke took the song solidly into the realm of danceable pop (◉ Sound Example 3.45). An unreleased 1962 Motown single fronted by Hattie Littles also takes the half-time melody over black pop groove approach. A well-trained daughter of Motown, Littles sings "You and I / We sweat and strain" (◉ Sound Example 3.46). Cher's 1966 version puts a half-time vocal over a folk pop, Byrds-ish texture (◉ Sound Example 3.47). And, at the end of the decade, the Satisfactions ride a soulful groove, among the last Ol' Man Rhythms made for the pop market (◉ Sound Example 3.48). This version, with an almost militant snare-drum beat, served as the B side for the single "This Bitter Earth," which was marketed as a critical response to the Vietnam War.

While all of this rhythmic exploration of "Ol' Man River" was going on, Bing Crosby was still singing the song. His 1956 studio recording with the Buddy Cole Trio—in the easy mid-1920s bpm and paired with "In a Little Spanish Town"—was described by one professional listener this way: "These sides are by far the best things Crosby has done in the last year. Either side, or both, could make it all the way. Crosby seems to be enjoying himself more than usual."[26] Indeed, fun remains the keynote with Crosby and "Ol' Man River" to the very end of his career. He topped out tempo-wise at about 150 bpm during a concert at the London Palladium in 1976, where Crosby concluded a thirty-minute, thirty-three song medley of signature tunes with a full chorus of "Ol' Man River" (⊛ Sound Example 3.49). The audience, as *Variety* reported, was "predominantly middleaged to elderly."[27] The number had served as an effective act closer—"good for solid returns on his bowoff"—at the London Palladium two decades earlier as well.[28] This audience was accustomed to hearing an up-tempo "Ol' Man River," and with their—and Crosby's—inevitable passing, an approach to Hammerstein and Kern's song that was familiar fare for years was largely lost. For many twenty-first-century listeners, all of the Ol' Man Rhythms noted here might sound strange—like sounds hailing the ear from a different country, which, indeed and in so many ways, they are.

Only Rosemary Clooney, a close associate of Crosby's and on the bill with him at the London Palladium in 1976, hung on to the Crosby-style "River" in the decades after his death. Clooney recorded it fast (160 bpm) in 1994 and sang it live on television on *The Rosie O'Donnell Show* a bit quicker (162 bpm). Clooney always sings the Crosby bridge with that signature blue note on the word "land," yet another instance of an approach to the song being transferred from performer to performer by example (⊛ Sound Example 3.50). And at the very end of her career, Clooney sang "Ol' Man River" even faster (164 bpm) during her last live concert appearance in 2001 (captured on the disc *The Last Concert*). When the drummer lays down the beat, Clooney comments, "That's a hell of a tempo"; when it's all over she says, "That's so much fun to do."

Why is "Ol' Man River" done fast so much fun to do? For starters, up-tempo treatment brings out the inherent snap and drive of Kern's tune. Not known for writing syncopated songs, Kern's patterned, riff-like melody pops out at fast tempos, making "Ol' Man River" his most convincing dance song. Rhythm singers of "Ol' Man River" don't dwell on the words. There isn't time. The words must be tossed off and in that throwing away "Ol' Man River" becomes just another song. It's important to note that musicians and singers, black and white, have consistently enjoyed "Ol' Man River" at this level, bracketing out any deep meaning in the song and just having fun with a good tune. In the process, fast "Ol' Man Rivers" have revealed musical possibilities latent in Kern's tune when, in defiance of the composer's tastes, it's played for dancers. It's unlikely these aspects of "Ol' Man River" would have been discovered had musicians treated the song as some kind of sacred cow.

Some fast versions do, however, comment on the song—both by way of rewritten words and choices of musical style and expression. The target, most often, is the stoic black pose of noble suffering. The most pointed of these, versions that cross the line into satire, have been saved for subsequent chapters.

Given the persistent connections drawn between "Ol' Man River" and more sanguine (and stereotypical) representations of the "South" in popular music, up-tempo performances run the risk of reproducing the manic energy of minstrelsy. American performers have generally steered clear of this by updating the tune with contemporary dance rhythms. (Whiteman's 1928 version with Robeson, which treats the song's verse as a levee dance, is an anomaly.) But a version made for foreign consumption in 1974 goes all the way. Italian television star Raffaella Carrà inserted "Ol' Man River" into a full-out blackface minstrel dance number, complete with prop banjos (⊙ Sound Example 3.51; the televised version can usually be found on YouTube). Carrà's routine draws directly on the lavish Hollywood minstrel numbers found across the history of the studio-era film musical, a context where it's unlikely "Ol' Man River" would have been used (and where Hammerstein and Kern could have prevented its use). Carrà's production number hints at creative lines performers entertaining mass audiences in the U.S. did not cross. (Blackface was fading from the scene in the late 1920s but some blackface performers did try out "Ol' Man River" on vaudeville in the song's earliest years. Some "shuffled" their way through the song but most seem to have treated the song in a serious manner, as a chance to show off their vocal abilities.[29] For example, Al Jolson recorded "Ol' Man River" in a serious manner as considered in chapter 6. There's no evidence Jolson sang the song live while in blackface. Britain's Black and White Minstrels, a stage and television revue performed by men in blackface that ran into the late 1970s, did perform and record "Ol' Man River." Their approach is serious, generally in the Robeson vein—an unsurprising choice given how revered Robeson remained in Britain.)

A contrasting take on Ol' Man Rhythm, also from beyond US shores, brings this chapter to a close. Japanese singer Kasagi Shizuko, a pop singer known as "the Japanese queen of boogie" recorded a fast "Ol' Man River" in the early 1950s to the accompaniment of a big band.[30] Kasagi doesn't require a full Japanese translation of Hammerstein's text. For all the A phrases, she simply fits the English words of the title to Kern's riff-like melody. On paper, it goes something like this.

> Ol' Man River
> The Ol' Man River
> The Ol' Man River
> The Ol' Man River
> River.

Japanese lyrics are heard only once, on Kasagi's single pass through the bridge. Anticipating approaches that appeared in the United States some years later, a long stretch of Kasagi's version sits on a single chord. She sings or chants "Ol' Man River" in call-and-response fashion with the members of the band, who shout it back at her to the accompaniment of clapping (⊙ Sound Example 3.52).

In the immediate postwar years, Kasagi's American-style Japanese pop music expressed her and her listeners' full embrace of American culture and consumerism, often in songs about shopping. Her utterly unique "Ol' Man River" reinvents the song as a party record designed to get the audience clapping, dancing, and shouting along. The talismanic words "Ol' Man River" are repeated more than fifty times in under three minutes: in live performance, the interaction could have gone on much longer. For Kasagi and her Japanese audience, "Ol' Man River" *was* American music. Repeating the title phrase to a boogie beat was a musical act that declared a new historical moment in a Japan turning toward the United States, until recently its enemy. This reaction, far removed from any questions of content or meaning, constitutes a foreign dividend paid out to the astonishingly malleable "Ol' Man River" from its very ubiquity in American popular music.

4

cVo

Ol' Man Parody

A few lines of Hammerstein's lyric have been linked to literary sources. Critic Gary Giddins has noted a phrase from Augustine's *Confessions*—"thoroughly tired of living and extremely frightened of dying"—and, in a letter to his daughter, Hammerstein acknowledged a "similar" idea in a line from Alfred Lord Tennyson's poem "The Brook"—"Men may come, men may go / But I go on forever."[1] (Hammerstein was recalling the act two reprise of "Ol' Man River," sung by Joe, which includes the line "New things come an' old things go.") These connections point less toward Hammerstein's actual sources and more toward the rather generic philosophical notions of human existence that "Ol' Man River" taps into—one source of the song's seriousness in the context of both *Show Boat* and popular music.

But where did Hammerstein get the phrase "Ol' Man River"? One source might be the title of a short story by Edna Ferber. Her "Old Man Minick" was published in 1924 and adapted as a Broadway play the same year. The lyric's other signature phrase—"he jes' keeps rollin' along"—was perhaps suggested to Hammerstein by a familiar military song, dating to 1908, the chorus for which closes with the line "and the caissons keep rolling along."

Once "Ol' Man River" came on the scene, other songs picked up the title phrase, changing the noun as perhaps Hammerstein himself had done. Johnny Mercer penned the lyrics to "Old Man Rhythm," the title song for a 1935 Paramount Pictures college musical. Ethel Waters, among many others, recorded "Old Man Harlem" in the late 1930s, and the novelty song "Old Man Mose" also bounced around swing bands and band singers in those years.

"Ol' Man River" inspired more than a few full-blown parodies, with complete alternate lyrics for Kern's tune. Some stray far from the song's original intent but most take off from some element of Hammerstein's richly varied original. Four parodies—one from the 1940s, two from the 1950s, and a final example from the 2000s—open this chapter, illustrating how "Ol' Man River" was put to work in various contexts.

In the weeks after the Japanese attack on Pearl Harbor, with the US military struggling to defend its position in the Philippines, an amateur lyricist penned an "Ol' Man River" parody in tribute to General Douglas MacArthur, leader of the remaining US forces on Corregidor Island in Manila Bay. Setting the long version of the verse and the complete chorus, this parody is in deadly earnest. The *New York Times* printed the full text, assuming its readers knew both verse and chorus melodies. The verse begins,

> Fightin' out there in the Bataan jungle
> Fightin' out there in the green hell's heat
> Shootin' down Japs from the dawn till sunset
> Makin' 'em die if they don't retreat.[2]

The author doesn't call the general old but instead sets the opening phrases of Kern's chorus to MacArthur's name, suggesting an intimacy between the nation singing his praises and the tough old soldier fighting for them.

> Doug MacArthur,
> That's Doug MacArthur.
> A soldier's soldier
> He don't say nuthin'
> He just keeps fightin'
> He just keeps fightin' along.

The *Times* reported that MacArthur's men "heard the song rendered by the Deep River Boys, professional Negro quartet." Even in the midst of the Pacific War, the segregated armed forces of the United States could produce a group of professional black singers to serenade the general and his (white) fighting men in a song all would have recognized was at its best when sung by black voices. And "Ol' Man River" was exactly the right tune for the moment, with its artful simplicity, rising resolve, and, in the parodist's setting, defiant ending. Some fifteen years after its appearance, "Ol' Man River" was still a song everyone knew. Ironically, the day the "Doug MacArthur" parody was published President Franklin D. Roosevelt ordered MacArthur to withdraw from the Philippines. One wonders if the parodist would have revised Hammerstein's line "he don't say nuthin'" after MacArthur escaped to Australia and uttered the phrase "I shall return."

Hammerstein's lyric repeats the title phrase so many times it's practically an invitation to parody. Change "river" to something else and the song opens up to almost any topic. "Ol' Man Eisn'h'r" was penned by a Democratic US senator to taunt a Republican senator in the days before General Dwight Eisenhower signaled he would accept the Republican nomination for president. (The Democratic Party was also courting Eisenhower.) The parody adopts a full-out black dialect—just as Hammerstein did some twenty-five years earlier—and even replaces "Tote dat barge!" and "Lift dat bale!" with similarly framed quotations.[3] Again, an "Ol' Man River" parody assumes universal knowledge of the tune and a sense for how the song was typically performed.

Frank Sinatra sang a parody version in the early 1950s, just as he was emerging from a career slump. After offering his signature serious rendition of "Ol' Man River," Sinatra went into a verse that described the target of the parody.

> There's a guy owns quite a lot of horses
> Real estate, and the Pirates, too.
> He plays a lot of golf
> On a lot of courses.
> I love the guy
> And so do you.

For those in the audience unfamiliar with the business and recreational resumé just summarized, Sinatra decorates the final "you" with a musical embellishment that leaves no doubt as to who the "guy" is: a familiar turn tells anyone with ears it's Bing Crosby. On the audience's laugh of recognition, Sinatra jokes, "That's right—Frankie Laine." By mentioning Laine—a still new pop male vocalist—Sinatra sets up the joke, for this parody, titled "Ol' Man Crosby," centers on Crosby's staying power some twenty-five years after he first appeared on the scene. "Ol' Man River" provides an easy way to sing this joke in the first A phrase.

> Old Man Crosby
> That Old Man Crosby.
> He don't say nothin'
> But he must know somethin'
> Cause' he keeps on singing.
> He keeps on singing.
> He keeps on singing.
>
> [big pause]
>
> He keeps on singing along.

After this Sinatra whispers, "I wish he'd quit." Indeed, the song is as much about Sinatra and other "younger fellas" in the singing game as it is about Crosby, and Sinatra ruefully notes the joke of lumping himself in with "younger fellas." This parody, not all that funny—as even Sinatra notes in the introduction—builds on the "Ol' Man" in Hammerstein's lyric and, like most parodies, is a historical curiosity tied to a specific moment. It doesn't say much about Hammerstein and Kern's song—beyond, again, its universal familiarity.

And that familiarity didn't end after the key year of 1970. While hosting the 2003 Academy Awards, comedian Billy Crystal sang a full chorus of "Ol' Man River" to roast the Clint Eastwood-directed best picture nominee *Mystic River*. The title fits Kern's tune all too well: "Mys-tic Ri-ver." Turning the song into a chance to celebrate the film's director, Crystal descended into the audience and seated himself on Eastwood's lap for the bridge, which ends with the humorous request: "You sang in *Paint Your Wagon* / Please don't sing no more." The final A phrase demonstrates Crystal's sure knowledge of the original.

> We get weary
> And sick of tryin'
> Most men your age
> Are either dead or dyin'
> But not Clint Eastwood
> You just keep rollin' along.

Countless casual salutes to elder figures have used the phrase "jes' keeps rollin' along," as any online media search shows. With his generosity of spirit and direct address to the man being honored—intimate despite being telecast live to a global audience—Crystal puts "Ol' Man River" to terrific use, showing that even in the twenty-first century, the song still works a kind of magic.

These parodies leverage the public's familiarity with "Ol' Man River" in ways unrelated to Hammerstein's exploration of the thoughts and feelings of a black male laborer and Kern's expansion of musical idioms drawn from Negro spirituals. Such parodies do little more than mark the song's place in American culture, for only a very well-known song could bear such treatment. But some parodies do have a point. Singers and comedians have typically changed the lyrics with the intent to undermine "Ol' Man River" by taking apart the song's core assumptions, a markedly different strategy from rhythm versions that skate over the song's content or Robeson's revisions, which taken together make up a partial parody with serious intent that seeks to correct perceived faults in the lyric. Several parodies intent on undermining or disfiguring the original are discussed here. Versions that engage with the song in a satirical or deconstructive manner without changing the lyrics are also discussed in this chapter. Parodies and satires alike exploit the resources of performance style and performer persona to take down the song's stoic pose.

Perhaps the best-planned attack on "Ol' Man River" is Stan Freberg's "Elderly Man River." Freberg began his career doing comic voices for cartoons in the 1940s. In the 1950s, he began creating comedy records that sold very well and sometimes included pointed political satire. In 1957, Freberg briefly had a sketch-comedy show on CBS radio called *The Stan Freberg Show*. The show failed to win a sponsor and lasted only fifteen episodes. Recorded for radio with a live studio audience, "Elderly Man River" is a radio sketch, not a stand-alone musical performance. (It was included on a two-LP box set released in 1958.)

Across the 1950s, Freberg dismantled the pieties and absurdities of popular music with the weapon of exaggeration. For example, for a lush version of Cole Porter's "I've Got You under My Skin" Freberg paired an overheated, out-of-control singer who keeps forgetting the words with a saccharine mixed choir, typical of Fifties high-gloss pop, who repeat back the soloist's mistakes, never breaking their supremely rehearsed, super- or inhuman composure. The gag works because of Freberg's own production values—with crack musicianship and expert accompaniment, this is pop music of the highest quality taking pop music of the highest quality as its target. In a version of "Heartbreak Hotel," Freberg played Elvis Presley. By turning up the slapback echo applied to Elvis's voice to the point of distortion, Freberg made plain to the ear why the pop music establishment of 1956 thought rock and roll was an aesthetic mess made by, in Sinatra's words, "cretinous goons." But Freberg's pop music parodies don't destroy the originals. Instead, Freberg draws out the distinctive qualities of whatever style or song he's sending up, helping the listener hear the creative choices in the original in a new light. Freberg's "Elderly Man River" works this way, too, with some important elements left for listeners to contextualize in the larger realm of race that always surrounds the song.

"Elderly Man River" puts Freberg as a singer in conflict with a certain Mr. Tweedly (played by Freberg regular Daws Butler) from the "Citizen's Radio Committee." Censorship by ultra-proper community groups—perhaps such as those targeting rock and roll in the 1950s—is the apparent target of the entire exercise although Freberg positioned the joke differently in a 2003 interview, saying of the sketch, "I did this thirty years before anyone invented political correctness."[4] Tweedly presents himself as the guardian of the "tiny tots" in the listening audience and repeatedly interrupts Freberg's singing with his "little horn," a comically loud, sonically rude buzzer that punctuates the supremely well-paced timing of the sketch.

Tweedly attacks from the first line of the chorus, stating "the word *old* has a connotation some of the more elderly people find distasteful." He suggests "elderly" as an appropriate "substitution" and, with his sustained insistence on politeness, makes Freberg thank him for forcing the change. Tweedly's first target pokes fun at excessive political correctness a good four decades *avant le lettre*. But the joke works precisely because "Ol' Man River" had always been a song where controversies and substitutions of single words—such as the n-word—were not seen as excessive but rather as essential. Objecting to "old" raises this sensitivity to the highest level.

As the song proceeds, Tweedly turns his critique toward issues of grammar and usage. He objects to the missing final –g in the word "somethin'." Freberg protests: "That's authentic—somethin'—somethin'—that's the way the people talk." Tweedly insists and Freberg gives in. The issue of who "the people" embedded in the lyric are is never brought up. The Southern-ness or black-ness of Hammerstein's lyrical diction goes unmentioned. Tweedly corrects the double negative "don't say nothin'," opining that what Freberg really means is "doesn't say anything." Freberg accepts the change but his singing of "doesn't say anything" comes off as predictably prissy, the antithesis of the hipness inherent in black popular music slang that permits a line like the original "don't say nothin'." Freberg corrects himself with minimal prodding from Tweedley through the second A phrase, fixing "don't say" to "doesn't say" and "dem" to "dese" then "those" without losing the beat in a display of emergent self-censorship. He's internalized Tweedly's lesson but at the expense of unselfconscious immersion in the song (⊙ Sound Example 4.1).

Then Freberg and company arrive at the bridge lyric "You and me," to which Tweedly applies a good long buzz. No need to detail the necessary change: bandleader Billy May repeats the lead in—a tight row of short brass chords—and Freberg and chorus grandly sing "you and I." Here, the change registers as a joke. For many black singers, proper pronoun usage on Hammerstein's bridge lyric was a standard substitution that made the song singable. The first to record the line this way was the Ravens on their influential 1947 version: they did not mean the change to be funny. In the context of Freberg's sketch, correcting "you and me" to "you and I" becomes just another fussy change that takes the life—specifically, the blackness—out of the lyric.

The bridge continues without incident—Freberg changes "sweat" to "perspire"—until a big *ritardando* on the line "get a little..." Freberg breaks off before the word *drunk* and surrenders unconditionally: "Take your finger off the button, Mr. Tweedly. We know when we're licked." And with that, "Elderly Man River" abruptly ends. No big finish, no musical payoff courtesy of Kern's tune, just the lingering notion that part of "Ol' Man River" is irredeemable. The line "get a little drunk" is—of course—exactly the part many black critics and performers had objected to. Freberg takes its power so seriously it makes the song unsingable. Of course, in context Freberg is only dealing with drink, not with race.

What joke lies at the heart of "Elderly Man River"? Popular song lyrics often dispense with proper grammar, offering evidence for the pervasive influence of stylized black dialect and singing personas from minstrelsy onward. Tweedly's grammar policing takes the life—the American language, the *black* American language, "the way those people talk"—out of "Ol' Man River," in the process producing a "white" version, underlining the truth that anyone who sings "Ol' Man River" in some measure takes on a stereotypical black voice. (Freberg's vocal performance of "he jes' keeps rollin' along" consistently slips into an exaggerated delivery that suggests a Jolson-esque, blackface mammy singer.) This is the case in many, many popular songs of the same vintage. But given the serious nature of its lyric—in particular, the explicit references to blacks and whites in the verse, which Freberg omits—the blackness behind popular song becomes audible each time "Ol' Man River" is sung by anyone. Performances by white singers always brush up against the black voice embedded in the lyric.

A satirist for the mainstream, and so only modestly transgressive, if ever even that, Freberg avoids any and all race questions. His satire of "Ol' Man River" proceeds from a place where whites can sing and even deconstruct the details of black music without raising racial questions directly. Most every revision Tweedly demands can be traced back to the origins of American popular culture in racial mimicry. This turning toward issues of race—even when those issues go unnamed *as* racial—has been central to the historic role "Ol' Man River" has played. The fundamental question of how the song should be arranged or performed leads to a confrontation with racial histories that popular culture products typically seek to avoid. As a prism for the performance of blackness in popular music, "Ol' Man River" refracts the light of popular culture more subtly than most any similar song.

Freberg's parody corrects the lyric's "bad" grammar. Comedian Phil Silvers also had an "Ol' Man River" sketch but his turned on the need to instruct the singer in how to sing in dialect. Developed during private parties at musical movie star Gene Kelly's home—where a circle of Hollywood stars met regularly—and first performed as part of Silver's cabaret act at Charley Foy's nightclub in Los Angeles in the mid-1940s, the skit had

Silvers as Kern trying to convince a Paul Robeson stand-in (played initially by white songwriter Saul Chaplin) to sing "Ol' Man River." In his autobiography, Silvers claimed the premise behind the satire was this:

> Give a singer a choice and he'll inevitably pick the wrong song. "Ol' Man River" is one of the greatest dramatic numbers of our time. My assumption: Robeson would rather have sung "Captain Andy," the only song in that great score that never achieved much popularity. (Later, both Robeson and Kern told me I didn't know how close I was to the truth.) I honestly feel this was the most brilliant piece of material I ever conceived. My so-called liberal friends told me it had anti-Negro overtones. *Nuts.*[5]

Kern biographer Gerald Bordman claims that Kern loved the sketch so much he memorized it and "when [Kern] met Silvers at a party he had no trouble playing himself to Silvers' Robeson."[6] The sketch stayed in Silvers's repertoire into the 1950s. He performed it on television on *The Ed Sullivan Show* in 1956: *Variety* described it as "a skit on 'Ol' Man River' at a *Show Boat* rehearsal that hit a peak in comedics."[7] Silvers repeated the skit on his TV special *Phil Silvers on Broadway* in 1958: an industry reviewer described it as a "brilliant flash of inspired wit."[8] And he did it yet again in 1964, when a black newspaper described the routine this way: "Phil Silvers portrayed Paul Robeson objecting to composer Kern that 'Ol' Man River' was inconsequential."[9] Silvers approached the song from the opposite angle as Freberg—bad grammar is taught instead of corrected—and highlighted the artificiality of Kern's sophisticated tune being paired with Hammerstein's untutored poetic diction. Silvers's declared intent—that the sketch was about singers and not this particular song—suggests an understanding on his part that audiences would view the connection between Robeson and "Ol' Man River" as inevitable. In fact, as the history of *Show Boat* suggests, it wasn't. Robeson resisted the song. Silvers's sketch unknowingly and unintentionally revisits this scene, staging it for white audiences and for laughs.

Parodies and satires often open up hidden meanings. Television writer and producer Stan Daniels's "Ol' Man River," captured on videotape in the mid-1970s, effectively recast the racial stereotypes of the song, pointing the listener toward Jewish instead of black stereotypes. Performing for a private, sociable event and not before a public, paying audience, Daniels trades the nobly suffering Joe for the always kvetching Jew.

Daniels speaks rather than sings Hammerstein's words and there is no musical accompaniment. He begins with the verse—"Dere's an ol' man..."—the better to set up the distinction Daniels will make between himself and the "ol' man." Lacking the grandeur of Kern's melody, the "ol' man" comes across not as a river but, indeed, as a man. This version dispenses with the theme of nature's indifference; instead Daniels adopts the persona of a schlemiel and compares himself to a luckier guy who manages to "roll along."

Freed from Kern's tune, Daniels can emphasize specific words in Hammerstein's lyric as no singer could. The first such moment comes with the first complaint:

> He don't DO nothin'.
> He don't SAY nothin'.

Daniels punctuates "do" and "say" with small hand gestures that add to both the effectiveness of his delivery and the racial stereotype on offer. The humorous contrast between Daniels's Seventies sideburns and open red shirt and his evocation of an unreconstructed Old World persona clicks at just this moment, as audience reaction suggests (⊙ Sound Example 4.2).

Emphasis on nouns rather than verbs—"Tote dat BARGE! / Lift dat BALE!"—sets up Daniels's throwaway delivery of the chorus's most controversial line: "You get a LITTLE drunk you land in jail" scans like a comic complaint that can be read any number of ways, remaking the lyric as so much overstatement from a perhaps untrustworthy character. Daniels isn't overwhelmed by work: indeed, he could easily be a shirker who gets away with being lazy, beset by a world of imagined troubles he takes verbal pleasure in rehearsing. The stereotypical burden of the black experience dematerializes when taken up by a Jewish stereotype of excessive complaint whose voice evokes an entire world of racial experience distant from the song's original context. Daniels trades the black man's noble suffering beside a silent river for the Jewish trope of inevitable suffering and endless complaining about a river that gets all the breaks. The moral earnestness of Joe's statuesque, largely speechless figure—a powerful, racially defined Broadway character—is handed over to a Tevye-like, world-weary yet wise comic Jew—another powerful, racially defined Broadway character type. When Daniels did his spoof, the Jewish type was recently embodied in *Fiddler on the Roof*, like *Show Boat* a super-successful musical noted for its blend of comedy and tragedy.

Daniels doesn't sing and doesn't alter a single word of the lyric. Another Jewish parody, also from a semi-private space, changes every one of Hammerstein's words as a means to reclaim the song for a Jewish singer in the twenty-first century. The Internet makes this second version accessible. Cantor Henry Rosenblum of Toronto's Beth Tzedec Synagogue sang his own

"Ol' Man River" in 2010. Someone from the Beth Tzedec Men's Club posted the clip on voobys.com, inviting those who found it to check out the synagogue's website and, if in the area, to check out the congregation, which looks like a fun group able to share a laugh.

The event appears to be a fundraiser. With dinner over, Rosenblum steps to the microphone and delivers something he introduces as "Ol' Man River NOT," a complete revision of the lyric titled "Cold Chopped Liver." It's a paean to gustatory overindulgence in a tasty shabbas dish that bites back.

In the second A phrase, Rosenblum sings of passing up the "taters" and "finger lickin' chicken" on offer: all he wants is cold chopped liver. Replacing "cotton" with "chicken" elides all mention of the South and also suggests the long racial history of food in popular song. An insatiable appetite for chicken was central to racist caricatures of blacks at the turn of the twentieth century, the time of the "coon" song. Among the best-known "coon" songs was "Who Dat Say Chicken in Dis Crowd?," just one indication of the ubiquity of the connection between blacks and chicken in this particularly offensive period for mainstream popular music. While there was no obvious place for it in his lyric, had Hammerstein included a reference to chicken—almost as bad as watermelon—in "Ol' Man River," the chorus would have been genuinely unsingable, crossing a line beyond "get a little drunk." As Rosenblum's version suggests, a Jewish man of stature doing self-deprecating comedy can sing about chicken all he wants. At the end of the bridge, Rosenblum even suppresses a burp.

Rosenblum is a cantor, a singer by profession—and a good one. His is a voice that should sing "Ol' Man River." But if he's going to sing the song— in 2010—it will have to be a completely changed version, a comic parody of Jewish masculinity sung in a clubby setting. Before he begins to sing, Rosenblum offers apologies to Kern; Hammerstein might be more deserving of mention. Both Kern and Hammerstein would have likely gotten the joke.

The Internet lets listeners outside the Beth Tzedec community in on the joke. How many other "Ol' Man River" parodies have escaped notice in similar closed rooms? The Internet has opened many such rooms. Before that newspapers served a similar purpose.

In late 1991, members of the Monmouth County, New Jersey, Bar Association staged a skit intending to skewer African American law professor Anita Hill, who had recently gained national attention in the confirmation hearings of Supreme Court Justice Clarence Thomas. The skit featured a white man as Hill in blackface and drag—exactly the getup worn by some white minstrel performers in the nineteenth century—who entered singing "Ol'

Man River."[10] The president of the Garden State Bar Association, an organization of minority lawyers, said of the skit: "Anita Hill is an articulate, attractive, well-spoken attorney. By ignoring that and depicting a Black in a stereotyped manner, well, that can be called racist, really." This episode serves as a reminder that Hammerstein's words have, on occasion, been put to use by unsympathetic performers.

The Monmouth Bar's skit wielded the racial content of Hammerstein's lyric so crudely the question *what were they thinking?* seems all too obvious. With other targets in their sights, Daniels and Rosenblum's Jewish versions sidestep the original racial questions at the heart of "Ol' Man River," replacing them with other jokes. Freberg and Silvers's scenes of instruction get closer to the issue of race and representation but neither sketch crosses the line into critique. In contrast to all of the above—all made by white performers—a parody version of "Ol' Man River" from 1938 by Cootie Williams and his Rug Cutters, a group of moonlighting sidemen from the Duke Ellington Orchestra—with Ellington at the piano—takes on the noble black suffering lodged so deeply in Hammerstein's lyric. This recording is a prime example of signifying: using a rhythm tune approach to take down "Ol' Man River," turning small group swing into an instrument of racial critique without losing the attraction of hearing great players play. It's a have-your-cake-and-eat-it-too recording. And—to Williams and his singer Jerry Kruger's credit—the critique offered here embraces both musical and lyrical dimensions.

Williams was a key member of Ellington's orchestra, and his signature muted playing brought a new, modern, knowing black voice to popular music. His growling trumpet kicks off the group's "Ol' Man River" with a sound that mocks "serious" vocal performance. Playing with an edgy impatience not typical of his other late Thirties records, Williams plays Kern's tune without alteration in a manner that suggests Hammerstein's lyric is a bunch of whining (◉ Sound Example 4.3). The spirit of black swing gives the lie to Jazz Age pieties of submissive if noble blackness embodied in "Ol' Man River" as performed in *Show Boat*.

On the vocal chorus, Kruger sings an alternate lyric that amplifies the spirit of Williams's played chorus.

> Ol' Man River,
> That Ol' Man River,
> Don't say nothin'
> Must know somethin'.
> He's been there for years shedding his tears.
> The old oaken bucket is a dunkin' again.

He don' a plant a taters
And he don' plant cotton.
Them that plants 'em are squares
And they're forgotten.
But Ol' Man River, he keeps on—
I want some Lyonnaise potatoes and some pork chops.

You and me we sweat an' strain.
Body all weary and wracked with pain.
Totin' the barge,
Liftin' up the bale.
Smoke a little tea
And sing o sole mio.

I'm weary
And I'm sick of tryin'.
Tired of livin'
And I feel like dyin'.
But Ol' Man River,
He keeps on rollin' along.

Kruger's attention to the song-identifying phrase "jes' keeps rollin' along" falters both times in the first half of the tune. In effect, she denies the listener a signature moment, replacing it in the first A phrase with a reference to "The Old Oaken Bucket," an early nineteenth-century poem turned into a well-known folk-like tune. Kruger resolutely refuses to haul "Ol' Man River's" "old oaken bucket" of existential weariness. The second time "jes' keeps rolling along" comes up, Kruger reveals a very concrete hunger, as she abruptly gets the urge for some "Lyonnaise potatoes and some pork chops." On the bridge, the most morally intense stretch of the lyric, Kruger downplays the words of the boss and dismisses those who labor as "squares," not exactly an expression of racial solidarity with working folks but instead a claim that the song's lyric doesn't apply to her.

Indeed, as the bridge unfolds the singer's identity is revealed: the line "Smoke a little tea and sing o sole mio" confirms our suspicion that a hip jazz singer has taken Joe's place, earning this track inclusion on the CD *Reefer Madness*, a compilation of pro-pot pop. As the voice of the band, Kruger complains a bit but she's enjoying life to the full, smoking marijuana and *not* getting sent to jail, as Hammerstein's original lyric imagined was the inevitable result of even slight intoxication. On her repeat of the second half of the chorus, Kruger adjusts the final A phrase and sings "Tired of givin', tired of livin' / But I don't feel like dyin'," further assuring the listener that this song doesn't speak for her or the boys playing hot jazz behind her.

Cootie Williams's version, with its mocking trumpet solo and pointedly rewritten, even smug take on the lyric, deconstructs "Ol' Man River" from the inside, giving the lie to its reverent poses. It's a Thirties answer to the Twenties: no more noble suffering on the shores of the muddy Mississippi; today, Williams's disc proclaims, we're enjoying life and remaking the sound of popular music. Underwriting this version is the liberating performance location of a low-stakes recording session where the fact that Kruger was white and the players black could go unnoted by the uninformed listener.

Other recordings by black jazz groups from the 1930s and 1940s used the technique of partial parody to reject the terms on which Hammerstein's lyric defined blackness. Snub Mosley's 1940 take on the tune also mentions getting high:

> You and I—oh
> Get high. Land in jail.
> Ain't gonna do that no more.
> No one to go my bail.

Mosley's critique isn't as thoroughgoing as Williams's. In all likelihood, Mosley is signifying on Williams's earlier version, extending the theme of getting high.

The Loumell Morgan Trio called on the Ol' Man to get in step with the present. At the close of their 1946 recording, the already fast tempo abruptly speeds up for a final chorus with parody lyrics. The second A phrase ends with the cry,

> What's a matter with ya river
> Get up a there
> Roll up boy and ya jump for joy.

"Jump for joy" was a catch line at the time, an optimistic expression passed around within the black community and used by Duke Ellington as the title for his 1941 musical, a show that attempted to eliminate long-standing black stereotypes from the musical stage. On the bridge, the singer makes fun of the white man boss by turning his cries of "tote" and "lift" into nonsense babbling. Morgan's group reminds their black listeners that the boss is far away and it's time to celebrate. This urban "Ol' Man River" has no interest in recreating the rural South.

In a similar vein, the 1933 song "Old Man Harlem"—an answer song, not a parody—abstracted the "Ol' Man" and "rollin' along" phrases and built a new black persona: the Harlem resident whose life is defined not by noble suffering on the land or longing for the release of heaven. This singer has a relationship with the black urban North, which gives her "Sunday headaches" from dancing till dawn, keeps her "skimpin'" and saving, and leaves her "old and gray" before she's really lived. With no nostalgia for, nor mention of, the South, "Old Man Harlem" gives a remarkably sober assessment of the North. The "Old Man" and the singer are connected: the former drives on the latter in the absence of any sort of "white man boss." Without sentiment, the singer describes the pace, expense, and personal wear and tear of the city. There's no fatalism here and, it must be said, very little fun. Like "Ol' Man River," "Old Man Harlem" remains ambiguous, open in its meanings.

"Old Man Harlem" was written by Rudy Vallee and Hoagy Carmichael. Like "Ol' Man River," it's a song about the black experience penned by white popular musicians. White and black performers recorded it. Whites—such as the Dorsey Brothers band and Carmichael himself—took a fast tempo, using the music to express the driving energy of Harlem. Black singing star Ethel Waters recorded a very different take—on the slow side, bringing an exhausted but content persona that suggests Waters found a kernel of truth in the lyric. (Waters sang "Ol' Man River" in her specialty act during the national tour of the Broadway show *Rhapsody in Black* in 1932. Her version featured a male quartet and combined the song with the tune "River Stay Away from My Door." One reviewer described the effect as "very unique indeed.")[11]

The parodies, satires, and answer songs discussed in this chapter argue against the status of "Ol' Man River" as an anthem or hymn and—importantly—several refuse to uncritically reinforce the song's connection to an imagined popular music South. In that respect, the parodic impulse calls out the easy simplifications of performers who lump "Ol' Man River" together with less complex tunes, insisting, instead, that the song and the imaginary South be opened up as the musical and theatrical constructions they are. The urge to make small or wholesale changes to the lyrics of "Ol' Man River" has been common. In this chapter, most of my examples have been drawn from before the most intense years of the civil rights movement. Parody versions from that period—the song's high season, from the late 1950s to the close of the 1960s—and after by African American artists, all of whom use language or performance choices that are overtly political, have been saved for the final chapter of the book.

5

cᐯɔ

Ol' Man Easy Listening

S ome recorded versions of "Ol' Man River" are best heard as items from a case of curiosities.

Item One. Recording in the mid-1940s, guitarist Marcel Bianchi plays the tune Hawaiian guitar-style without embellishment to the accompaniment of strings and piano. On the second chorus, the piano, then the violins, take the tune, while Bianchi plays swooping, quivering chords, before coming to a close on a vibrato-heavy upswing (⊙ Sound Example 5.1). It's a lovely record—"Ol' Man River" as Hawaiian lounge music, the Mississippi flowing through a tropical paradise. (Recordings by Santo and Johnny, with slide guitar and strings, and Italian pop saxophonist Fausto Papetti— both from the 1960s—offer similar pleasures.)

Item Two. The 2011 version by the Berlin Philharmonic Horn Quartet takes a deliberate, slow tempo. These exquisitely skilled classical musicians turn in a creamy smooth "Ol' Man River," complete with a very low solo section and a finely calibrated build to the close. The effect is quasi-Wagnerian—Ol' Man Rhinegold?—but remains in the popular vein because of Kern's supple, singable tune (⊙ Sound Example 5.2). The Berlin players don't puff the song up into something epic or operatic: any listener who cares about "Ol' Man River" as "one of America's great light classics" will likely nod in approval at this tasteful recording. (Another twenty-first century instrumental version by classical players—the London Double Bass Sound, a chorus of double basses with a harp—achieves much the same effect.)

Item Three. Giora Feidman's solo version on bass clarinet appears on his 1996 CD *To You!*, an eclectic disc—perhaps a compilation of encores—that includes Schubert's "Ave Maria," a rag by Scott Joplin, a tango by Astor Piazzolla, and Leonard Bernstein's overture to *Candide.* Feidman, born in

Argentina to Jewish immigrants from Bessarabia, moved to Israel in 1957 and played clarinet in the Israeli Philharmonic for eighteen years. In Israel, Feidman began playing klezmer, delving deeply into this Eastern European musical style which his website calls "Jewish Soul."[1] Beginning in the 1970s, Feidman was at the forefront of a global klezmer revival. But Feidman doesn't play "Ol' Man River" as a klezmer tune—although how such an approach might sound can be imagined by analogy with the Dixieland recordings of the song. Instead, Feidman turns his supple melodic powers to Kern's melody, singing "Ol' Man River" by way of the bass clarinet, further underlining the song's historic affinity with soloing in the bass register (◉ Sound Example 5.3). Feidman's "River" is restrained, quiet, reserved, and mellow. In a Robeson-esque style, Feidman puts his faith in Kern's melody and makes no stylistic argument that "Ol' Man River" has its roots in Jewish music.

Item Four. Guitarist John Fahey pairs "Ol' Man River" with the spiritual "Deep River" on *Of Rivers and Religion*, a disc *Time* magazine listed among the top ten albums of 1972. Fahey draws a resonant, slightly metallic sound from his guitar that might suggest the banjo, or perhaps autoharp—except it's clearly a guitar. This is no nostalgic recreation of the old South: it's remaking of acoustic guitar in a clangorous yet spare style Fahey called "American Primitive" (◉ Sound Example 5.4). Prior to *Of Rivers and Religion*, Fahey had mostly played folk songs and blues tunes. With a degree in folklore and a philosophical bent, Fahey might seem an unlikely musician to play a Broadway show tune but "Ol' Man River" manages to fit right in—again showing the tremendous generic flexibility of Kern and Hammerstein's song. As music critic Nat Hentoff writes on the album's jacket, "Fahey gives you a lot of room in which to feel. Space is an integral part of his music; and moving into that space, surrounded by the music, becomes a different journey each time. Backwards, forwards, now." Fahey's "River"—played without drama in a lilting fashion (like some jazz players, he uses Kern's first A phrase throughout, simplifying the melody's overall shape) and recorded with a lot of presence and reverb—renders the song at once strange and familiar, starkly beautiful, utterly unique.

Item Five. Finally, there's Brazilian pop star Milton Nascimento's version from 1997. From the downward rippling piano chords that start the track, Nascimento's "River" is shrouded in fog—or, perhaps, Amazonian mist (◉ Sound Example 5.5). Nascimento sings the tune wordlessly, surrounding it with expansive, sonically transparent, colorful, overlapping sounds. It's not a conventionally recorded or mixed orchestra. Individual voices—a closely-miked flute, for example—come forward here and there. At the close, a choir joins the mix, but not with the heavy-handed approach a version out of Hollywood might have taken. Keeping the mix as hazy and lustrous as possible seems to be Nascimento's goal, and "Ol' Man River" serves as an appropriate vessel for the effort.

Indeed, making as beautiful a "River" as possible seems to be the central priority of all these versions, none of which fit the Ol' Man Rhythm category. These easy-to-listen-to versions are on the slow side, with a reflective affect, frequently striving to create a mood or musical atmosphere more than anything else. Kern's melody remains central; the listener's desire to hum along is never frustrated. If rhythmic versions exploit the riff-like rhythms in Kern's tune, easy listening versions bring out the song's long, long line.

With so much attentiveness to the melody, presented in a singing idiom, it's hard not to hear these typically quite gentle versions as somehow responding to the content of Hammerstein's lyrics. What is "Ol' Man River" saying in these versions geared for easy listening? All these recordings minimize the dramatic tension of the song's bridge: even Feidman doesn't wail on these phrases. The cries of "tote" and "lift"—standout features in vocal performances in this tempo range (see Chapter 6)—are absorbed into a generalized dreaminess without depth. There is no sense of longing to cross over the River Jordan; no desire for much of anything. And so, these varied versions—however lovely they might be—give the listener an easy escape from the complexities of Hammerstein and Kern's song. Hammerstein put conflict into the words and Kern put struggle into the melody, but Ol' Man Easy Listening never sweats or strains.

Another sort of easy listening "Ol' Man River" hails from the middle decades of the twentieth century, when the category of mood music emerged as part of music industry efforts to sell adult listeners on the long-playing record and high-fidelity stereo equipment. For several prominent arrangers and mood music maestros, "Ol' Man River" seemed a good song to demonstrate the superior highs and lows and louds and softs of the new world of high-end home audio.

Arranger Neal Hefti included "Ol' Man River" on his 1957 disc *Concert Miniatures*, described on its liner as "a group of classical or semi-classical warhorses" made into "modern miniature concert pieces, and jazz-oriented ones at that." "Ol' Man River" is the sole show tune among famous light classical themes—several by Tchaikovsky—and selections like Gershwin's *Rhapsody in Blue* and Debussy's "The Girl with the Flaxen Hair." Throughout the arrangement, Hefti breaks Kern's tune into sharply distinct, directly juxtaposed textures: for example, a chorus of flutes is suddenly replaced by passionate high-register strings during the verse. On the chorus, what sounds like a mellow bassoon—a minor miracle of sound engineering?—plays the tune against endlessly cycling scales in the strings (Hefti may have borrowed this slightly tedious accompaniment idea from Stan Kenton's 1940s version where it's also heard). The bridge erupts in dramatic, even operatic, style, perhaps hinting at Hammerstein's lyrics. But with no unified character to the arrangement, the effect is just abrupt (☉ Sound Example 5.6). Hefti's sharp shifts in volume and character would have offered a dramatic test of the era's new home audio equipment. "Ol' Man River" also shows up in the catalog of the 101 Strings—an unsurprising entry in the song's discography given the huge output of this studio-based, easy-listening brand name orchestra whose peak years ran from the late 1950s to the early 1970s. The 101 Strings' version turns "Ol' Man River" into epic movie music suggestive of a widescreen, Technicolor western, with a super legato rendering of the A phrases in the strings (a broad love theme), jaunty woodwinds on the verse (music for the comic relief), and a huge cymbal-crash conclusion announcing "The End" (☉ Sound Example 5.7). As the 101 Strings version suggests, not all these stereo recordings were slow. Marty Gold's version on the 1963 disc *Sounds Unlimited* is an almost comically kaleidoscopic demonstration of "the magnificent new sound" of the Dynagroove technology developed by RCA Victor. The opening accompaniment figure—nervous strings—heralds a schizophrenic arrangement that never settles into any single idea (☉ Sound Example 5.8). The effect is dizzying, drawing the ear to sounds for their own sake—which was, of course, the whole point. Still, the subtle construction of Kern's tune can be heard to enable Gold's approach again and again. It also permits that rarity in any genre: the tuba solo.

The Hefti, 101 Strings, and Gold arrangements, among several others from this era in LP history, remade "Ol' Man River" as a pop symphony fitted to the still new space of the audiophile's living room. The musical variety of Kern's tune, the song's inherent grandeur—its quasi-classical pretentions—and, of course, its familiarity to all listeners surely recommended "Ol' Man River" for this sort of elaborately produced treatment.

The notion that "Ol' Man River" could bear the weight of symphonic treatment has more traditional symphonic roots in the previous decade. In the early 1940s, Kern himself was enlisted by conductor Artur Rodzinski to create a tone poem on themes from *Show Boat* for the Cleveland Orchestra. The result was Kern's *Scenario for Orchestra*. This twenty-two-minute work opens with the bridge from "Ol' Man River," hauntingly scored for violas and bass clarinet, dropping the listener midstream into the musical world of the show's score by way of a highly familiar melody (☉ Sound Example 5.9). The effect is pictorial throughout: akin to movie music of the least subtle, theme-heavy sort, the *Scenario* paints a broad canvas, rewarding listeners who know the words and can sing along in their minds while freely associating with any aspect of *Show Boat*'s characters and plot. And while a tune like "Can't Help Lovin' Dat Man" can evoke tropes of blackness by way of orchestration or accompaniment figures—muted horns, bending blue notes—"Ol' Man River," with its less common, less musically specific conceit of noble suffering and natural grandeur, comes off as generically tragic and grand, as an American tune dressed up in the fancy clothes of European art music.

The Cleveland Orchestra might play Kern on occasion but "America's great light classics" were not at the center of their repertory. In commissioning Kern's *Scenario*, Rodzinski was working toward that magical, hall-filling midcentury category of middlebrow music, dipping downward to pull a venerable Broadway score up into the concert hall. *Show Boat*, especially with "Ol' Man River" in tow, has been a safe bet for such efforts almost since its 1927 premiere.

Working the same middlebrow crowd—or market—from the other side was popular symphonist Andre Kostelanetz, whose capacious catalog of recordings provided musical uplift to culturally aspiring phonograph-owning households. Kostelanetz's series of instrumental albums from the late 1940s included *Show Boat* among Rodgers and Hammerstein and Gershwin hits, anointing the Broadway musical as solid cultural stuff. Indeed, Kostelanetz recorded Kern's *Scenario* beside similar "scenarios" of *South Pacific* and *Porgy and Bess*. For Kostelanetz, "Ol' Man River" was best sold as part of *Show Boat*. His 1945 album of four 45s titled *Music by Jerome Kern* includes a three-song medley of *Show Boat* songs: "Ol' Man River" comes last. When Columbia reissued the Kern recordings as an LP in 1955, the *Show Boat* medley and "Ol' Man River" ended side two, a structurally strong position that would be repeated on many later LPs (multiple examples crossing several genre boundaries are discussed in subsequent chapters). Kostelanetz's arrangement offers a bland benchmark of sorts for easy listening versions of "Ol' Man River." The string section carries the tune: initially the low-register cellos (an obvious choice); at the bridge, the violins take over (◉ Sound Example 5.10). Transitions are smoother than in later pop symphonic versions for the hi-fi and the whole effect is one of dynamic and orchestral expansion. Like Kern's *Scenario*, Kostelanetz's "River" paints a big canvas, a landscape that celebrates the broad expanse of the river.

Another popular purveyor of Ol' Man Middlebrow was Fred Waring, like Kostelanetz a successful brand name in easy listening for decades. Waring's band, the Pennsylvanians, was distinguished from competitors by the inclusion of a full mixed chorus: the Glee Club. Waring himself was known on radio and records as "the man who taught America to sing."[2] And so, Waring's easy listening arrangement of "Ol' Man River"—he recorded the same one twice—forced a confrontation with Hammerstein's lyrics.

Waring's first recording—from a 1946 album of 45s titled *Program Time* (reissued as an LP in 1950)—uses the "Darkies all work" version of the verse. White Broadway baritone Walter Scheff is featured as soloist (⊕ Sound Example 5.11). Waring's second recording—from the 1957 LP *Fred Waring in Hi-Fi* (another home stereo-exploiting disc)—changes the verse text, sung by the chorus this time, to "Here we all work on the Mississippi / Here we all work while the other folks play" (⊕ Sound Example 5.12). The soloist on this version is Frank Davis, an African American bass. A surprising story of interracial performance lies behind Waring's substitution of a black for a white soloist and "here we all work" for "darkies all work." This rather innocuous sounding "Ol' Man River" facilitated a crossing of the color line in the waning years of Jim Crow.

Waring had a television show in the early 1950s. *The Fred Waring Show* featured a recurring spot called Varsity Showcase which gave soloists from colleges and universities around the nation the chance to sing on television and, perhaps, be selected to join Waring's group. Frank Davis, a senior at Xavier University in New Orleans—described by Waring as "America's only Catholic college for Negro students"—appeared on the Varsity Showcase in 1952. He was, according to Waring, the "unanimous choice for the season's outstanding candidate." Davis joined Waring's organization as a bass soloist and remained with the group through the end of the 1950s (returning for limited appearances in 1962 and 1968–69). He was frequently featured on television in dramatically lit renditions of spirituals and even did a costumed version of "It Ain't Necessarily So," interacting with the all-white singers of the Waring chorus as if in an interracial production of *Porgy and Bess*.

When the television show ended in 1954, Waring's outfit, with Davis a much-featured soloist, began what the leader's wife Virginia Waring describes as "long, long road tours," during which "problems of housing and restaurants surfaced for Frank." Waring took a strong and strategic stand against any attempt to exclude Davis. If a restaurant refused to serve Davis, then all fifty-five Pennsylvanians would rise from their seats and exit the establishment. On some routes, members of the group formed a committee to provide food for all instead of relying on roadside diners, the entire company traveling like many African Americans did in the segregated South, minimizing the number of necessary encounters with discriminatory, perhaps dangerous local "customs." On other occasions, Waring would hold off entering a restaurant with Davis until everyone else in the group was seated. If Davis was refused a place in the dining room, Waring—the nationally famous guest of honor—would eat in the kitchen with Frank and the "help." Waring also played hardball with city-owned auditoriums that objected to Davis appearing onstage with a white group. Told that the mayor of Memphis refused permission to "raise the curtain" if he "insisted on using the black singer," Waring reportedly replied, "Well, that's fine with me. You don't need to raise the curtain. We'll do the show in back of the curtain. Our contract is to do the show, and they knew we had a black performer before they signed the contract. You just tell the mayor that it is OK with me—fine—they don't need to raise the curtain." Having called the segregationist's bluff, Waring and Davis would go on—sometimes Waring recounted the trouble to the audience before starting the music—but Southern cities that caused this kind of problem were typically struck from future tour itineraries.[3] One can only imagine Davis's experience of these tours, which he endured for half a decade.

"Ol' Man River" was an all-but-inevitable choice for a singer like Davis in a group like Waring's. Indeed, Davis sang the number on his first television appearance—his Varsity Showcase tryout in March 1952. After joining the

Frank Davis soloing while surrounded by Fred Waring's all-white Glee Club on television in the early 1950s. (Fred Waring's America, Penn State University Special Collections Library)

group, Davis sang "Ol' Man River" twice more on television in 1952. He also sang the song during the 1953 festivities for Dwight Eisenhower's inauguration as president of the United States. Black newspapers savored the image of the governor of South Carolina "applauding lustily" after Davis sang "with an all-white chorus" and noted that after "Ol' Man River," Waring "did a turnabout and directed the 100-voice Howard University Choir!" from the well-known, historically black institution.[4]

It's easy to judge a revision like "Here we all work while the other folks play" as just so much dodging of the racial issue at the song's heart. But given the context—a black bass welcomed as featured soloist in a high-profile white chorus in the early 1950s—the change poetically marks an incremental shift in race relations. Waring wasn't afraid to make an issue of Davis's full inclusion on stage, but he apparently did not want to complicate Davis's musical contribution in the midst of enjoying the baritone's considerable talent. And so, racial words in Hammerstein's lyric were removed in favor of an unraced pronoun—"Here we all work"—and a two-syllable substitution for the word *white*—"the other folks play"—that even necessitated a change in the rhythm of Kern's tune. Later listeners, unaware of the interracial nature of Waring and Davis's 1957 recording of "Ol' Man River," might judge the recording as bland or even intentionally dodging the issue of race when, in historical perspective, this version fairly crackles with the potential of changes to come in American race relations (◉ Sound Example 5.13).

Davis and Waring's 1957 "Ol' Man River" shows up on the 1970s LP *This Is My Country*, a special product released by the Longines Symphonette Society, producers of *The Family Library of Beautiful Listening* and other LPs designed to edify and delight home listeners across the generations (but probably only pleasing to the old folks). "Ol' Man River" appears on *This Is My Country* as one of ten patriotic songs: such placement is far from unusual in midcentury LPs (as shown in Chapter 6). "Ol' Man River" is, after all, sort of a folk song, a song to know even if you don't know music, even if you don't like Broadway musicals or Negro spirituals. And while Hammerstein and Kern's tune doesn't have the obvious public function of a song like Berlin's "God Bless America," it is of similar stature as a song in the popular vein, produced by music industry professionals, that has transcended its origins and entered national life. And while it's probably too hard musically for most children to sing, knowing Kern's melody and the repeated catch-phrases of Hammerstein's lyric can be understood as part of basic cultural knowledge for Americans—at least to the 1970s. (The All-American Boys Chorus made a valiant effort to record "Ol' Man River" in 1997 but the expansive range of the tune proves too much for the young voices. The chorus's arrangement finesses the peak of the melody, letting the boys drop the octave at the climax of the final A phrase, the same spot where older singers dropped down in 1928 [◉ Sound Example 5.14].)

Two CDs from 2002 offer evidence that the producers of "special products" still place "Ol' Man River" in the category of American songs everyone should know in the twenty-first century. The disc *Mark Twain's America* places a sung version of "Ol' Man River" by black American operatic bass Simon Estes among songs like "Battle Hymn of the Republic," favorites by Stephen Foster sung by smooth sounding baritones, and instrumental favorites like Joplin's "The Entertainer" and Aaron Copland's uber-American *Appalachian Spring* and *Rodeo*. The disc *Celebration of America*, produced by the children's record label Music for Little People, takes a similar if more inclusive—even liberal—approach. As the disc's promotional materials state, "The tone of the record is reverent, yet light enough to keep young listeners interested. Perfect for the Fourth of July." *Celebration of America* lumps "Ol' Man River" among songs kids should just know—and helps parents teach it as well. Robeson singing "Ol' Man River" is followed by The Weavers singing Woody Guthrie's "This Land Is Your Land"—a nice juxtaposition that should get the reflective listener thinking. Both songs speak of the landscape and labor. Guthrie's completely singable tune, an answer to Berlin's "God Bless America," hits one end of the anthem spectrum: it's a tune to be sung by the masses. Hammerstein and Kern's song is not easily bent to such a purpose. As the example of Robeson suggests, "Ol' Man River" remains an anthem to be listened to, a song to be heard, not sung. Although—and there is always an example to be found in the history of this song—there was at least one semi-patriotic sing-along to "Ol' Man River." Summertime productions of *Show Boat* under the stars at the massive Jones Beach amphitheater near New York City in the 1950s ended with the complete cast of the show—an interracial group—leading the audience in a sing-along of "Ol' Man River" while fireworks rose above the stage, which looked out over the waters of the Atlantic Ocean. It's hard to imagine what the mostly white audience thought about while singing "Ol' Man River" in such a setting—but it's safe to say Hammerstein's fraught meditation on the experience of being black was not uppermost in most minds.

Easy listening versions that leverage the song for quasi-patriotic ends are best heard as just so much scene painting, grand panoramas of the nation's past dressed in expensive musical materials, so large in scale the figures in the landscape become little more than decorative detail. The river—an important, but crucially a silent, character in the lyric—drowns out the voices of those working on its banks, silencing the "I" and the "you and me" who sing Hammerstein's words. Joe, inevitably, shrinks in stature in such a scene.

To the resistant ear, symphonic or overly pictorial versions of "Ol' Man River" are easily heard as "pastoral scenes of the gallant South" (to quote a line from the anti-lynching song "Strange Fruit"), tableaux that miss the point of Hammerstein's lyric as an expression of historical suffering—noble but suffering nonetheless. The emotionally and intellectually complex black persona embedded in Hammerstein's words is silenced when his setting is too grand. Similarly, the texture and grain of any human voice struggling with Kern's wide-ranging melody is lost when played with surpassing technical skill by a full orchestra.

One moment in *Show Boat* anticipates the pseudo-symphonic and atmospheric treatments of "Ol' Man River" discussed in this chapter. In act one's penultimate scene, the dashing Gaylord Ravenal contrives to meet his leading lady Magnolia Hawks for a few moments of romantic bliss in the moonlight at the water barrel on the boat's top deck. The musical evocation of this moment involved the members of *Show Boat*'s black chorus humming "Ol' Man River" from offstage. And so, even *Show Boat* put "Ol' Man River" to use as just another component of the moonlight-and-magnolia South, a world where blacks are content to croon soft and low in the shadows while white lovers relish the joys of youth and spring.

A final stream of easy listening versions takes Hammerstein and Kern's song to an unlikely place beyond US shores. In 1968, the first reggae treatment of "Ol' Man River" was recorded by the Silvertones, a vocal group, with Tommy McCook and the Supersonics providing instrumental backup. The Silvertones set fragments of Kern's A phrase over an oscillating two-chord groove. Tempo-wise, this "River" rolls in the 70s bpm, where all subsequent reggae versions would ride (◉ Sound Example 5.15). Surviving members of the group re-recorded their easy-flowing "Ol' Man River" for a 2013 digital album titled *Keep Rolling Along*.

Like the Ravens R&B-defining 1947 groove, the Silvertones' approach was widely copied and adapted, with new versions appearing for more than a decade. Reggae pioneer Leroy "Scratch" Perry and his band the Upsetters turned the Silvertones' basic elements into an instrumental featuring the Hammond B3 organ on a track called "Django (Ol' Man River)" on the 1970 LP *Eastwood Rides Again* (◉ Sound Example 5.16). Prince Alla's track from 1982, with some new lyrics, suggests the tendency of reggae versions to get caught in a "rolling along" aesthetic that seems to have little to say: in one stretch of his recording, Prince Alla, uniquely in the song's history, reduces Hammerstein's lyric to little more than "he keeps on rolling along" (◉ Sound Example 5.17). At least one reggae musician explored the entirely of Kern's tune: trumpeter Eddie "Tan Tan" Thornton recorded a grooving instrumental of the complete chorus in 1981, reminiscent of earlier Latin groove versions except for its relaxed tempo (right at 70 bpm). Thornton's mellow trumpet finds easy melodic pleasure in the chorus and he even improvises a bit over the verse, played by another trumpet in a sonically complex, transparent yet rich, passage (◉ Sound Example 5.18).

The majority of Ol' Man Reggae versions fall in the easy listening category for their relaxed tempo and untroubled use of select elements. But the reggae tradition did produce one version that offers an interpretation of the song that speaks to the black experience—something the committed reggae listener might expect given the music's long connection to political and social expression. "Crown Prince of Reggae" Dennis Brown's "Ol' Man River" reached number one on the reggae disco charts in Britain's *New Musical Express* for several weeks in 1985. Brown stays true to the reggae tempo (73 bpm) and even uses Perry's version of the chorus tune. But Brown digs deeper into Hammerstein and Kern's original and draws on the verse, adding a contrasting melodic idea to that same rocking bass groove. And, like so many before him, Brown rewrites Hammerstein's troubling first words. Brown's track begins by hailing a specifically black audience, advising the listener to leave the land and the river behind (◉ Sound Example 5.19).

Negro man, come away from the Mississippi.
Negro man, come away from the sinking sand.

Brown signifies on Hammerstein's chorus lyric throughout, mentioning being scared "of dying," "to fly free," and "of sighing." Brown's call to "come away" echoes several very different sounding versions of "Ol' Man River" made in the United States in the 1960s (see Chapter 10) and also shows that an easy groove can serve as the vessel for serious reflection on the complex issues lying in wait in Hammerstein's text.

6

୦୴ଚ

Ol' Man Metaphor

Norma Terris was among the first women to perform "Ol' Man River." A minor star of vaudeville and musical comedy in the 1920s, Terris originated the white ingénue role of Magnolia in the debut production of *Show Boat*. My book on *Show Boat* describes how Terris influenced the musical content of Magnolia's part.[1] Terris's claim to fame was doing musical imitations of established stars—she managed to shoe-horn some imitations into *Show Boat*—and she certainly knew how Jules Bledsoe, the original Joe, sang "Ol' Man River." But when Terris added "Ol' Man River" to her 1931 solo act at the Palace Theatre in New York City, the premiere vaudeville venue in the nation, she evidently didn't imitate a man singing the song. A critic reported, "In her own style she sings 'Ol' Man River,' the campus song back in the old days at Sixth Avenue and Fifty-fourth Street [site of the Ziegfeld Theatre where *Show Boat* ran], and then submits an impression of—yes—Ethel Barrymore, wearily rendering the same ballad."[2] Terris's "own style" was to sing prettily in her rather pretty soprano voice: such a take on "Ol' Man River" would have been unusual for any era. Her imitation of Barrymore would have been a joke inside a joke. Barrymore was the *grande dame* of the American theater in her fourth decade on the stage: a Broadway theater had been named in her honor in 1928. Terris's version of Barrymore singing "Ol' Man River" likely empha-sized themes of age and endurance: how she negotiated the overriding maleness of the lyric, not to mention questions of physical labor and black-ness, remain a mystery.

Terris evidently did not do "Ol' Man River" in a comic or up-tempo rhythm style. Later women who took up the number seem to have favored a mix of both—although it's impossible to know for sure. More than a few female singers on the variety stage and nightclub circuit included "Ol' Man River" in their acts. Almost none recorded the number. White comedienne and singer Martha Raye did, however, record a two-tempo "Ol' Man River" in 1939: after an initial chorus at a bluesy pace, Raye bursts into a very fast second chorus—including scat singing in the breaks—with the added line "shoot the liquor to me, john boy" (⊙ Sound Example 6.1). But Raye's recording was exceptional. Most women who sang "Ol' Man River" before the advent of rock and roll left behind only terse descriptions of their performances found in reviews written for entertainment industry insiders in the pages of *Variety* and *Billboard*. These glimpses of a largely lost approach to the song bear some consideration.

In the mid-1930s, Caroline Snowden, a black singer and dancer known as the "Josephine Baker of the West," sang "Ol' Man River" in burlesque— adult-oriented theaters associated with strippers and risqué comics. As Snowden remembered two decades later, "I sang dramatic numbers like 'Ol' Man River' which usually opened the second part of the show. You know, there were some great people with Minsky's [the best-known burlesque producers]...Jules Bledsoe, among others."[3]

Snowden seems not to have played "Ol' Man River" for comedy: most subsequent black female singers did—for example, Ann Robinson, described by *Variety* in 1943 as a "colored comedy songstress." Playing Le Ruban Bleu, a midtown Manhattan nightclub with a white clientele, Robinson was "given to gut-bucket rhythmic and riff-roughouse [sic] vocalizing....a hoyden Harlem comedienne who will do better in the classier spots, although OK for the general café circuit." Her "Ol' Man River" was "further fortified by good accomp[animent]."[4] Robinson played the number for comedy but delivered musical pleasure as well.

Annabelle Hill earned this review in *Variety* based on three songs sung onstage at the Apollo Theater in Harlem in 1945:

> This huskily built Negro femme has a baritone voice deep enough for a male singer, but it's pretty hard for her to control it and consequently during her turn there's a great deal of tittering. While a downtown audience might feel uncomfortable during her turn, audience here wouldn't let her off. Miss Hill gives out with three numbers in the masculine vein, "Ol' Man River," "Road to Mandalay," and "[Begin the] Beguine." Delivery, mannerisms and conception of tunes are not at all feminine.[5]

Several years later, Hill would introduce the song "Another Openin', Another Show" in the first scene of Cole Porter's *Kiss Me, Kate* on Broadway. Her remarkable voice can be heard on the show's original cast album, giving an explanation of sorts for why Hill thought "Ol' Man River" was right for her. The disjunction between Hill's female body and very low voice would create a genuine novelty effect on a song like "Ol' Man River," associated so closely with the sound of baritones and basses.

June Richmond, a black singer who often worked with white bands, earned these comments in a nightclub review from 1946: "June Richmond, hefty comic, builds her routine nicely after a slow start, bringing some good yocks as well as showing nifty pipes in 'Ol' Man River.' Depends heavily on little bits of business, especially facial expressions, to get across. Also, she smartly lays off overplaying the sight end of her comedy by draping herself with tasteful costuming."[6] This review toggles between the comic element—Richmond's size and expressions—and her abilities as a singer—those "nifty pipes." Her evident skill singing "Ol' Man River" is balanced by the disjunctions inherent in her treating the serious song as an opportunity for "good yocks." In 1945, Richmond sang "Ol' Man River" with the Count Basie Orchestra on the radio show *Jubilee*, a program of mostly black artists designed for broadcast to soldiers around the world. Richmond sings an original lyric for the verse.

> Everyone likes to sing "Ol' Man River"
> But I would like to get in the groove.
> Everyone wants to be so dramatic
> But here's how I'd like to sing that song for you.

Having set the terms, Richmond launches into a very fast chorus: 162 bpm. Her second chorus shifts tempo several times: cooling down to make room for some scat vocalizing; going into a deliberate pace for the big finish, which is drawn out—"routined" in the show biz sense—for maximum impact. Indeed, Richmond ends with a long high G-sharp. The audience of GIs loves it (⊛ Sound Example 6.2).

Finally, back in Harlem at the Apollo in 1954: "Topliner Big Maybelle, in the closing niche, is a beefy bounce stylist. Garbed in a petite pink frock, she makes a striking appearance as she skips through 'Ol' Man River' [and other tunes]. She's got a fine rhythmic style and some unusual offbeat phrasing that makes her the delight of the hepsters."[7] Big Maybelle's recorded output is large and gives a taste of how she might have done "Ol' Man River" in a thoroughly rhythm-and-blues style. Also on the bill with Maybelle was black comedienne Jackie "Moms" Mabley, whose 1960s revision of "Ol' Man River" captured live before a boisterous black audience is discussed in the final chapter.

The four women described here—only Richmond can be heard singing the song—suggest a kind of geologically hidden oxbow lake: "Ol' Man River" as a comic song sung by a deep-voiced, physically large, black woman. This way with the tune never made it on to records but, as the pages of *Variety* suggest, was a viable option for performers filling a particular niche in mid-century nightlife.

In 1973, fresh off a long run as Julie in *Show Boat* in London's West End, British singing star Cleo Laine traveled to America to record a live LP at Carnegie Hall. In the process, Laine added another episode to the history of "Ol' Man River" as sung by women and as performed in America's premiere concert hall. Laine didn't sing "Ol' Man River" per se. Instead, Hammerstein and Kern's tune shows up in a virtuoso novelty arrangement of the 1950s song "Control Yourself," the lyric for which exhorts the listener to control, contain, restrict, and restrain the self in a search for tranquility and serenity. The repeat of the chorus has Laine herself losing control by slipping briefly into popular standards associated with overheated and overblown performance. Laine bursts forth in lines from "I Got Rhythm" and "Secret Love" only to abruptly regain control with a return to the cool delivery of the "Control Yourself" groove. The advice on offer is something the singer herself needs to hear, no surprise to anyone who knows Laine's idiosyncratic work. Her most extended insertion—and loss of control—is the last: the final A phrase from "Ol' Man River," beginning at "I gets weary..." The audience starts laughing immediately; the joke works instantly, better than either of the earlier two interpolated snippets. Laine gets worked up quickly in volume and affect, laughing somewhat crazily after the line "sick of trying." Sailing up to the peak of Kern's tune—in a tantalizing hint of how she would *really* sing it—Laine cuts herself off: "but Ol' Man...Control Yourself" (◉ Sound Example 6.3).

Laine's "Control Yourself" effectively spoofs the emotional artifice behind any and all singing. Singers often express big emotions, apparently losing themselves in the musical moment but in fact exercising exquisite control (except, of course, for guitar and vocal cord-destroying rockers—although even that requires technique of a sort). The joke lying just beneath the comic surface of "Control Yourself" is Laine's complete technical control, which allows her to perform a loss of emotional control. She turns the emotion on and off, revealing in the process that none of it is real. It's all a performance.

Laine's dip into "Ol' Man River" is a solid historical joke. Singers had been losing control while singing the song for decades. Rowan and Martin, later of *Laugh In* fame on 1960s television, had an "Ol' Man River" sketch in their nightclub act in the late 1950s, described by one reviewer as "Martin's impresh of a pompous basso sweating out an offkey 'Ol' Man River.'"[8] Comic Buddy Lester engaged in a "spoofing of Met baritone singing 'Ol'

Man River'" in his 1948 vaudeville act, judged by *Variety* to be a "rib-tickler."[9] And at Lewisohn Stadium in 1947, musical satirist Alec Templeton offered up one of "his famous specialties," described in the *Times* as "a vocal rendition of 'Ol' Man River' as most baritones sing it."[10] Templeton probably wasn't satirizing Robeson: his take on the song was too staid for comedy. The baritones being targeted by these comics were most likely white singers who treated the song as a serious soliloquy. As June Richmond noted in her reflexive revision of the verse, "Everyone wants to be so dramatic": white baritones and basses have, as a group, fit this description best. Such singers have tended to overdo it, to push on the song, indeed to push on specific bits. White singers correctly perceived Kern's tune as song that could display vocal power and emotional range and command thunderous, outsized—knee jerk?—applause. The drama inherent in the lyric also provides a chance to do some acting—in some cases, an opportunity to overact.

But there's a problem. If "Ol' Man River" is taken seriously as an expression of sincere emotions and authentic thought, then it's tough to frame the song as anything but a protest against something specific—for example, the actual and existential predicament of black laborers in the South. How else explain "taters" and "cotton" and a river understood to be the Mississippi in the chorus and named outright in the verse? And given the verse lyric's mention of the "white man boss," it only makes sense for black singers to sing it.

Some sorts of white singers might be imagined as closer to "Ol' Man River" than others. White rock and roll singers with an affinity for the blues might pick it up: only a few have with any real commitment—the most famous being Rod Stewart on guitarist Jeff Beck's 1968 album *Truth* (see Chapter 8). One can imagine a socially conscious rocker like Bruce Springsteen resonating with Hammerstein's lyric, a notion developed further in a later chapter as well. But Springsteen and his like typically sing their own material and—unlike singers from earlier generations, such as Robeson—are unlikely to allow a Broadway show tune into the corpus of genuine folk songs they do choose to sing.

The white male singers who took up "Ol' Man River" in a serious manner have been of two kinds: opera, light opera, and musical theater singers who are professionally invested in big songs, emotions, and drama; and popular male vocalists who want to show interpretive range, to sing something profound that's not about romantic love. The first category includes a roll call of famous voices, some better remembered today than others: Lawrence Tibbett, Leonard Warren, George London, John Charles Thomas, Robert Merrill, Gordon MacRae, Samuel Ramey, Sherrill Milnes, and Davis Gaines. The second group is smaller but much more famous: Al Jolson and Frank

Sinatra both sang "Ol' Man River" multiple times. This chapter treats all these men except for Sinatra, whose history with the song warrants its own chapter.

The historical window for white men to sing "Ol' Man River" in a serious manner closed in the 1990s. The most active period for this approach ran from 1928 to about 1970, the same four decades that saw the flourishing of Ol' Man Rhythm. Jolson started the practice in 1928.

To think about these white performers singing a black song, I'd like to borrow an idea from dance history scholar Susan Manning. Writing about white modern dancers in the Thirties, Manning describes their attempts to embody the black experience as "metaphorical minstrelsy."[11] Frequently dancing to spirituals, sometimes as sung by black singers, these white dancers assumed black identities—literally took them upon their bodies without blacking up their faces—at a time when black dancers and chore- ographers were denied opportunities with modern dance companies and were just beginning to articulate a practice of black self-representation in modern dance. By the early Forties, white dancers dancing the black expe- rience were effectively displaced by blacks dancing their own blackness, a development that culminated in the work of Alvin Ailey and other African American choreographers and dancers. The historical window for "meta- phorical minstrelsy" in modern dance was brief.

Adapting Manning's idea, this chapter brings together what we might call "metaphorical Joes," white singers who approach "Ol' Man River" in a serious tone with the intent of embodying its expression of dignified black suffering. These performances typically combine a few key interpretive choices: a slow tempo with a lot of rubato allowing for displays of dynamic variety and breath control; alteration of key words such as "white folks" in the verse; orchestral accompaniment in a quasi-symphonic style, with min- imal, if any, suggestion of a rhythm section; supporting choral voices that act as a musical halo, typically over the climax; and bombastic vocal and emotional release at the close intended to elicit wild applause. Audiences proved quite willing to oblige. A 1930 review of operatic baritone John Charles Thomas singing "Ol' Man River" in Manhattan's Town Hall cap- tures the interpretive strategy and typical crowd response: Thomas "[began] in a dramatic whisper and carried to a shout. The waiting audience . . . came back with an answering roar."[12] The whisper-to-shout approach worked similarly for many, many singers.

Metaphorical Joes might be best described as singers who could never play Joe in *Show Boat* but who want—perhaps desperately want—to embody this exceptionally serious, exceptionally popular song and hitch a ride on the historically outsized reaction white audiences give it again and

again. Metaphorical performance of "Ol' Man River" also offered an opportunity to show interpretive range that crossed racial lines without a loss of
dignity. One white baritone recitalist who sang "Ol' Man River" and several
spirituals as encores for a varied classical program was praised for skillfully
singing "in the Negro manner."[13] "Ol' Man River" gave these white singers
the chance to embody serious black emotions while also singing a wildly
popular song. At the same time, "Ol' Man River" offered pop singers like
Jolson and Sinatra the chance to sing something that sounded slightly
operatic, something that called up big emotions and smacked of serious, or
at least middlebrow, art.

Three serious solo singers recorded the original opening of the verse in
the early years of the song's history. Besides Robeson in his 1930 recording,
Al Jolson and Lawrence Tibbett both waxed the line "Niggers all work on de
Mississippi." Jolson and Tibbett, a popular singing star and a beloved operatic star, form an interesting pair.

Twelve weeks before *Show Boat* opened on Broadway, Jolson inaugurated
the age of synchronized sound in the cinema: *The Jazz Singer* featured Jolson
singing popular songs, in and out of blackface. Jolson's persona was a mix of
energetic, frenetic rousers and sentimental, overwrought weepies: in *The
Jazz Singer* he caromed from "Toot-Toot Tootsie Goodbye" to "Mammy" and
also sang Jewish liturgical music. Jolson's film career would end up emphasizing the sentimental side, with most of his film plots involving the death
of loved ones and the loss of children or love. Jolson was no stranger to
serious emotions and tragic scenarios. With a career-long investment in
performing in blackface and moving his audience to tears with emotional
songs, "Ol' Man River" must have been irresistible to Jolson.

Jolson's two recorded versions, made twenty years apart, are remarkably similar. Both are utterly serious: Jolson puts on a concert hall persona
and tries to rely solely on the power of his voice to interpret the lyric and
melody. Both recordings would work just fine as part of a production of
Show Boat. Indeed, Jolson—who surely saw *Show Boat* during its initial
Broadway run—could have seen Joe as a part he might someday play.
Around that time Jolson expressed his desire to star in a musical version of
the play *Porgy*, which ran concurrently with *Show Boat* on Broadway and
was later turned into a black-cast opera by Gershwin. Kern and Hammerstein
were Jolson's first choices to write the score for his imagined *Porgy*
vehicle.

Jolson sings "Ol' Man River" in a dignified manner, with only a few
touches that might be chalked up to his forceful show biz style: for example, he rewrites the end of the first two A phrases with a short three-
note descent—at times blurred into a slide—that adds just a touch of

Broadway styling (◉ Sound Example 6.4). No other singer adopted this small touch—except for Frank Sinatra, who consistently incorporated Jolson's three-note slide (◉ Sound Example 6.5 includes short clips from two Sinatra recordings: his 1944 V-Disc recording and his 1963 LP *The Concert Sinatra*). Jolson sings the lyrics without alteration and embodies the black persona completely. At the bridge, he speaks the lines "'Tote dat barge!' / 'Lif' dat bale!'" in a way that suggests the black laborer singing is imitating the cries of the white man boss through his own experience of having to do the work. Jolson doesn't slip into the boss persona but remains in the mind of the black singing subject—a significant difference between his attempt to channel Joe and that of the trained white singers coming out of the opera house.

Jolson's 1948 "Ol' Man River" was captured as part of a radio appearance. He introduces the number as from Jerome Kern's "greatest score." The arrangement is more elaborate than on his 1928 version: wordless chorus and overactive orchestral textures distract a bit from Jolson's singing. Here, Jolson's limitations as a singer are more audible: he doesn't really have the pipes to sing "Ol' Man River" in this way (◉ Sound Example 6.6). Will Friedwald disagrees, calling Jolson's performance "indisputably the greatest Jewish performance of the song," adding "his intonation and his attitude are unmistakably Hebraic. Jolson underscores the universality of the text by showing how it applies as much to the plight of the Jews as it does to blacks in the American south."[14]

Jolson's recordings of "Ol' Man River" reveal a performer known for manic energy striving for a more "legitimate" dramatic and musical effect. His sincerity should not be discounted—nor should that of the other white male singers profiled in this chapter. These baritones recognized the power of this song written for Robeson, a major singing talent with whom, in practical terms in an age of segregation, none of them had to compete for work or audiences. Their desire to sing this beloved song makes transparent sense: they all liked to please their audiences. And "Ol' Man River" offered an interpretive challenge: to perform the noble suffering of black Americans in a popular song with the potential to show off a great voice.

Lawrence Tibbett's recording from 1932 is the historical point of origin for a string of white opera singers who recorded "Ol' Man River," adding this show tune to their public persona as captured on record in an era when singers' stage careers were represented on recordings by way of excerpts only. Tibbett was a famous American-born baritone and Metropolitan Opera mainstay when he recorded "Ol' Man River" and the song was something of a signature for him. He sang it twice on the Met stage in special concerts of popular American favorites in 1932 and 1934. Tibbett wore blackface at the Met in 1933 while playing the operatic version of Robeson's signature dramatic role, Brutus Jones, in the premiere of Louis Gruenberg's opera *The Emperor Jones*. Tibbett's performances of "Ol' Man River" and appearances in *The Emperor Jones* both pointed toward Robeson, the great African American dramatic and musical artist of the day. At the first Met concert, Tibbett sang "Ol' Man River" solo early on and then led all the featured artists in a sing-along of the tune to close the evening. The *Times* noted how many of the songs on the program "brought a catch to the throat and a tear to the eye of every hearer, stirred by strangely familiar word and refrain of universal sentiment and memory."[15] Just five years old and "Ol' Man River" could already fulfill this nostalgic task for white audiences. The second concert was described as "given in minstrel style" although it was noted that neither "Old Folks at Home" nor "Dixie" were offered. "Ol' Man River," however, held its place in this context.[16]

(Jules Bledsoe also sang "Ol' Man River" in the Metropolitan Opera House at another special event featuring American music: the 1935 opera ball. With the stage set representing the portico of a gracious Southern mansion—described in the *Times* as "a luxurious setting reflecting the benign atmosphere of plantation days in the 'deep South' of the pre-Civil War era"—attendees donned antebellum costumes and assumed new identities, their character and real names listed in the paper as if playing roles in a drama.[17] Musical performances were integrated seamlessly into the festivities: Met stars impersonated famous opera singers of the earlier age, for example, Rose Bampton as Jenny Lind. Bledsoe played an entirely predictable part in this historical pageant. As the paper reported, "Jules Bledsoe, Negro baritone, was cast as Jules, butler of the La Grange family, and he sang the famous old Foster song 'Massa's in the Cold, Cold Ground.' As an encore, Bledsoe offered 'Ol' Man River.'")

"Ol' Man River" remained a radio favorite through the 1930s and 1940s. For example, Ezio Pinza, the operatic bass for whom Rodgers and Hammerstein wrote the male lead Emile Lebec in *South Pacific*, sang it on the radio as part of an otherwise all classical concert in 1930.[18] These performances are largely lost beyond the radio listings preserved in newspapers. Any regular listener to classical and light classical singers on the radio could have heard "Ol' Man River" several times a year.

After World War II, during the first decade of the long-playing record, many opera and light opera singers recorded "Ol' Man River" as part of an album of popular favorites. These song anthologies where "Ol' Man River" found inclusion suggest how white, male, trained singers and their record labels understood the song's usefulness, how it could be made to fit into their vocal personas, their careers, and the imagination of their desired audiences. Among the many studio-cast recordings of *Show Boat* produced in these years, several stand out for letting white opera or operetta singers play Joe on record in a way they never could have on stage. Before considering the overwhelmingly similar manner in which these men sang the song, the vocalists' backgrounds and how they positioned "Ol' Man River" in their recorded output deserve some attention.

- Leonard Warren, American baritone and Met regular, placed "Ol' Man River" next to last on side two of his 1951 disc *Songs for Everyone,* which opens with "America the Beautiful" and closes with "Battle Hymn of the Republic." Between these, Warren offers ballads sentimental ("Love's Old Sweet Song"), rustic ("Home on the Range"), and historical (a setting of Kipling's "On the Road to Mandalay"). "Ol' Man River" is the only Broadway show tune: in this company, it functions as a folk song—a song, as the album title suggests, everyone knows and loves outside the trends of popular music. *Billboard* judged the disc "should appeal to the older folks, sentimentalists and collectors who have a special interest in Metopera [*sic*] baritone Warren."[19] "Ol' Man River" was one of only two tracks singled out as potentially viable as a single 45.
- George London, a Canadian-born bass-baritone also known for his Met appearances, positioned "Ol' Man River" exclusively among show tunes on his 1957 disc *George London on Broadway.* London's choices all welcome his lyric baritone, even though some—like "On the Street Where You Live"—were originally written for the tenor range. In this company, "Ol' Man River" is a lush melody among similarly smooth lines.
- Robert Merrill, another American baritone and Met star, recorded "Ol' Man River" three times: a Red Seal version from 1949, pressed on red vinyl with "The Lord's Prayer" as the flip side, and two studio-cast versions of the *Show Boat* score, 1949 and 1956, respectively, on both of which Merrill sang Joe's part as well as the solos and duets for the show's romantic leading man Gaylord Ravenal. Casting Merrill as Joe and Ravenal brings to the surface the issues of race and masculinity present for all these white men singing a black man's song. Merrill also sang "Ol' Man River" during a 1954 stint in the lounge at the Hotel Sands in Las Vegas, part of a program mixing "long-hair and semi-classical numbers selected to please everyone who might wander in."[20]
- Gordon MacRae stands out among this group as an American baritone who did not have an opera career. With "a clear lyric baritone voice with attractive masculine, yet non-operatic qualities," MacRae is best known for playing the leading male roles in the film adaptations of *Oklahoma!* (1955) and *Carousel* (1956).[21] (On the latter, MacRae replaced Sinatra in

the part of Billy Bigelow: both men regularly performed the dramatic "Soliloquy" from this Rodgers and Hammerstein score.) MacRae sang "Ol' Man River" as early as 1949 on *The Railroad Hour*, an NBC radio show that featured condensed versions of famous Broadway musicals. MacRae was the show's baritone star. MacRae recorded "Ol' Man River" twice, in 1951 and 1958. The later recording appears on an LP titled *Gordon MacRae in Concert*. The liner notes define the album as filled with examples of "the 'big' song—the lasting Broadway hit, the time-proven ballad, the song that closes an act." The choices are eclectic, with more than a few written specifically for black characters ("Lost in the Stars," "Summertime") and one, besides "Ol' Man River," suggesting Robeson ("Water Boy"). The others are big Broadway and Hollywood ballads, like "Begin the Beguine" and "Stranger in Paradise," or emotional pop songs, like "I Believe." The liner notes define MacRae as an unaffected singer: "His technique (if directness and simplicity can be so termed) derives its strength from a voice warm and sensitive, yet powerful and compelling. But most important of all, people sense that here is a singer who loves to sing, who lives to sing."

When taken up by experienced opera and operetta singers, the dramatic possibilities of Kern and Hammerstein's song are brought to the front. The opportunity to project with passion provided by the tune's melodic climax also finds new punch when sung by these trained voices. The tune's peak, as well the depths plumbed at the opening, would be vocally familiar territory for singers of opera and operetta, who gravitated to this popular song which has a range that's too big for most normal voices.

Part of the dramatic attraction of the song is the verse: all these singers recorded it. Predictably, changes to the lyrics are made. Only Tibbett, recording in 1932, sings the original lyric, complete with "niggers all work... white folks play... [and] white man boss." Thomas sings "darkies" in 1931. White singers in the 1950s sang "here we all work," in part because of an effective campaign by black civil rights groups to rid the air waves of the word "darkies" (discussed later). Merrill and London alike left "white folks play" and "white man boss" unchanged. MacRae's approach—"here we all work while the big boss plays"—uniquely dodges any mention of race at the cost of the non-threatening, upon reflection potentially nonsensical image of the big boss at play: how threatening could his commands to "tote" and "lift" be? MacRae was the only member of this cohort to remove all the racial markers in the lyric.

The elimination of "darkies" was a recent change, as suggested by a controversy involving Merrill that was generated by a black newspaper. In 1947, as part of an effort to ban "all racial epithets on the air," the *Afro-American* sent a letter to RCA Victor, Merrill's label, requesting that the singer "not use the song, 'Ol' Man River,' or, if he uses it, to omit the epithet 'd—' as applied to colored people." Recognizing that the song "has become established as an American classic," the newspaper felt that asking Merrill to "omit it from his repertoire" went a step too far. But, the paper noted,

> The world is moving forward. All of us recognize that the minstrels in the old fashioned popular songs, which used epithets, are out of date. We don't like the use of the word "shine" nor of the word "d—" on the radio and we propose to fight it with every means at our command. If RCA proposes to continue the use of the word "d—," then it will certainly have to use "Sheenie," "dago," "kike" and epithets applying to all other races.[22]

Merrill himself replied at length to the *Afro-American*.

> I want to thank you for calling my attention to the lines of the song "Ol' Man River" which might be construed as derogatory to colored people. I have made all necessary changes, and I am enclosing the lyrics that I now use. I will perform the song with these lyrics at all my concerts in the future. I am also scheduled to record this song in the very near future for RCA-Victor, and will use these lyrics at that recording date.... Please understand that when an artist sings a song, he looks at it only as a piece of great music. Unfortunately, he seldom takes the time to analyze the meaning of the song, and any implication it might carry which could be construed as derogatory to a race, color, creed, or individual. I have never done anything or thought any thoughts in my private life that could be considered as prejudiced action or thought toward anyone. I surely do not want to do anything in my musical life that would not be in keeping with my thinking in private life.[23]

Merrill meant what he said and black newspapers followed and praised his actions. In 1948, he duetted on the radio with black opera star Dorothy Maynor, violating what the *Pittsburgh Courier* called "a silent but effective ban on interracial duets." The *Courier* also reminded its black readership of Merrill's stand on "Ol' Man River," his choice to use "non-objectionable lyrics."[24] White singers who did not require prodding could expect to get recognized as well. In 1937, columnist Malcolm Fulcher wrote in the *Afro-American*, "Nelson Eddie [Eddy] endeared himself to me forever. When he sang 'Ol' Man River' he changed the word 'd-----' to 'Negro.' There are so many of the radio singers who seem to take a delight in making offensive remarks in songs and chatter about our people. I don't know if congratulations are in order, but here they are anyway."[25]

Metropolitan Opera star Robert Merrill responded positively to a public request by the *Baltimore Afro-American*, a national black newspaper, to eliminate the word "darkies" while singing "Ol' Man River." (Photofest)

And the *Afro-American* wasn't afraid of going after bigger targets than singers. When Hammerstein commented negatively on Robeson's revisions in 1949, the paper fired back to the lyricist "that he might at least eliminate the word 'darky.'" Hammerstein replied to the paper, "This is not my word but is the invention of some singer. The modern lyrics in 'Ol' Man River' as used in the recent production of *Show Boat* is [sic] 'colored folk work on the Mississippi.'"[26] This exchange shows, yet again, how refining the details has been at the center of the reception and survival of "Ol' Man River." Talking about those changes, making them an issue in newsprint, has been part of the process that kept the song "established as an American classic." This dialogue was initiated and sustained by black newspaper editors: whites who cared about these black voices—Merrill and Hammerstein among them—responded thoughtfully at the time.

The arrangements used by white baritones—custom-made for each singer—suggest a common understanding of "Ol' Man River" as a big song: both loud and important. (Tibbett's recording is the exception, using piano accompaniment only.) The 1950s versions all opt for a full orchestra on the bombastic side, although subtle touches—harps, even a celeste—are heard as well. Fanfare-like fortissimo openings and closings are common—this, they insist, is a substantial song worthy of symphonic treatment.

The rhythmic impulse backing the vocal line plays a major role in defining the overall mood of these versions. Tibbet's and MacRae's 1958 recordings share a relentless quality, with repeated chords, in the piano and low strings, respectively, driving on the A sections, forcing both men to fit themselves to the beat—an apt rhythmic treatment for a work song (⊙ Sound Example 6.7 includes Tibbet and MacRae on the same phrase). Other versions are more flexible, giving the singer room to shape how the melody unfolds and to draw attention to their own vocal artistry by drawing out select high notes.

The higher phrases of the song lend themselves to emphasis for these singers, who are looking to "Ol' Man River" to display beauty of line and tone. Tibbett finds this in both the verse—"don't look up and don't look down"—and the chorus—"soon forgotten" and from "scared of dyin'" to the close. The song's penultimate note—the "a" of the last "along"—gets extra time from every one of these singers.

But lyrical shape and dynamic climax aren't all these singers are after. They all also enhance the dynamic contrast between soft and loud by mixing in spoken and shouted, even barked, vocal deliveries. Indeed, in their search for emotion and drama in "Ol' Man River," every one of the white trained or "supported" singers who recorded the song between 1931 and the end of the 1950s attacked Hammerstein's bridge lyric in a particular manner. They all felt compelled to shout or speak—not to just sing—on the lines " 'Tote dat barge!' / 'Lif' dat bale!' " Tibbett does it and so does every serious singer after him (⊙ Sound Example 6.8 excerpts Tibbett, Thomas, Merrill [1949], Warren, London, and MacRae [1958] in order). This shared impulse among white male singers to enhance their singing with speaking or shouting is one historical marker of how "Ol' Man River"—a song sung by a black character about the black experience—challenged white performers to search for new interpretive strategies.

Two reasons for this universal expressive choice suggest themselves. The singers, working from printed music, are taking Hammerstein's quotation marks and exclamation points seriously. Shouting becomes a way to impersonate the white man or big man boss, a way to bring to life the dramatic nature of the bridge text. (We'll hear doo-wop groups in the 1960s taking a similar approach.) Alternately, the singers are responding to the directly physical nature of Hammerstein's lyric. This song's about manual labor: about work, not feelings. Bringing out these lyrics by briefly abandoning their characteristic cultivated and effortless vocal techniques becomes a way to highlight Hammerstein's rather unusual imagery—indeed, his abandonment of imagery in favor of emphatic commands to move. MacRae follows this logic by also shouting the word *pull* in "pull that rope" not as a command but as if saying it will help him do the task. It bears repeating that Robeson never dramatized these words. Singing them was enough for him. He didn't underscore their meaning, which he likely took as somewhat transparent for his white and black listeners when sung by a big, black man at a time in history when African Americans were understood, by most whites, as fit by nature and history for manual labor. Trained white male singers—by profession, paragons of refinement—felt the need to compensate by dipping into other vocal techniques. Some can be heard to overcompensate, for shouting or speak-singing on the bridge opens a slippery slope. Some of these singers modify their vocal style throughout the song. Often—as with Warren and London—they gravitate toward the line "I gets weary." Thomas carries the spoken quality throughout much of his recording (⊙ Sound Example 6.9 excerpts Thomas, Warren, and London in succession). Under what other circumstances do these white baritones speak rather than sing a musical line? Almost never. "Ol' Man River" elicits interpretive choices no other song does. And perhaps that's why they chose to sing it. In these white men's voices, "Ol' Man River" becomes both a song to show off a good voice and a vehicle for dramatic embodiment of a black character either implied or explicitly stated. This tension between the song as a vehicle for vocal display and the song as a dramatic soliloquy crossing the lines of race and class can be heard in all the trained white men's versions of "Ol' Man River."

There's another reason white singers were attracted to "Ol' Man River": its association with manliness. Two anecdotes from the late 1940s point toward the connection between unassailable masculinity and "Ol' Man River."[27]

In 1947, Robert Weede, yet another leading baritone at the Metropolitan Opera, appeared on the radio show *Guest Star*. The show's host, Win Elliot, humorously mistook Weede for an Irish tenor. When told Weede was a baritone,

Elliot replied "Well, if he's a baritone he's going to have to prove it to me." Without another word, Weede launched into "Ol' Man River" and the point was made. Anyone who knows music, the sketch implies, knows that "Ol' Man River" is the great test of baritones and basses. Like his white peers would do in their 1950s recordings, Weede spoke the "tote" and "lift" lines—he also spoke "bend your knees" in the verse—and used the penultimate high note to end the song by emphasizing his voice over the drama of the lyric.

In late 1948, Arthur Godfrey was ready to take his radio show onto the new medium of television. In a rehearsal for Godfrey's small-screen debut, John Evans, a white, not young but not too old, baritone, stepped to the microphone to sing "Ol' Man River." Evans had triumphed with the song in Godfrey's *Talent Scout* radio show the previous evening. Evans sang with a heavy, operatic vibrato but, unlike a trained singer, went straight to the consonants (-n, -m) and used overly bright vowels on dialect words like "jes'." Evans's style is a hybrid of classical and popular singing: perfectly suited to a song like "Ol' Man River," which sits easily on the border between trained and untrained singing. Godfrey praised Evans in gendered terms as a rarity on the radio. Evans had, Godfrey said, "a real, virile, legitimate baritone voice."

Assuming listeners agreed, they would have been likely comparing Evans to Robeson, who had recently recorded "Ol' Man River" for the final time in a recording studio. (This recording, with Robeson's alterations to the lyrics, was heard on the radio in 1948.)[28] In the case of "Ol' Man River," white male singers measured their virility against a black male model. Shortly after the controversies of 1949, Robeson was effectively removed from the musical scene: he never recorded for a major label again and sang a handful of major concerts in the late 1950s before retiring from public life. Did this silencing of Robeson open the door for Merrill, Warren, London, and MacRae to sing "Ol' Man River" without fear of comparison? In 1951, the radio show *Toast of the Town* devoted an entire episode to telling the story of Oscar Hammerstein. When it came time to salute *Show Boat*, the black star Lena Horne sang "Can't Help Lovin' Dat Man." "Ol' Man River" was next on the program. The announcer set it up this way, praising Hammerstein's lyric as central to the framing of *Show Boat*'s story: "The one force running through and dominating the lives of all the characters was the Mississippi River. . . . and telling the resignation of a race to the ruthlessness of its currents. Told best now by Robert Merrill." Only with Robeson excluded from the scene could a white singer be the "best" choice "now" to deliver "Ol' Man River."

A few white opera singers recorded or performed "Ol' Man River" after the 1960s—among them Sherrill Milnes, whose abortive attempt to sing the song at the US Capitol in the 1990s was discussed in Chapter 1, and Samuel Ramey, who found television venues in the 1990s that used a celebration of the history of the American musical to leverage performance of the song by a white opera star.

Milnes recorded "Ol' Man River" on a 1976 disc titled *The Songs America Loves*, a bicentennial descendant of the 1950s discs of popular favorites discussed earlier and a precursor to the twenty-first-century patriotic "special products" profiled in Chapter 5. Milnes's solo LP was produced by the General Federation of Women's Clubs, an organization working to enhance community funding for the arts. The Clubs' president articulated a high calling for the album and its buyers on the cover: "By buying and giving *The Songs America Loves* you have personally had a part in telling future generations what a great land we have. When we are gone, only *The Arts* will be here to tell the story." The album's story spotted "Ol' Man River" in a familiar prominent place: the end of side B. Milnes's participation in the project—he's described as the "All-American Superstar"—formed part of a familiar career strategy: success on the opera stage, however great, would never generate the popular success to be gained by singing popular favorites. Along a similar tack, Milnes had recently recorded three discs of sacred songs and hymns. *The Songs America Loves* opens with "The Star-Spangled Banner" and includes medleys of Armed Forces songs and Stephen Foster favorites, and even a setting of Lincoln's Gettysburg Address. It's largely the repertoire Milnes described as planned for his 1992 July Fourth concert at the Capitol. Supported by a full symphony orchestra and lush, almost superabundant arrangements, Milnes sings with tremendous line, evenness of tone, clarity of diction, and flexibility of sound. For an opera singer, he manages not to sound like an opera singer: the effect is light, rich, effortless; never heavy, wobbly, or labored. His "Ol' Man River" leans toward the lyrical rather than the dramatic. Milnes does shout "tote" and "lift," but there's a kind of cinematic grandeur to the whole that suggests a singer holding the song at arm's length (⊚ Sound Example 6.10). Milnes sings "Ol' Man River" as a "classic," departing significantly from the overly dramatic approach of earlier generations of white opera singers.

Samuel Ramey, a white American bass, recorded "Ol' Man River" in 1994, spotting it last on a CD of Broadway show tunes, and sang it twice on television in the 1990s, both times on PBS telecasts of concerts given in New York City. Both concerts connected Ramey's performance of "Ol' Man River" directly to *Show Boat*. Both also worked the old middlebrow magic: bringing American opera stars down and Broadway musicals up to a meeting place where PBS viewers might comfortably enjoy looking in on the scene from their living rooms.

American opera star Sherrill Milnes sang "Ol' Man River" with Arthur Fiedler and the Boston Pops on PBS in 1976. Milnes was prevented from singing the song on the steps of the US Capitol for PBS broadcast in 1992. (Photofest)

The 1990 telecast *Flicka and Friends* on the PBS series *Live from Lincoln Center* featured American mezzo-soprano Fredericka Von Stade, joined by Ramey and tenor Jerry Hadley. The first half was serious: the three sang opera arias, duets, and trios in their original foreign languages. The second half was familiar: the trio, joined by a chorus, offered selections from *Show*

Boat. Von Stade and Hadley had recently recorded the leading romantic roles of Magnolia and Ravenal on a three-disc *Show Boat* set conducted by John McGlinn, an expert in the reconstruction of original orchestrations for "classic" musicals. McGlinn's project attracted attention, criticism, and protest for its use of Hammerstein's original verse lyric at the opening of act one. The black chorus initially engaged for the recording walked out over the issue of singing the n-word: a white chorus, in the old practice of metaphorical blackface, sang their parts.[29] Only two black singers agreed to participate: one was black bass Bruce Hubbard as Joe. McGlinn could get away with a white chorus singing the black chorus parts but the option of hiring a white singer to deliver "Ol' Man River" in the context of so exalted a project was beyond the pale. Hubbard even provided a written explanation in the set's press packet for why he felt comfortable singing Hammerstein's original lyric. But on *Flicka and Friends*, Ramey sang Joe, supported by an almost entirely white chorus and conducted by African American conductor Henry Lewis. In context, Ramey was the obvious choice: the bass on hand to sing this obligatory bass feature in a setting where questions of race might still be elided, at least for the length of a song.

Ramey sang "Ol' Man River" in concert a second time on public television as part of the 1997 show *A Celebration of the American Musical.* This concert featured six American opera singers—all white—doing solos, duets, and trios, lending their heavy, trained voices to light numbers like "Sing for Your Supper" and "There Is Nothing Like a Dame," as well as Broadway tunes more friendly to trained singing, such as selections from the operetta *Kismet.* "Ol' Man River"—the only number written for a black character on the program—was a predictable choice as a song well suited to trained voices. Supported by a modest-sized, all-white men's chorus and following the form of the song as it appears in *Show Boat*, Ramey took a restrained approach—singing in thoroughly operatic fashion and not pushing the drama of the song like his 1950s opera peers had done. He does shout "tote" and "lift" but the sluggish tempo takes all the energy out of the performance. In this narrow context, a white singer could still metaphorically put on the character of Joe.

A final white male version of "Ol' Man River" from the 1990s is worth a listen, if only because it hints at how reliant serious performance of the song is on a particular kind of singing style derived, in part, from the concert hall and opera house. The sound of Broadway singing changed in the 1980s and the new, pop-style operetta voice—heard in the long-running "poperettas" of the time—proves a poor match for "Ol' Man River." American musical theater leading man Davis Gaines, veteran of over two thousand performances as the Phantom in Andrew Lloyd Webber's *The*

Phantom of the Opera, recorded "Ol' Man River" in 1996 on a disc of mostly Broadway selections. With the quavery vibrato and strained quality of late twentieth-century musical theater voices, Gaines sounds confusingly like the Phantom singing Joe. The multiple masks in play make for a disturbing effect. Manipulative, pop-derived modulations in the arrangement and a manneristic dramatic style—perfectly matched to Lloyd Webber's *Phantom*, a poor fit for Kern's tune—push Gaines's version across a kind of tastefulness line. Gaines adapts Robeson's revisions for his own big finish, changing the activist's proclamation "I must keep fightin' / Until I'm dying" to the shouted but mundane observation "I must keep livin' / Until I'm dying" (◉ Sound Example 6.11). The juxtaposition of two historically distant, racially distinct Broadway archetypes—the Joe in the song text; the Phantom in Gaines's voice—affords the ear an odd reminder that new approaches to singing don't always serve old songs.

How did black singers respond to the tradition of white singers singing "Ol' Man River" in this serious, metaphorical manner? Two recordings suggest answers.

In 1945, the Phil Moore Four, a hip jazz quartet fronted by singer, pianist, composer, arranger, and vocal coach Moore, recorded a rhythmic takedown of the song.[30] Moore attacks the lyric from the start, singing "Ol' Man Rib-bah"—perhaps recalling Robeson's "Ol' man ribber" from the 1936 film—and inserting the phrase "roll, roll, roll your boat, gently out to sea" in the breaks at the end of each A phrase. Moore takes aim at white serious singers' interpretations on the bridge. He overemphasizes the word *strain* and extravagantly rolls the "r" in "wracked." At the so often shouted commands to "tote" and "lift," Moore shifts to a high and fast, petite and prissy delivery. His "big man boss" gives orders in an unmistakeably swishy voice, suggesting that the shouting bosses heard in "serious" versions of the song are overcompensating, or at least engaging in a performance of masculinity that tries suspiciously too hard to be hard.

A 1991 recording—a full-blown satire—offers another possible reply to Ol' Man Metaphor. The uncategorizable pop crazy man Screamin' Jay Hawkins included "Ol' Man River" on his 1991 album *Black Music for White People*. Hawkins turns in a long, kaleidoscopic track—over six minutes in length—that touches on almost all the ways "Ol' Man River" has been performed.

At the start, piano octaves play the opening of the verse, boldly announcing the tune. Hawkins comes in on the chorus, sung very slowly with minimal accompaniment. His delivery is understated, even internalized. But at the second syllable of the word "along"—at the key phrase "he jes' keeps rollin' along"—Hawkins breaks into a completely unprepared scream: high and loud and full of gravel, with chaotic drum hits all out of meter. The beat stops during Hawkins's scream: there's no way to know how long it will go on. When it does end, Hawkins instantly returns to the calm, quiet, introspective delivery that began the chorus (⊚ Sound Example 6.12). When "rollin' along" returns at the end of the next phrase, the scream returns, too. What was a surprise the first time becomes something to dread or anticipate throughout the second A phrase. "Yes indeed, he did it again," the listener might think. Either Hawkins is schizophrenic, manic-depressive, or he's targeting any approach that hangs over-large emotions on the song.

On the bridge, Hawkins sings "you and I." "Tote" and "lift" are shouted, with a sax coming in for some bluesy obbligato commentary. Passing smoothly across the moment when others make changes or show off, Hawkins doesn't do much to the lines about getting drunk and going to jail. With the start of the final A phrase, a soulful and slow jazz beat starts up. The sax keeps up with the fills and Hawkins lets it go vocally, finally building up to the climaxing words in a way that feels familiar. But again at the second half of "along" he takes an unexpected turn. Instead of sustaining the more serious mood only recently set—or going back to his manic screams—Hawkins starts to scat. The scatting drops us into a bouncing rhythm version of the entire chorus. For the final A phrase, the beat slows back down, as Hawkins finally treats the phrase "rollin' along" with the dignity one might think it deserves.

Hawkins's original ambition was to be like Paul Robeson—to sing serious music in a dignified manner—and even to sing opera. Instead, he created a screaming rock and roll alter ego miles away from Robeson's stoic, smiling persona. Hawkins's approach to "Ol' Man River," like Cleo Laine's "Control Yourself," highlights the constructedness of musical emotions.

Hawkins's "Ol' Man River" does not come last on the album *Black Music for White People*. Instead it appears second to last, followed by a graphic ode to masturbation and sex called "Strokin'." Earlier songs on the disc include "Ignant and Shit" (a lengthy, one-sided rant directed at a silent figure sitting on the street eating watermelon, among other overstated stereotypical depictions of deviant blackness), "Swamp Gas" (a jungle number complete with fake tribal lyrics), "Voodoo Priestess" (a riff on the fear of ghosts and the supernatural), and "Ice Cream Man" (a double-entendre song sung by a well-endowed, smooth operator). *Black Music for White People* incorporates "Ol' Man River" sans changes to the lyric into a disturbingly funny exploration of pernicious racist stereotypes pushed to and beyond their limits.

When asked in 1990 to name the records that influenced him, Hawkins headed his list with Robeson's "Ol' Man River," lauding the singer as "a rebel who fought the system in the U.S. during the 20s and 30s, went to

Russia and made motion pictures there because he didn't get too much work here and refused to be an Uncle Tom like Stepin Fetchit, Eddie 'Rochester' Anderson, Lena Horne, Ethel Waters or Buckwheat."[31] Unafraid to satirize a song he loved and had recorded in a standard up-tempo idiom in 1958, Hawkins uses "Ol' Man River" to entertain—it's a funny recording—but also to undercut the pieties of any popular music performance that takes itself too seriously and especially those that seek to define African Americans in stereotypical terms. Hawkins's bigger target, as the album title says, is black music made for white people. The most obvious analogy to his version of "Ol' Man River" is the white, trained singers profiled in this chapter, all of whom looked on the song as a chance to get serious. At the end of his "Ol' Man River," Hawkins is overheard, as if the mikes remained on in the studio, saying "I got carried away. I got carried away. I apologize. I thought I was doing a live show." Cleo Laine might suggest that Hawkins control himself.

7

⚭

Sinatra's Way

Frank Sinatra sang "Ol' Man River" for almost fifty years. He recorded it three times in the studio, always using grand, orchestral arrangements. He included it in live shows at all sorts of venues, from Lewisohn Stadium to Las Vegas lounges to the White House. He sang it on film at the climax of the 1946 MGM film *Till the Clouds Roll By* and on television in the tumultuous mid-1960s. If "Ol' Man River" was a song for Paul Robeson, Frank Sinatra made it his song, too.

"Ol' Man River" isn't the only signature song of another artist that Sinatra refashioned for his own use. He similarly adopted and reimagined several songs introduced by Fred Astaire, most memorably "Night and Day," which Sinatra sang as both a tender ballad and a swinging showpiece. With a sure sense for what he could say and do with a song, Sinatra turned "Ol' Man River" and "Night and Day"—two standards composed for two iconic performers who could hardly be more different from each other and from Sinatra—into career-long vehicles for his own expressive purposes.

But, in Sinatra's eyes, "Ol' Man River" was special. Sinatra told composer Alec Wilder that he considered "Ol' Man River" to be an essential song in his repertoire.[1] This extraordinary statement deserves unpacking, as does the mystique that has attached itself to Sinatra as a singer of popular songs like "Ol' Man River."

Sinatra's first reviewed performance of "Ol' Man River" was at Lewisohn Stadium on August 3, 1943. This was sacred ground for the song: Robeson sang it there in 1928, 1940, and 1941 and would sing it there again in 1947. In 1943, Sinatra's primary audience—teenage girls; bobby-soxers, to use the contemporary term—were out in force at Lewisohn, where "their gleeful whoops, loud laughter and handclaps frequently almost drowned out the sad, sweet music of the singer."[2] Sinatra's performance of "Ol' Man River" that August night was roundly criticized by an unnamed *Times* reviewer: "Mr. Sinatra's baritone had little real volume and little carrying power beyond what the amplifier gave it, and it was utterly inadequate in 'Ol' Man River,' but the singing was definitely unique in the matter of style, and the singer's pleasant and friendly and somewhat dreamy personality matched it." Well, of course, Sinatra's voice had little carrying power: he was a microphone singer, the crooner reinvented. Singing "Ol' Man River" did, however, earn him description as a "baritone," a hint at what singing Hammerstein and Kern's song could do to enhance a pop singer's manliness. Still stateside and performing—when so many American men were overseas fighting—in 1943 Sinatra was "for millions of women . . . the romantic voice of the American homefront."[3] "Ol' Man River" was hardly typical fare for this often shrieking crowd. A live recording from a few years later at the Hollywood Bowl has Sinatra announce the song, after which girls scream then abruptly fall silent. They probably knew "Ol' Man River," too—not exactly the sort of swooning tune they favored from their Frankie, known to more dismissive listeners as "Swoonatra."

Sinatra included "Ol' Man River" on his first Hollywood Bowl appearance less than two weeks after the Lewisohn concert. According to music critic and Sinatra biographer Will Friedwald, on that occasion Sinatra sang the "darkies all work" version of the verse. He probably sang it that way at Lewisohn as well. And Sinatra was still singing "darkies all work" in October 1943, when his performance of the song on the CBS radio show *Broadway Bandbox* sparked letters of protest from the *Afro-American*, whose editors were always listening to the details. The CBS director of broadcasting responded with apologies: "Someone on our staff slipped in not advising Frank Sinatra of the revised lyrics we use in 'Ol' Man River,' which is just one of those mistakes that will happen in spite of anything we can do. We have been using our efforts over a long period of time to eliminate any questionable references to race, creed or color."[4] Recognizing the effect of their mini campaign, in early 1944 the *Afro-American* sent Sinatra virtual "Orchids" in their "kudos" column: "To Swooner-Crooner Sinatra, who replaced 'd . . . y' in his rendition of 'Ol' Man River' with 'Here we all work . . .' "[5]

The *Afro-American* made no comment about and seemed to have no problem with Sinatra singing other lines from the verse without change: "while the white folks play" and "let me go 'way from the white man boss." My students often ask, "Isn't Sinatra 'white folks'?" This is a fair question—to which we shall return—and one Sinatra seems to have finally asked himself when he sang "Ol' Man River" on television in 1967.

Sinatra's passage from "darkies all work" to "here we all work" adds another thread to the larger tale of how "Ol' Man River" negotiated the mid-twentieth century. Once again, the work of changing Hammerstein's verse lyric fell to black listeners with the inclination and the platform to challenge white institutions in the public sphere. As the stories told in this book show, in the 1940s white radio executives, singers like Robert Merrill and Frank Sinatra, and Hammerstein himself, all replied in good faith to these protests and changed the text of the song—thereby saving "Ol' Man River" for later performers and listeners. Friedwald credits Sinatra with being "the first singer to make a point of avoiding such expressions" as "darkies," adding "I'm sure the ever-perverse Sinatra would balk at being labeled the first 'politically correct' pop star." As shown here, sources drawn from African American media suggest otherwise. And the issue in 1943—indeed, at any time, for black audiences—wasn't political correctness: it was dignity. In the middle of World War II, as activism among black Americans was heating up, expunging the word "darkies" from the airwaves was part of the process that led to the end of legal segregation. It was accomplished, in part, by black listeners who complained about a song lyric. A decade later, such listeners were involved in more substantive actions: marches, boycotts, and sit-ins.

In his detailed consideration of Sinatra's recording career, Friedwald argues that Sinatra transcended the specific racial content of "Ol' Man River."

> If Sinatra's renditions of "River" and "Lost in the Stars" help those texts to transcend the time in which they were first staged, it's partly because he has divorced them from the specifically racial angles they were originally written to comment on. When Sinatra sings them, they no longer deal with the specific problems of one particular people, they confront the entire human condition. Sinatra transports these songs away from levee riverboats and Johannesburg prisons and universalizes them.[6]

Friedwald goes on to characterize Sinatra's 1945 recording of "Ol' Man River" as "so staggeringly definitive, it makes even Robeson's powerful production seem almost as dated as Jolson." Friedwald even speculates as to Kern's reaction to any and all of Sinatra's versions: "Still, the composer would have had to admit than an aura of majesty permeates the many Sinatra readings, even the visually overdecorated MGM version." Without a doubt, Friedwald thinks that Frank Sinatra should sing "Ol' Man River." But his discussion of Sinatra and "Ol' Man River" sets both singer and song outside of history. Friedwald avoids the unequal racial politics involved in Sinatra's singing the song in the first place, while also arguing that this particular white singer had the power to deliver transcendent truths, to universalize a song that puts forth a black perspective on American history.

Any reader who's gotten this far into this book knows I cannot hear Sinatra—indeed, any singer—in this way. Anyone who chooses to sing (or applaud) "Ol' Man River" is always embedded in history, specifically the history of the color line and racial discrimination, of demands for dignity and equality by and for African Americans, and of the powerfully symbolic realm of popular music and culture, where race has always played (and still plays) a defining role. Sinatra, just as much as Robeson, is part of this concrete history. And just as Sinatra's earliest performances find their place in the story of black activism targeting the lyrics of the verse, all of Sinatra's performances and recorded or filmed versions of "Ol' Man River" find their meaning in a particular place and time. This chapter looks at how Sinatra put "Ol' Man River" to work in the interests of his own career aspirations and also considers how he reshaped the tune for his own purposes. The racial questions raised by Sinatra's use of "Ol' Man River" are touched on here and in Chapter 9, where his 1967 television performance finds its place among other nationally telecast versions.

A semi-private performance of "Ol' Man River" evidently transformed Sinatra's career early on. Sinatra sang "Ol' Man River" at a benefit for the Jewish Home for the Aged in January 1944. Louis B. Mayer, head of Hollywood's premiere movie studio Metro-Goldwyn-Mayer, was in the audience, which was mostly made up of film industry Jews. Shortly after the event, Mayer signed Sinatra to an unprecedented contract at MGM. According to Sinatra biographer James Kaplan, Mayer himself insisted Sinatra sing "Ol' Man River" in the Jerome Kern biopic *Till the Clouds Roll By*, then in production at the studio. The many draft scripts for the film confirm that finding a spot for Sinatra to sing the song was an ongoing priority. Initially, he was to open the film singing it on a radio broadcast. Later, Sinatra's "River" was bumped to the end of the film, where it serves as the climax of a long musical sequence called "The Land Where the Good Songs Go."[7]

This easy-to-resist performance from Sinatra's earliest days at MGM has the singer attired in a white tuxedo, standing atop a white pillar high above a symphony orchestra, also dressed in white—a perfect example of the pompous style at Metro. Sinatra biographer Tom Santopietro, after noting that "in its very specificity, ['Ol' Man River'] resonates most powerfully when sung by an African-American artist," characterizes Sinatra's version as "wildly inappropriate, ludicrously overstaged, and yet somehow affecting."[8] Watching the number today, it's easy to forget that this was fairly standard stuff for the time. *Variety* described the sequence as "done in the best Culver City [the location of MGM's lot] production tradition...an eye-appealing, audience-arresting, surefire production."[9] And as shown in Chapter 6, "Ol' Man River" was frequently sung by white baritones. Sinatra makes his bid to be considered a "serious" singer by putting himself into their company on this one song (more on this later). *Variety* also compared Sinatra's version to that of black bass Caleb Peterson, who sang "Ol' Man River" as Joe in the condensed recreation of *Show Boat*'s opening night that opens *Till the Clouds Roll By*: "Both versions are creditably done and are calculated to meet any divergence of audience preference in the singing of 'Ol' Man River.' "[10] But there were naysayers at the time. *Times*' critic Bosley Crowther noted, "[MGM] could have done something different from the great big Te Deum of Kern songs which it uses to climax the picture and which concludes in a bath of blazing light with a pale, prim and pedestaled Frank Sinatra hymning 'Ol' Man River' horribly."[11] And *Life* magazine named Sinatra's "Ol' Man River" "the worst single moment" in a whole year's worth of films. Their critique latched on to the dissonance between Sinatra's "immaculate white suit" and the lyric "You an' me, we sweat an' strain." *Life* said, "MGM stifled the music with opulence [and] struck a high point in bad taste."[12] Sinatra can't really be blamed for the white suit and monumental set. In 1946, he was still getting his feet wet in Hollywood. And while he often didn't show up for work, when he did he did what he was told. His all-white "River"—like Robeson's shirtless "River" in the 1936 *Show Boat*—is best understood as Sinatra taking direction.

But on the musical side, Sinatra's filmed "Ol' Man River" closely reflects his lifelong approach to the song. Except for the significant omission of the verse—which he otherwise always sang—the MGM arrangement's huge forces and wide dynamic range and the way Sinatra phrases the melody match his 1944 and 1945 pop recordings (made for the Armed Forces V-Disc label and Columbia Records, respectively). These mid-1940s versions all capture Sinatra making "Ol' Man River" into *his* song. The tempo is deliberate, the mood is restrained, and his apparent vocal efforts are minimal. *Life* described him fairly as hardly breaking a sweat. Sinatra doesn't chew the scenery as so many white singers did—no shouts of "Tote dat barge! / Lif' dat bale!" for him—and he doesn't project much volume or create a long vocal line. His vocal approach generally works in contrast to the lush orchestral setting (⊙ Sound Example 7.1). Climactic moments, like the "a" of the last "along," do get some added volume and lengthening, but such touches are few. Sinatra unavoidably retains the freshness of youth. After all, he had yet to turn thirty years old when he began to sing "Ol' Man River" on a regular basis.

Why did Sinatra start singing "Ol' Man River" in the first place? Crosby may have pointed him toward the song. Around this time, Crosby was singing

"Ol' Man River" as a ballad: recordings from 1941 with Victor Young and 1945 with the Camarata Orchestra find Crosby singing with a light touch, putting his little vocal touches and turns on the song (⊕ Sound Example 7.2). (Crosby reverted to his 1920s rhythm tune approach in the 1950s.) But Crosby's slow versions—Friedwald calls them "the work of a crooner"—wouldn't have demonstrated the grand style Sinatra was after.[13] In the public imagination of the time, "Ol' Man River" was primarily a show piece for baritones with big voices. Such singers, black and white, sang "Ol' Man River" on the radio all the time, and Robeson—with the turning point of 1949 still in the future—remained the benchmark. Sinatra was not a natural fit for this group of singers. The typical Sinatra tune of the early 1940s was a sentimental weepy or song of dreamy romance pitched to the female audience. Typical Sinatra titles—"I Couldn't Sleep a Wink Last Night" and "If You Are but a Dream"—suggest a dazed young man caught in the thrill of love. These tunes did not exploit the lower reaches of the voice; nor did they tackle what might be called grown-up emotions or experiences. Whispered crooner-style into the microphone, such songs didn't draw out the power in Sinatra's voice. This intimate vocal persona, on which his early fame had been built, matched Sinatra's audience. Why would these listeners want to hear "Ol' Man River"?

Truth is, they didn't. In Sinatra's case, this song choice had little to do with the singer's primary audience: instead, "Ol' Man River" expressed Sinatra's sense of himself as a singer. Sinatra did not think of himself as merely a crooner—his ambitions were always larger than that. Finding the right song to demonstrate his vocal and interpretive prowess—and define himself anew for older fans, such as MGM's Mayer—would be difficult. Sinatra didn't have a trained voice and he wasn't about to sing opera arias. He was, fundamentally, a singer of popular songs. Sinatra did sing a duet from Mozart's *Don Giovanni* with operatic soprano Kathryn Grayson in the story context of the 1947 film *It Happened in Brooklyn*. With passable Italian diction, Sinatra keeps things light—both vocally and expressively, staying well within his brand of slightly daffy romantic comedy: no impersonations of an operatic baritone, mostly just puppy-dog eyes for Grayson. Nor did Sinatra have the pipes to take on the robust, full-voiced, Italian street singer persona, which, in the early 1940s, was typified by singers such as Tony Martin, who sang the operetta-style role of Ravenal with Grayson as Magnolia in the *Show Boat* scenes from *Till the Clouds Roll By*. Sinatra had neither the powerful physique, nor the conventionally handsome face, nor the generic leading man persona, nor the fully supported vocal style such songs and roles demanded. Indeed, operetta selections were as ill-suited to Sinatra as foreign-language opera arias. Both repertoires subordinate the singer's persona to historical standards of good vocal technique and convincing type casting.

Sinatra, like Crosby, needed to get beyond the crooner stereotype that earned him initial fame. He needed a song that sounded "operatic" (or serious or important or artistic), that was not broadly "romantic" (in the conventional "manly" sense), and that was still solidly in the popular vein (ideally something audiences would know already). "Ol' Man River" was the perfect choice—except for the racial dimension. But, given the timing, race questions raised few difficulties for Sinatra. As the previous chapter showed, mid-twentieth century white baritones enjoyed full access to this song written for a black singer and character.

Sinatra managed to shoehorn "Ol' Man River" into his repertory of popular love songs—just as Robeson, for different reasons, included Hammerstein and Kern's show tune in his folk song and spiritual repertory. Indeed, it's hard to think of any other song that could do for Sinatra what "Ol' Man River" did in the mid-1940s. It was a shrewd choice, made early in his career, demonstrating his instinct for creating an inimitable persona around his peculiar strengths and limitations. And, once Sinatra demonstrated to himself that he could sing it and that audiences would applaud it—the critics be damned—he kept on singing "Ol' Man River," but not, like Robeson, because he *had* to. Sinatra needed "Ol' Man River" to make a point about himself as a singer—a point no dreamy love song or, in later decades, swinging tune could drive home to listeners. With "Ol' Man River," Sinatra—known from early on as The Voice—declared in no uncertain terms that he could deliver a challenging melody and a serious lyric that dealt with life's biggest questions. Once installed in Sinatra's songbook, "Ol' Man River" ceased to be anything more (or less) than a Sinatra song, applauded like any other signature tune. Sinatra's subsequent stature allowed him to keep on singing "Ol' Man River" into the late 1980s, well past the point when it had passed out of most white singers' repertories. Sinatra sang "Ol' Man River" for the last time in public during his Ultimate Event tour in 1989. (He ceased performing in 1994 and died four years later.)

"Ol' Man River" was different from just about everything else in Sinatra's mid-1940s repertoire—except for one other song also not about romantic love. "The House I Live In"—music by Earl Robinson; lyrics by Lewis Allan (the pen name of Abel Meeropol, who also wrote the anti-lynching song "Strange Fruit")—expresses the democratic ideals used by the administration of Franklin D. Roosevelt to explain why the war against Nazi Germany had to be fought and won. Sinatra sang the song in a short film from 1945, for which he was awarded a special Academy Award. The verse for

"The House I Live In" begins and ends with a question: "What is America to me?" The answers given in the chorus are intentionally prosaic: the landscapes of everyday living, the common events of life, "but especially the people / That's America to me." In only a few places does political language intrude on this idyll of daily life: the singer defines "the right to speak my mind out" and "all races and religions" as also "America to me."

As dramatized in the film that won Sinatra an Oscar, the emphasis falls on religious tolerance. Stepping into the alley behind a recording studio for a smoke, Sinatra encounters a pack of kids preparing to beat up a boy because, they finally admit, "we don't like his religion." Sinatra immediately lumps the gang in with "those Nazi werewolfs I been reading about." He turns the boys toward democracy with tales of blood banks and bomber crews cooperating across religious divides to save American lives and win the war. Pointedly excluded from the discussion is any mention of race—it's all about religion, although the only two groups mentioned by name are Presbyterians and Jews. And, of course, understandings of Jews as a race were central to Nazi ideology and current thought in the United States as well. The pack of boys does not include a black face.

For 1945, this was laudably liberal stuff, and Sinatra was serious about advocating racial tolerance. Just before making *The House I Live In*, he sang and spoke in Gary, Indiana, during a high school integration crisis. James Kaplan aptly frames these moves as both sincere on Sinatra's part and calculated on the part of Sinatra's publicist. Any interpretation of Sinatra's performances of "Ol' Man River" should include some acknowledgment of the singer's efforts to promote interracial understanding. There is, however, little evidence Sinatra thought of "Ol' Man River" and "The House I Live In" as sharing any expressive agenda. The latter was an admittedly political song; the former was a "classic" song.

Paul Robeson also sang "The House I Live In" and included a forcefully sung version on his 1947 album *Songs of Free Men*—which, as noted earlier, did not include "Ol' Man River." Always sensitive to song texts in these years, Robeson sings a different set of lyrics from Sinatra's on the chorus to "The House I Live In," including the line "my neighbors white and black," which, in the late 1940s, pointed toward the fight against restrictive covenants, which kept blacks from moving into white neighborhoods. Lyricist Meeropohl had penned an alternate text, including the "neighbors" line, and Robeson, as was his wont, assembled his own version, freely drawing on Meeropohl's and making up some new lines as well. Sinatra's recording and the published sheet music didn't stray into such contentious territory. Meeropohl stated that the published version expressed "a promise for tomorrow." He wrote several alternate versions over the years, including one performed by Robeson and Sinatra at a labor rally and another for Sammy Davis Jr. to sing on television in the 1960s.[14]

Sinatra and Robeson, at almost the same time, were pushing popular singing into the realm of politics—Sinatra, of course, much less forcefully and without the controversy surrounding Robeson's much more assertive activism. "The House I Live In" is a modest statement which—in its modesty— argues for the common sense behind the ideas in the lyric. In the end, it's a tender song for a tender moment in Sinatra's career—as the film suggests, it's a song kids can understand. In that respect, it differs from "Ol' Man River," which, when turned to political ends as Robeson did, translated into a confrontational stance. When Sinatra sings "Ol' Man River" he generally leans toward the tender side as well. This approach, regardless of the accompaniment (discussed later), avoids the histrionics of the white opera and operetta singers explored in the previous chapter. Sinatra does not impersonate the white man boss on the bridge lyric " 'Tote dat barge!' / 'Lif' dat bale!,' " nor does he adopt a spoken or shouted quality. Instead, he sings. "Ol' Man River" for Sinatra was always, first and foremost, a display of fine singing and subtle interpretation of a song he understood to be a challenging classic: as early as 1945 he introduced the song at the Hollywood Bowl as "one of the greatest American songs we have today, I think you'll agree with me"; as late as 1989 he was still reminding the audience, in his introduction, that the song was "one of the great American classic songs."

Sinatra employed two sorts of musical arrangements for "Ol' Man River": orchestral and intimate. In the 1940s, Sinatra sang "River" with a full orchestra in full-on dramatic mode; his vocal style, calculated to sound effortless and natural, receives a splendid setting that would not be out of place for a fully supported, trained singer. As described, this approach subtly moved Sinatra from a crooner for screaming girls to a serious singer for more sophisticated listeners. Sinatra's arranger and close creative collaborator Axel Stordahl orchestrated his 1945 recording for Columbia (also used for his 1944 V-Disc recording, made for non-commercial release among soldiers overseas). The MGM arrangement for *Till the Clouds Roll By* follows suit. In 1963, Sinatra's close creative associate Nelson Riddle made an even grander orchestral arrangement for the album *The Concert Sinatra*. This LP parallels *Gordon MacRae in Concert* from 1958 in several respects: both are products of Capitol Records; both present male singers in performances of self-consciously "big" songs with lush symphonic accompaniment; both include versions of "Ol' Man River" done up for maximum effect on the home hi-fi.

Like many singers, Sinatra developed small touches that made the melody his own. One of these touches—a three-note descent, sung by Sinatra to

Frank Sinatra in the 1940s, rehearsing at the Hollywood Bowl—a venue where he sang "Ol' Man River" on several occasions. (Photofest)

end the second A phrase—was borrowed from Jolson, as noted earlier. But it's worth revisiting here from Sinatra's side (see ⊙ Sound Examples 6.4 and 6.5). While Jolson brings a schmaltzy feel to this added melodic touch—it's laden with unsubtle showmanship for the benefit of the balcony—Sinatra, as always, brings an understated approach. Sinatra uses the addition to bring a bit of informality to the vocal line: he tapers off the phrase, shaping the melody for a microphone singer who, unlike trained singers, tends to go to the consonant—the "n"—rather than sustain the vowel—the "aw" sound in "along," which an opera singer would modify to a lovely, open "ah." (◉ Sound Example 7.3 excerpts Sinatra singing with the Stordahl and Riddle arrangements.)

A more pronounced change to the song, consistent across his almost half century singing "Ol' Man River," allows Sinatra to display his superior breath control at a key moment in the tune. At the end of the bridge, Sinatra holds the word "jail"—the beat stops, the accompaniment waits or falls silent, the song hangs on the singer alone. Still sustaining his sound, Sinatra slides right into "Ah gits weary," after which he takes a big breath before "an' sick of tryin'." In one of his few substantial changes to the song, after 1950 Sinatra added an element that made the held note seem longer and also suggested a more mature depth to his range. Holding on to "jail," he drops to a lower note, then slides back up and sings "Ah gits weary," before finally taking a breath. (◉ Sound Example 7.4 gives Sinatra's sustained note on the bridge as captured in *Till the Clouds Roll By* in 1946, live in Blackpool, England, in 1953 [the added low note was a new addition at this time], live in Paris in 1962, and on *The Concert Sinatra* in 1963.)

The likely origin for this choice—which Friedwald calls a "Dorsey-style long-breath"—goes back to Sinatra's apprenticeship in the Tommy Dorsey big band.[15] Dorsey had legendary powers to sustain a beautiful tone on his trombone apparently without breathing. (He was a master at sneaking a breath.) Every member of Dorsey's organization was expected to cultivate this technical skill. Sinatra followed suit. His treatment of the end of the bridge in "Ol' Man River" makes this ability to sustain a musical line on a single breath into the reason he's singing. There's no interpretive reason why carrying over adds to the listener's understanding of the song. It even necessitates awkward breaths in the middle of two lines: "Git a little drunk / An' you land [breath] in jail. / Ah gits weary [breath] / an' sick of tryin'." Listen closely and Sinatra can be heard to take a big breath just before the word *in* on "in jail" that gets him through to "weary." An audible gasp for air follows "weary." In other words, this interpretive choice isn't driven by lyrical considerations so much as the taking of a musical opportunity to display a technical skill. Singer Harry Connick Jr. was impressed, calling "Ol' Man River" on *The Concert Sinatra* the "best example" of the singer's legendary breath control, adding jealously, "He must have an extra set of lungs. I wish he kept them in my chest."[16] Friedwald singled out the "ability to hold a note in 'Ol' Man River'" as the singer's "sole display of strength" at a time when "America's idea of maleness was John Wayne."[17] Here, again, the link between "Ol' Man River" and manliness crops up. Of course, concert and opera singers were accustomed—trained, in fact—to sustain long phrases, while also projecting without the aid of a microphone. Sinatra's held note over the bridge and into the final A phrase is very soft, barely there. Without the microphone, his approach to this passage wouldn't work.

For a non-technical audience and for listeners not predisposed to be automatically enthralled by Sinatra—for example, contemporary undergrads who never learned to revere The Voice—this moment can easily be heard as a gimmick. By any measure, Sinatra stops singing the lyric and instead displays his technical prowess, a self-indulgent, and rather surprising, choice that makes the singer—rather than the song—the center of Sinatra's "River." Sinatra was among the most famous singers in the world but not many singers copied his sustained breath across the end of the bridge. Gordon MacRae, tellingly, *does* sing the Sinatra connection on both his 1950s recordings. He was surely listening closely to Sinatra's approach in the late 1940s. (As mentioned earlier, such listening likely went both ways. *The Concert Sinatra* has more than a little in common with MacRae's *In Concert*.)

A 1951 recording by Al Hibbler features a black singer in a mild lampoon of Sinatra's approach to the bridge of "Ol' Man River." Hibbler, a pop stylist with a smooth, seductive, sometimes mannered delivery, sang with Duke Ellington's band briefly in the early 1950s. His resonant, true bass voice fits "Ol' Man River" well but several strange performance choices raise questions about how seriously Hibbler and Ellington, providing accompaniment at the piano, mean for the listener to take their efforts. Hibbler phrases against the melody in several places: for example, he overemphasizes the word "but" each time it occurs, yielding, at the second A phrase, the odd interpretive choice, "An' dem dat plants 'em / Is soon forgotten, / BUT." At the end of the bridge, Hibbler carries over—just like Sinatra—making an ostentatious display of his breath control while Ellington strikes the same pitch at octaves all up and down the keyboard. However, instead of connecting all the way to "weary" Hibbler gasps for air after "I," sounding like he barely made it that far (◉ Sound Example 7.5). This singularly odd phrasing completely interrupts the flow of the music, leaving the suave Hibbler in a position of undermining what could be his greatest stylistic asset for the song. Ellington's all-over-the-keyboard pianism, which includes abrupt and extreme highs and lows, and a dissonant, even atonal approach to harmony, especially in the final A phrase—Friedwald calls it "bizarro" and "deliberately arch"—also hints that the recording is, in part, a satire.[18] Sinatra's way with the bridge seems to be one target of Hibbler and Ellington's disc.

Starting in the early 1950s, Sinatra introduced an alternate "River" arrangement—a quiet approach, with intimate piano accompaniment only until the final A phrase, when whatever backing he had to hand came in to support a big finish (a choice Kern's ascending melodic trajectory effectively forces on most any singer). Sinatra never recorded this approach in the studio, but he performed it live for decades. He sang it this way in London (1950), Blackpool, England (1953), again in London (1962, at a royal command performance aired on the BBC), in Paris (1962, on a World Tour for Children, a performance available on the disc *Sinatra and Sextet*), in Carnegie Hall (1963), on American television (1967, Sinatra's own special), once again in London (1970, for a benefit at the Royal Festival Hall accompanied by Count Basie and His Orchestra), and, finally, at the Nixon White House (1973, a state dinner for the Italian president where the song received a standing ovation).[19] There's tremendous tenderness in these versions of the song. Sinatra employs his characteristic changes to the melody within a hushed context, quietly centered on Hammerstein's words. Minimal accompaniment and the microphone allow Sinatra to be powerful without pushing—until, that is, the final phrase, where he lets out what power he has in the appeal for applause that Kern wrote into the tune.

Sinatra's intimate approach takes his initial strategy with "Ol' Man River" a step further, reducing the scale of the accompaniment to the level of his microphone-assisted voice, with no need for elaborate orchestral arrangement to consecrate his efforts. "Ol' Man River," written for Robeson's reserved and unamplified vocal technique, made perfect sense when sung in more heated fashion by trained voices in the concert hall or on disc with an orchestra. Sinatra dodges both options—neither of which would have worked for him anyway—and redirects the tune toward the intimacy of the saloon. This approach, like the orchestral, still ignores the racial issues at the heart of the text. Sinatra's innovative approach to "Ol' Man River"—in some passages arguably self-indulgent—nonetheless finds a way to sing the tune without overdramatizing it (as white opera singers did) and without trivializing it (as rhythm singers did) and, crucially, without evoking Robeson's iconic pose of noble suffering nobly borne. Sinatra's rather stripped-down, low-key, modest approach—a pose, for sure, but one developed in songs like "The House I Live In"—allows him to get away with "Ol' Man River." In that respect, and again across much of the same time frame, Sinatra serves as a historical counterweight to Robeson, their contrasting ways with the song clarifying the different fates of black and white singers who both tried, on some level, to play a role in the social and political life of the nation. Robeson, who put aside noble resignation for defiant declaration, paid a profound price and was silenced. Sinatra, who turned "Ol' Man River" into an oddly contentless vehicle for the fashioning of a serious yet still always popular singer persona, sang "Ol' Man River" for decades, long after other white singers had ceased to sing lines like "let me go way from the white man boss." Sinatra—an artist given special allowances by most audiences (and authors)—got away with the Ol' Man Metaphor approach longer than any other white singer, indeed almost to the end of his life. On a bootleg of his 1989 performance, Sinatra—for the first time—actually sounds old. It's the only recorded time he didn't sustain that long note at the end of the bridge: he just didn't have the breath anymore. This late version reveals, by contrast, just how facile, supple, and youthful his characteristic approach to this work song had always been.

Perhaps Sinatra's core audience—whites, mostly, of a certain era; forced, like him, to endure the rock and roll juggernaut—appreciated the chance to savor "Ol' Man River" in this way into the 1960s, 1970s, and 1980s without having to be confronted by a black singer singing about racial injustice and without being pointed toward the sharper aspects of Hammerstein's—or Robeson's even sharper—vision. To return to the matter of small details, it is telling that Sinatra only eliminated "white folks play" and "white man boss" from the verse on one recorded occasion: in 1967, in the midst of the so-called Civil Rights Era—better understood as the period when white Americans were awakened by black Americans to a struggle for dignity and equality that had been ongoing for decades. The next chapter turns to this period, which coincides with the remarkable high season of "Ol' Man River."

8

⊷

The High Season on Records

squib from the February 4, 1948, issue of *Variety*.

[Mississippi's] Gov. Fielding, who's not so old, didn't like being introduced to the accompaniment of "Ol' Man River" a few months ago at the Governors' Conference and as a result will soon submit a new song to the state legislature for okay as Mississippi's official melody. It seems that at the Conference the introduction of each governor was heralded by a state song— "The Eyes of Texas are Upon You," "Georgia on my Mind," et al. When [Fielding] took the spotlight to Jerome Kern's "River" he didn't like it, although the coupling seemed fair enough.

Contrary to *Variety*'s reporting, "Ol' Man River" was never an official Mississippi state song: there was no need for the governor to request a new "official melody." The musical organizers of the conference made an ill-advised choice, which *Variety* didn't register with much insight either, as only the most cursory reflection on Hammerstein's lyric could lead anyone to imagine the governor of Mississippi might appreciate being introduced to the strains of a pseudo-spiritual including complaints about the "white man boss" written by two New York Jews for a famous black performer to sing in a Broadway show. Still, the report and incident raises the question of how "Ol' Man River" might enter the world of politics.

Hammerstein's "Oklahoma!" provides an illuminating counterexample. In the original 1943 Broadway production, the title song from Rodgers and Hammerstein's transformative hit *Oklahoma!* was staged—by Hammerstein— in a bold, positive, rousing manner. At the end of the song, sung near the end of act two, the entire cast—the farmers *and* the cowmen—rushed to the front of the stage, crossing the barrier of the footlights in a spirit of unstoppable optimism and enthusiasm: manifest destiny joyfully performed on a Broadway stage. No wonder the Oklahoma legislature adopted "Oklahoma!" as the official state song in 1953. Drivers along Oklahoma interstates are exhorted by signs to "keep our land grand"; the state's anti-littering campaign adapting Hammerstein's exultant lyric, in which the show's cast declares they "belong" to a "grand" "land." In this song about *white* Americans and the American landscape, Hammerstein celebrates spiritual connection and possession. The contrast with "Ol' Man River"—Hammerstein's lyric laments physical hardship and calls out racial dispossession—is profound. Imagine "Oklahoma!" rewritten along the lines of "Ol' Man River," as a song of noble suffering voiced by a Native American version of Joe, whose claims to what was once called Indian Country were definitively displaced around the time Oklahoma became a "brand new state." The absence of Native Americans from the all-white cast of *Oklahoma!* stands in sharp contrast to *Show Boat*'s complicated setting of black and white in the same national landscape.

No, indeed—"Ol' Man River" is an unlikely song to greet the governor of Mississippi, in the 1940s or any time. It is—quite simply—too contentiously political in its content to serve the purposes of establishment politics (for which "Oklahoma!" is supremely well fit). As previous chapters have shown, "Ol' Man River" entered the concrete political struggle of African Americans against the racism described and descried—and, for some, expressed—in the lyric as early as the 1930s. The years when Robeson put "Ol' Man River" to political use—the late 1940s to the end of the 1950s—coincided with small shifts in the song's larger cultural meaning, changes expressed independent of any performer's choices about how to sing it. Three news items reported in the national press mark this transition, when "Ol' Man River," a song everyone knew and which happened to be about the lived experience of racial intolerance and discrimination, started resonating in a new political and social environment where these same issues finally came to the forefront of national life. These vignettes hint at the high season to come.

In 1957, Levittown, Pennsylvania—the original suburb—was integrated by, in press terms of the time, a "Negro family" when William and Daisy Myers successfully purchased a home. White residents were prevented by community rules from staging protests on the sidewalk or in the street, so they drove by in their cars, honking and singing "Old Black Joe," "Dixie," and "Ol' Man River." The protesters also staged ongoing harassment of their new neighbors in an empty house next door from which they flew Confederate flags and "repeatedly [played] a recording of Paul Robeson singing 'Ol' Man River.'" If it was Robeson's 1948 version, then perhaps the new residents drew strength from Robeson's words about laughing instead of crying and fighting to the point of dying. William Myers told the press that he and his wife were "determined to remain residents of Levittown." Local police and state troopers were called in to protect the black family and maintain calm. The attorney general of Pennsylvania personally handled an injunction against eight harassing neighbors.[1]

A cartoon from late 1956 in the *Milwaukee Journal*, reprinted in the *New York Times*, took the revolutionary step of reversing the relationship between blacks and nature in Hammerstein's lyric, while simultaneously expressing an assurance that the days of the Jim Crow South were already numbered. The drawing shows the Mississippi bursting a levee while a lone white figure stands—broom in hand—trying to sweep back the flow, which carries the text "high court rulings against segregation." The caption is one, very familiar line: "Old man river, he just keeps rolling along." Here—finally—nature is on the side of racial equality and "Ol' Man River" is saying something pretty clear: segregation is doomed. The barriers against it, which white Southerners pretended were part of nature but which were, in truth, the product of centuries of de facto and de jure discrimination, were breached. All that remained was the flood to come.

African American activists saw the changes coming sooner—they must have, for the end of Jim Crow came only at their insistence—and one among their number reached for Hammerstein's "rollin' along." In a 1949 address at Fisk University, the eminent black intellectual and statesman Ralph Bunche looked toward the future in realistic terms, misquoting Hammerstein with a purpose along the way.

> We Negroes must be great realists.... The barriers of race are formidable, but they can be surmounted. Indeed, the entire history of the Negro in this country has been a history of continuous, relentless progress over these barriers. Like "Ol' Man River," the Negro keeps "movin' along," and if I know my people, the Negro will keep moving resolutely along until his goal of complete and unequivocal equality is attained.[2]

The change of verb—"movin'" in place of "rollin'"—has big consequences. Bunche's "River" is not an impersonal force of nature but instead a metaphorical embodiment of the resolutely realistic character of African Americans, who would settle for nothing less than a full claim in the promise of the nation. Bunche's words echo in Robeson's statement in his testimony to Congress some years later. Asked why he didn't leave the United States and move to Russia, Robeson replied, "Because my father was a slave, and my

Lewis in The Milwaukee Journal

"Old man river, he just keeps rolling along."

Cartoon originally appearing in the *Milwaukee Journal*, reproduced in the *New York Times*, December 2, 1956, illustrating the article "Organized Resistance to Racial Laws Grows" by John N. Popham.

people died to build this country, and I am going to stay here and have my part of it just like you."[3]

Neither the Levittown protest nor the levee-break cartoon nor Bunche's revision of the lyrics constitute interpretations of "Ol' Man River" the song. But all three do suggest that times were changing and that "Ol' Man River" retained its relevance in the age of racial transformation that began in earnest with the Supreme Court's decision to strike down "separate but equal" in 1954 and ended, after many victories, including the Voting Rights Act, in the turmoil of assassinations and riots in the late 1960s.

Singers and musicians agreed that "Ol' Man River" could still carry meaning in these changing times. Based on the sheer number and expressive variety of recordings and documented performances, the most prolific and engaged era for "Ol' Man River" was the late 1950s to the end of the 1960s. This rich stretch of years was, without a doubt, the high season for Hammerstein and Kern's song. This chapter and the next explore the high season: initially by listening to Hammerstein and Kern's song as recorded in several realms of popular music; second, by watching and listening to television variety shows, where very famous performers made the song their own in a high-stakes live medium that brought the nation together into one audience.

The cover of bandleader Lester Lanin's 1957 LP *At the Tiffany Ball* pictures high-class couples swirling beneath a massive chandelier. On this disc made for dancing, Lanin leads his orchestra through a string of familiar songs arranged in strict-time medleys. The muffled sounds of a busy ballroom added to the mix—the hubbub of voices, appreciative clapping—lend the record the quality of a live radio hookup from a sophisticated nightspot. "Ol' Man River" shows up after several *Show Boat* tunes go fleetingly by, ending what seems to be a typical Broadway medley. But Lanin has a novel close to his *Show Boat* potpourri: after "Ol' Man River," the band segues into "Dixie" (⊕ Sound Example 8.1).

Lanin's disc puts "Ol' Man River" in the supposedly genteel world of the gracious South, appending a Confederate marching song to Hammerstein and Kern's very different tune for Joe. Also pairing these tunes at an imagined all-white occasion, the *Afro-American* commented on the reappearance of Confederate flags and hats in Baltimore in the early 1950s by sarcastically imagining the graves of prominent white supremacist politicians, "Rebel heroes, the sepulchers of exponents of racial hatred and bigotry" joining in "the chorus of 'Dixie' and 'Ol' Man River' as their ideas 'go marching on.'"[4] The refrain of the "Battle Hymn of the Republic"—"his truth is marching on"—gets mixed up with Hammerstein's "jes' keeps rollin' along" in this angry reference to a song otherwise defended by the same paper in other contexts.

Lanin's rhythm "River," included on an LP meant for social dancing in the home, raises two interlocking questions. The first concerns form: where was "Ol' Man River" positioned on concept albums? The second deals with content: what did the Southern-ness of "Ol' Man River" come to mean in an era when the South was associated in the public mind with non-violent resistance by blacks and frequently violent responses by whites. Form and content alike carry political weight in the realm of the concept LP, a still-new, long-format popular music product that opens a window on where "Ol' Man River" fit within various song categories during the high season.

In the later 1950s, jazz producer and promoter Norman Granz, creator of Jazz at the Philharmonic, introduced the "song book" concept album, a creative and marketing strategy that organized LPs around the work of Broadway and Hollywood songwriters of the prewar decades, dressing familiar and obscure tunes in modern musical clothing and helping solidify the category of popular song "standards" for a new generation of listeners.[5] "Ol' Man River" didn't need help in this regard, as previous chapters have abundantly shown, and the tune turns up only sporadically on LP tributes to Jerome Kern, an indication of the extent to which the song had escaped association with its composer or its *Show Boat* origins, persisting on its own popularity and creative back-and-forth among all sorts of singers and musicians. Ella Fitzgerald's *Jerome Kern Song Book*, from 1963, did not include "Ol' Man River," although one can imagine how her wide range might have negotiated the tune. Margaret Whiting, like Fitzgerald recording for Granz's Verve Records, also left "Ol' Man River" off her 1960 double-LP Kern songbook. Female jazz-pop singers like Fitzgerald and Whiting generally avoided the song (although studio logs show that Whiting recorded an "Ol' Man River" at her Kern sessions that went unissued). André Previn and Oscar Peterson, white and black jazz pianists, respectively, each made a Jerome Kern disc including "Ol' Man River" in 1959. Peterson's piano version, mentioned in Chapter 3, is fast and showy, unusual for taking even the verse at a quick tempo. Previn's six-minute meditation for solo piano is slow, contemplative, dark, and moody, an expressively innovative take that can be heard as exploring the human tragedy lodged inside the world "Ol' Man River" describes (⊚ Sound Example 8.2).

"Ol' Man River" appears on five albums of "Southern" songs released between 1959 and 1964: banjoist John Cali's *Banjo on My Knee*, the Dukes of Dixieland's *Up the Mississippi*, and the Dave Brubeck Quartet's *Gone with the Wind*—all from 1959; singer Lou Rawls's *Tobacco Road* from 1963; and saxophonist Albert Ayler's *Goin' Home* from 1964. These concept albums, featuring widely divergent performers and targeting different audiences, use "Ol' Man River" to buttress different notions of the South during a period when the region was in turmoil and in the papers. Made during a crucial period of the civil rights movement and given the larger context of these performers' careers—Brubeck, Rawls, and Ayler, especially—it makes sense to listen to these discs as a group, linked together by their common inclusion of Hammerstein and Kern's song.

"Ol' Man River" is the only point of contact between all five discs. Cali's *Banjo on My Knee* (recorded in 1955) shares no other tune with the other four. The Dukes of Dixieland's *Up the Mississippi* and Lou Rawls's *Tobacco Road* both include "St. Louis Blues." The CD re-release of *Tobacco Road* includes a South song recorded but not included on the original LP—"When It's Sleepy Time Down South"—which is also on *Up the Mississippi*. *Tobacco Road* and Brubeck's *Gone with the Wind* share "Georgia on My Mind." *Up the Mississippi* and Ayler's *Goin' Home* offer different takes on "Down by the Riverside" and "Deep River" (the latter heard on *Up the Mississippi* as part of "Dear Old Southland"). These shared songs—hailing from different sources: Tin Pan Alley, Broadway, Negro spirituals—complicate the collective engagement of these discs with the idea of the South as a musical location and point to further repertories. *Banjo on My Knee*, filled with nineteenth-century tunes like "Turkey in the Straw," finds Cali targeting the nostalgia market for old-timey evocations of minstrelsy sans blackface. *Up the Mississippi* features river songs: "Ol' Man River," especially given its history as a jam tune, finds easy company among other Dixieland standards. *Goin' Home* digs into the spiritual repertory, where, again, "Ol' Man River" has connections along many lines. *Tobacco Road* brings in black-identified jazz standards, including "Stormy Weather." Given the foundational association of "Ol' Man River" with black male singers, Rawls's inclusion of it on his album makes sense. Brubeck's *Gone with the Wind*, the most eclectic of the five, puts nineteenth-century minstrel tunes beside forgotten Tin Pan Alley spirituals, pop standards, and one Brubeck original—the title track, which closes side two. Listeners might anticipate hearing the sentimental "Theme from Tara," from Max Steiner's motion picture score for *Gone with the Wind*. But Brubeck's "Gone with the Wind" is a cool modern instrumental that rewards the informed jazz listener (saxophonist Paul Desmond quotes "St. Thomas," the opening track on Sonny Rollins's 1956 LP *Saxophone Colossus*). "Ol' Man River" finds a place on all these discs. How these artists perform "Ol' Man River" and how they fit it into their chosen song lists demonstrate on yet another stretch of aesthetic terrain the tremendous openness of Hammerstein and Kern's song to different interpretations and uses.

The Dukes of Dixieland and Cali, his banjo supplemented by a small, minstrel-style combo, offer nostalgia that can be heard as little else. There's no room for irony or satire on these stylistically conservative LPs that appeal to a longing for an idealized Southern past that would not be out of place at Disneyland, which erected a sanitized simulacrum of the old South, sans slave cabins but including a singing Aunt Jemima serving stacks of pancakes, in the mid-1950s. From the start, Dixieland jazz was, and remains, part of the so-called Magic Kingdom. Indeed, the Dukes of Dixieland played there and recorded a disc titled *The Dukes at Disneyland* in 1963.

The Dukes of Dixieland began as a father-and-sons trio in 1948. A traditional New Orleans revival band, they released a flood of LPs in the late 1950s—including *Minstrel Time*, *Mardi Gras Time*, and *Circus Time*—on the small Audio Fidelity label, which marketed their retro music as an ideal way to show off the newest hi-fidelity stereo equipment. Just after making *Up the Mississippi*, the all-white group began a recording studio collaboration with Louis Armstrong, which yielded Armstrong's only recording of "Dixie."

On *Up the Mississippi*, their ninth LP in three years, the group plays the two-tempo version of "Ol' Man River" adopted by many trad jazz players at the time (versions by Eddie Condon and others were discussed in Chapter 3). The Dukes' version opens with horns only on a restrained, slow verse. A driving beat from the drums opens up a robust, quick tempo chorus. The group divides Kern's eight-bar A phrases into two halves, creating a kind of call and response effect. For the first four bars, the trumpet plays the tune while the trombone bounces around. For the second four bars, on the words "but Ol' Man River he jes' keeps rollin' along," the whole band comes in with full-blown group improvisation (⊙ Sound Example 8.3). The Dukes repeat this division on every A phrase and it works every time because of Hammerstein's use of the same lyric in that spot. The Dukes invite the listener to raucously join in on the easy-to-pick-up "rollin' along" aspect of the tune. Everything else can be safely ignored. "Ol' Man River" is the only song from a Broadway musical on *Up the Mississippi*, and almost the only Tin Pan Alley–type popular song. Others in the second category are "Mississippi Mud"—first recorded by a very young Bing Crosby in the summer of 1927 (when "Ol' Man River" had been written but was yet to be released)—and "When It's Sleepy Time Down South," Louis Armstrong's theme song (which, as noted, garnered much criticism for Armstrong in the early 1950s when he recorded it using the word "darkies"). All the tracks on *Up the Mississippi* are rhythm tunes and the Dukes generally stay within a range of tempos from medium fast to driving.

In similar fashion, Cali's *Banjo on My Knee* uncomplicatedly puts "Ol' Man River" among songs like "Rock-a-bye Your Baby with a Dixie Melody" (a Jolson tune also recorded by Aretha Franklin in the 1960s) and "Waiting for the Robert E. Lee." The latter offers an interesting counterpoint to "Ol' Man River"—if the lyrics of both are considered. "Waiting for the Robert E. Lee," a Tin Pan Alley song dating to 1912 and given full blackface minstrel treatment by Mickey Rooney and Judy Garland in the 1941 film *Babes on Broadway*, celebrates the arrival of a steamboat on a Mississippi levee. In the lyric, which assumes a black voice, the listener is invited to "watch them shufflin' along" and also to "join that shufflin' throng" as they welcome the arrival of the Robert E. Lee. This stereotypical river scene, with blacks dancing and singing with enthusiasm, is described by Edna Ferber in *Show Boat* but was not replicated in Kern and Hammerstein's *Show Boat*, which begins with blacks working, and not dancing, on a levee where, they pointedly comment, "the white folks play." In "Ol' Man River," a historically innovative "levee" song, the listener is invited by the black voice of the singer to think on the realities of living and working "on the Mississippi," where power and leisure are expressed in racial terms. Lumping "Ol' Man River" among happy South songs, as Cali does, fundamentally misrepresents Hammerstein's lyric. In 1959, *Billboard* saw "Very Strong Sales Potential" for Cali's disc.[6]

The Dave Brubeck Quartet's *Gone with the Wind,* also 1959, paints a very different South from these two nostalgic portraits. When the interracial group of Brubeck, Desmond (alto sax), Joe Morello (drums), and Eugene Wright (bass) recorded the disc in two sessions in 1959, the quartet was in the midst of a concert cancellation controversy. Scheduled to tour the South, with many dates at colleges and universities, the group refused to appear in halls that required the audience to be segregated by race. Brubeck's quartet had been integrated since late 1957 with the addition of Wright, the group's African American member. Southern papers attended closely to this chronology, wanting to be sure Wright hadn't been added to provoke controversy.

Gone with the Wind was the album before Brubeck's signature disc *Take Five,* which features the same personnel. The origin of *Gone with the Wind* is obscure. Brubeck biographer Fred M. Hall says it was a matter of each member picking a favorite.[7] Yet there's no evidence the group had ever played these songs before. Were these favorites the quartet didn't know? Known more for jazz originals, here Brubeck offers songs that all connect to the South. Tin Pan Alley tunes like "Georgia on My Mind" and "Basin Street Blues" are combined with an "Ol' Man River" shadow hit of 1927, the composed spiritual "The Lonesome Road" (recorded by Robeson, Armstrong, Crosby, and Sam Cooke, among others), and Stephen Foster's "Old Folks at Home" (titled "Swanee River" on the liner). Two nineteenth-century rhythm songs, which can be heard as minstrel tunes—Foster's "Camptown Races" and "Short'nin' Bread"—and the Brubeck original, the title track, round out the disc. Most of these are not jazz standards; few jazz players played these tunes then or ever. How much irony attends song choice on Brubeck's disc? Certainly Brubeck's equivocal, minor mode opening to "Swanee River"—which opens side one with an ambivalent fanfare—drops the listener into a slightly nervous, less than happy South (⊙ Sound Example 8.4). "Ol' Man River" serves as a bass solo—the only track without Desmond's sax—and harkens back to the Jazz at the Philharmonic version described earlier: solo choruses for Wright in two quick tempos, followed by an unaccompanied cadenza with a quiet close. Brubeck and Morello provide minimal support (⊙ Sound Example 8.5).

Reviewers heard the Southern connection linking the songs on *Gone with the Wind. Billboard* gave the disc five stars, writing, "In this collection of southern songs, the quartet achieves a looseness and rapport of greater degree than their previous albums. And how these men listen to each other!... This is a happy, swingin' LP lacking in pretentiousness and played by a group of men who obviously enjoy their work and each other."[8] *Billboard* describes exactly the kind of shared respect and labor the South's Jim Crow laws and traditions attempted to prevent and police. Brubeck's foursome demonstrated interracial comity on songs about a South that would never have permitted this kind of respectful, affectionate mixing of the races. The song choices and their execution by the group in this time and place are a rebuke in themselves. Whatever it is, *Gone with the Wind* is not an exercise in nostalgia like *Up the Mississippi* and *Banjo on My Knee*. The tension between old South songs and Brubeck's urbane, cool jazz—associated with its own regional fantasy of the West Coast—is felt throughout.

In the months after *Gone with the Wind*, as the civil rights movement continued to heat up, Brubeck remained adamant about appearing only before integrated audiences. The group released a follow-up LP in 1960 titled *The Southern Scene*, which, like *Gone with the Wind*, took South songs and made them modern and cool. The cover image for *The Southern Scene* pictured the interracial quartet sitting side by side, with stylized drawings of a plantation big house and a Mississippi paddle wheeler, easily mistakable for *Show Boat*'s Cotton Blossom Floating Palace Theater. Among the songs on that disc are "When It's Sleepy Time Down South" and "Nobody Knows the Trouble I've Seen." The visual provocation continued with the group's other 1960 disc, *Brubeck a la Mode*, which pictured the smiling quartet sharing ice cream sodas at a picture-perfect soda fountain and was released at the height of the sit-in movement at Southern lunch counters and soda fountains.

Last among the instrumental discs, Albert Ayler's 1964 *Goin' Home* gives "Ol' Man River" unabashedly serious treatment. Here, as with Robeson, it's a fully invested spiritual. Ayler was a young saxophone player forging his own path in the 1960s. Often using a plastic reed, and switching between soprano and tenor sax, Ayler has a unique sound to say the least. *Goin' Home* finds him midway on his journey toward free jazz—his next albums would abandon traditional notions of rhythm, melody, and harmony. But on *Goin' Home*, Ayler turns one final time to singable melodies. All the songs—except for "Ol' Man River" and the Dvorak-derived title track—are traditional tunes of the sort his audience could be expected to hum along with. As noted back in Chapter 2, Kern's bridge for "River" builds on the angular melody of "Goin' Home": Ayler surely heard the connection. "Ol' Man River" and the spirituals "Swing Low, Sweet Chariot" and "Deep River" receive similar treatment as ballads here: all three begin with Ayler unaccompanied. When bass, drums, and piano come in, each plays freely. There's no beat coordinating the whole: the four men play together but not as one. Ayler, who sticks to the melody throughout the record, uses intonation to expressive effect. His approach can sound out of tune if heard out of context (⊚ Sound Example 8.6). Ayler's disc puts "Ol' Man River" solidly back into Robeson's repertoire as reassembled by a black jazz loner playing in his own way. The spiritual dimension is there for listeners willing to embrace it—this is not commercial music by any stretch of the imagination—and clearly Ayler found Kern's tune to be as inspiring as the more authentic material he chose to record.

Ayler's strenuous and serious disc, like Brubeck's tongue-in-cheek but still biting record, recontextualized "Ol' Man River" and its surrounding repertories by way of musical approaches that made these old songs new. Shortly after working through this heritage of South songs, Ayler and Brubeck both left the repertory behind. Coming from contrasting musical approaches, their discs similarly play these songs, "Ol' Man River" among them, out of the book of jazz. Cali and the Dukes of Dixieland's South discs had less forward-looking musical work in mind, appealing as they did to unreflective nostalgia. These backward-looking efforts would quickly date themselves as relics of the supposed 1950s consensus, which masked the inequality of the status quo and a misremembering of the nation's past behind a facile longing for the good old days that never were. Hammerstein, of course, made this point about the South way back in 1926 when he penned the lyric to "Ol' Man River."

Like Ayler and Brubeck's LPs, Lou Rawls's *Tobacco Road* aggressively works out the present by reimagining old South songs. Rawls's richly ambiguous record uses these tunes to explore African Americans' love/hate relationship with the South. Ironically, Rawls begins by appropriating the song "Tobacco Road." Written by the bizarre early rocker John D. Loudermilk in 1960, and using the name of a famous novel, play, and film from the 1930s that told a bittersweet story of poor white Southern sharecroppers, Rawls heard the voices of poor black farmers in the song and reached across the racial divide in a spirit of class solidarity. Unlike Hammerstein's lyric, which lays out a racially divided South, nothing in Loudermilk's lyric except for the intertextual associations of the title speaks directly to race.

On his fairly swinging "Ol' Man River," Rawls reshapes several of Kern's downward-tending lines into upward, questioning, or resisting trajectories. He refuses to let the tune shape the track. Rawls does not ride one big crescendo to the close: "Ol' Man River" must serve the groove even if Rawls's vocal calls forth an intensity of emotion unusual in versions with a bpm in the mid 140s. Rawls riffs on the bridge lyric, singing "I said now, you and me, a well, we sweat, we sweat, we sweat and we strain." His repetitions of "we sweat" enact the labor described. Rawls wastes no energy on the "tote" and "lift" lines, sliding past them into a recomposed melody for "land in the jail" (◉ Sound Example 8.7). It's hip—cool, if you will—but also decidedly physical. Coming a few songs after the tune "Cotton Fields," which also explicitly describes manual labor, Rawls makes the bridge of "Ol' Man River" into a grooving work song, integrating urban musical energy and the lyric's investment in actual labor, synthesizing rather than separating the two, as Cootie Williams's 1938 "Ol' Man River," which dismissed farm workers as "squares," had done.

Rawls's "Ol' Man River" brings a complex approach to the vocal and its setting. The musical context is swinging—Sinatra-esque, perhaps, if grittier than Sinatra's contemporary LPs. (Sinatra and Rawls were both recording for Capitol Records at the time.) The ongoing electric guitar line in Onzy Matthews's big band arrangement adds a soulful element. Matthews, an unsung African American bandleader and arranger/composer based in Los Angeles, brings a heady mix of blues and elegance to the recording. (Matthews and Rawls had teamed up in 1963 on the disc *Black and Blue*, which, like *Tobacco Road*, explored in a direct manner the experience of being black. That disc closes with the rarely recorded "Strange Fruit.") But Rawls's vocals go beyond Sinatra's in their masculine emotional range. Or, perhaps, the effect comes from Rawls tapping into a black masculinity that's inaccessible to the sensitive Sinatra. Rawls is unafraid to roughen up his supper club-ready voice and he chooses songs that paint pictures of poverty Sinatra wouldn't have touched. Sinatra was willing to sing a liberal anthem like "The House I Live In": Rawls goes into deeper territory, taking the listener beyond interracial understanding and into the experience of being black. (Black singer Joe Williams recorded a much less "black" "Ol' Man River" with big band accompaniment in 1965, staying within Sinatra-style bounds and offering a nice contrast to Rawls's raw approach [◉ Sound Example 8.8].)

"Ol' Man River" ends *Tobacco Road*'s side one—the same position it holds on *The Concert Sinatra* and Ray Charles's *Ingredients in a Recipe for Soul* (all three discs released in 1963). Rawls's side one begins with Loudermilk's "Tobacco Road," which has the singer describe being "born in a dump": his mother dead, his father "drunk." This is no idyllic cabin in the cotton, safe in "Mammy's arms." The bridge lyric calls Tobacco Road "home" but by the close the singer's ready to blow the loathed place up, recognizing there's nothing to be done but start completely over. Explicitly stated ambiguity— love and hate, home and hell—marks most every track on Rawls's album. Song after song interrogates the physical world of the South, whether the lyrics are sentimental or direct. Rawls puts "Ol' Man River" in company with an intentionally combative mix of standards: the saccharine "Sentimental Journey," the bluesy "Stormy Weather," and the original blues hit "St. Louis Blues." As noted, Rawls recorded but did not end up including Louis Armstrong's theme song "When It's Sleepy Time Down South" on *Tobacco Road* as released in 1963. Armstrong was a difficult figure, easy to dismiss when Rawls was making his album, and Armstrong's theme song—problematic in the 1930s—was beyond the pale in the 1960s, with its images of a "life of ease" and "Mammy's arms" (even with the word "darkies" removed.) Rawls evidently tried to keep Armstrong's song in the musical conversation but balked at the last, even though he had changed "darkies singing soft and low" to "folks are crooning songs soft and low." "Ol' Man River" and "When It's Sleepy Time Down South" needed such small changes to survive. The latter song lacked the former's complexity.

Like Ayler's *Goin' Home* and Brubeck's *Gone with the Wind* but with the greater directness that comes from a singer delivering lyrics, Rawls's *Tobacco Road* explores a complicated construction of the South in popular music at a time when the real South was undergoing historic struggles. To Hammerstein and Kern's credit, "Ol' Man River" fits on all three of these albums that capture the contradictions of the high season.

There were many, many rhythm versions of "Ol' Man River" made and released during the song's high season: more than a few were mentioned in Chapter 3. These records tap into practices around the tune reaching back to the 1920s, all more or less fitting "Ol' Man River" to the prevailing dance beat of the moment. In that sense, most of the high season rhythm versions of "Ol' Man River" continued established musical practices. But there were also more than a few expressively innovative takes on the song released into the volatile and diverse 1960s musical marketplace. This chapter concludes with a listen to several recorded versions by white artists. More than historical curiosities, these recordings mark the song's passage through various pop music centers of the decade—Nashville, Los Angeles, London—as well as regional scenes (Southern rock) and emerging trends (progressive rock). Mapping these versions across the Anglo-American popular music world shows yet another generation of singers and musicians trying to refresh the old song—not always with success. Their efforts are worth contemplating, in part because they suggest the level of experimentation that marks the high season, but also as a means to explain why "Ol' Man River" ceased to satisfy, getting close to the historical question of why pop musicians finally set the old song aside.

Pianist Floyd Cramer is best known for his work with Elvis Presley. Cramer can be heard on Presley's 1956 hit "Heartbreak Hotel" and he toured with the rock and roll singer before Presley's stardom hit the nation, and the music business, like an earthquake. In the later 1950s and 1960s, Cramer was a much sought-after session musician who helped define the Nashville Sound: a slick sort of country music that, with musicians like Cramer in the mix, increasingly incorporated piano together with rafts of violins and ooh-ing backing vocals. Cramer—who sounds the piano notes at the start of Patsy Cline's signature 1961 hit "Crazy"—enjoyed a moment in the spotlight in 1960 with the instrumental "Last Date," which reached #11 on the country chart and #2 on *Billboard*'s Hot 100 chart. He was, for a time, *America's Biggest Selling Pianist* (as the title of his 1962 LP declared). Cramer, a country artist, did what black artists were doing on the R&B side: he crossed over and became a pop star. (Cramer has been inducted into both the Country Music and Rock and Roll Halls of Fame.) Finding a middle point between the diverging adult and youth markets while also bridging the country-pop gap, Cramer made many LPs of easy listening mood music—no need to reset the volume knob—with rafts of strings, wordless female vocals, and his own low key, slip note piano style.

On his 1963 LP *Comin' On*, Cramer applied his approach to "Ol' Man River." He begins with the verse, opening the track in a plaintive style with no beat and sticking closely to the tune. Many "Ol' Man River" instrumentals begin this way. With the start of the chorus, Cramer plays the tune unaltered in the right hand in the upper half of the keyboard, while the left provides a distinctive answering syncopation down low. Distance between the hands opens up a sonic space that was typical of Cramer's mood music creations, which combine familiar acoustic timbres and the modern recording studio to produce novel soundscapes. As the chorus unfolds, the key elements of the Nashville Sound enter the arrangement one by one, building up a layered, transparent but thick texture (⊛ Sound Example 8.9). By the start of the bridge, lush strings and voices take over the tune in full force. But Cramer reasserts his primacy for the second half of the bridge and plays his divided right hand/left hand texture, emphasizing a passage the informed listener knows speaks of "landing in jail." Indeed, the total trajectory of the recording is one of dynamic and expressive crescendo, exactly the approach favored by so many singers. But most such singers didn't sing with a strong backbeat and, in mood music fashion, Cramer keeps the dynamic range of the recording within limits. Nor, once the beat begins at the chorus, does the tempo ever flag—Cramer's "Ol' Man River" might even invite slow dancing. The overall effect isn't jazzy or bluesy (he's not a creative improviser), nor is it obviously a country record (any instrumentally implied twang is kept to a minimum), nor is this innocuous mood music (anyone who knows the song's words can follow Cramer's emotional trajectory, however restrained its range). This sophisticated record cries out for a singer to magnetize its layers into a specific interpretive take.

Elvis Presley recorded gospel tunes and hymns in arrangements much like Cramer's for "Ol' Man River." It's too bad the two never combined on Hammerstein and Kern's song. The result might have found a less-than-completely-credible place on Presley's 1967 LP *How Great Thou Art*, which features well-known religious songs and hymns. Presley gets even closer to "Ol' Man River" on his 1968 single of Rodgers and Hammerstein's "You'll Never Walk Alone," a song with connections to "Ol' Man River" across the 1960s and after. All these inspirational recordings feature fairly innocuous, slightly country instrumental backgrounds setting off Presley's earnest vocals, many of which follow the whisper-to-shout trajectory of so many versions of "Ol' Man River." Especially "You'll Never Walk Alone"—a combination hymn/Broadway anthem and among the few show tunes Presley recorded—hints at how he might have risen to the heights of "Ol' Man River" (◉ Sound Example 8.10).

There were other ways for a white Southerner to approach "Ol' Man River" in the 1960s. The same year as Cramer's piano version, country singer Charlie Rich recorded "Ol' Man River" at a healthy 160 bpm. With a slight sneer and a slighter twang in his voice and backed up by wordless female voices, Rich gives another answer to the question of how Presley might have sung the song, inflecting "Ol' Man River" not through religious music—with which the song has a real affinity—but rather through the attitude of a rebellious young man. Rich sings with cool contempt over a minor-mode groove. There's emotion here but it's suppressed and slightly ironic rather than nobly borne (◉ Sound Example 8.11). Presley was likely too well behaved and too conscious of the song's religious overtones to have treated "Ol' Man River" so dismissively. That Presley did *not* sing "Ol' Man River"—at a time when so many others were doing so—in itself marks a transition: all previous male pop singers of Presley's stature—that is, Crosby and Sinatra—included the song in their repertoires.

Out in Los Angeles, the Righteous Brothers put "Ol' Man River" on a 1965 LP capitalizing on the white duo's breakthrough hit "You've Lost That Lovin' Feelin'." Here, "Ol' Man River" serves as a vehicle for some so-called "blue-eyed soul" framed by producer Phil Spector. The track serves as a solo feature for Bill Medley, the bass in the pair. Singing only the chorus, Medley traces the well-worn path from very soft to very loud. With each successive phrase, more elements are added to the arrangement, which begins with minimal piano comping in a gospel style, adds back beat and horns, and finally brings in wordless backing vocals. Medley doesn't emote much, even on the bridge: no spoken "tote" and "lift" for him. Only at the height of the tune does he let loose and there he doesn't explore the tune: a two-chord vamp cycles a few times while Medley improvises, finally sounding invested in the moment (⊛ Sound Example 8.12). Medley's added words are hard to catch—on the order of "I don't know how he [the eponymous 'ol' man'] do it, yeah"—and by this point the performance is about vocal power and Spector's signature "Wall of Sound." The track fades out abruptly. Did Medley and Spector choose "Ol' Man River" because of its historic status as a feature for the bass voice? Given Medley's range and "soulful" style, it would seem to be an obvious choice but Medley apparently had little to say by singing it. This oddly perfunctory track reminds the listener that effective performance at this tempo demands investment in Hammerstein's lyrical content. White baritones knew how to make the song "dramatic" but by the 1960s this approach was dated and out of step with Medley's persona. Still, "Ol' Man River" remained a possible song choice. Medley and Spector were not alone in giving it a try.

In a similarly unlikely recording from the same years, pop singer Cher included "Ol' Man River" on her second LP, *The Sonny Side of Cher* from 1966. Also on the album was Cher's first Top 10 single, "Bang Bang (My Baby Shot Me Down)." As with the Righteous Brothers' disc, fans who bought these albums to get "Bang Bang" or "You've Lost That Lovin' Feeling" also got "Ol' Man River." LP turntable technology meant the listener either let the track play or executed a delicate move to skip it. Cher's version, produced by Sonny Bono, surrounds "Ol' Man River" with a lively and lovely folk rock texture, complete with harpsichord and tambourine. The tempo's not terribly fast—about 100 bpm—although the double time, jangly beat gives the whole track a rhythmic density. Cher's voice is strong but detached. She struggles a bit with the highest notes—like Crosby did back in 1928—and comes up with a new shaping of the tune that backs off emotionally when other singers typically go full throttle. Cher's track, like Medley's, abruptly fades out, leaving her still holding the last note (⊛ Sound Example 8.13). Cher's "River" exemplifies her vocal persona as a powerful singer who can, at times, project a kind of emotional opacity. Her relation to the song remains unclear: there's a quality of rote repetition of a well-known, slightly folk-like song but there's also the sheer power of her voice, which Kern's tune audibly challenges. One of a small group of female singers to record "Ol' Man River," Cher provides the listener with a version that packs no emotional punch but instead offers removed self-possession. (Her willingness to more aggressively shape classic pop standards into vehicles of personal emotion would be demonstrated again and again on her 1973 LP *Bittersweet White Light*, a commercial failure.) As the following chapter shows, in the mid-1960s Judy Garland—a different sort of singer approaching "Ol'

Man River" at the end rather than the start of her career—used Hammerstein and Kern's song to much more explicit emotional ends. Another big voice from the 1960s, Aretha Franklin, offers a third example of how a strong woman sings "Ol' Man River." Franklin's gospel approach to "Ol' Man River" is treated in the final chapter.

At the end of the 1960s, "Ol' Man River" made it to Abbey Road—the famous London recording studios frequented by the Beatles—where Jeff Beck, Rod Stewart, and Keith Moon crafted a somewhat spooky version for the Jeff Beck Group's 1968 album *Truth*. Here, "Ol' Man River" received full-on rock vocal treatment. *Truth* was guitarist Beck's first venture after leaving the Yardbirds—the LP was billed as a Jeff Beck solo—but the real interest on the recording is Stewart's vocal. In his autobiography, Stewart claimed the decision to record "Ol' Man River" was "my very cheeky sugges-tion."[9] His take on the vocal, like most all of *Truth*, looks into but doesn't quite enter the land of heavy metal just over the musical horizon. "Ol' Man River" appears in a prime spot on *Truth*: the end of side one, a placement that echoes *The Concert Sinatra*, Rawls's *Tobacco Road*, and Ray Charles's *Ingredients in a Recipe for Soul* (discussed at the close of the book). Stewart's alteration to the second A phrase—he sings "and we all know he don't plant cotton"—suggests he had been listening to the recent *Temptations Live!*, a Motown LP released in 1967 (also discussed later). Like the Righteous Brothers' version—which Beck and company might have known—the track proceeds once through the chorus at a moderately slow tempo and rounds out with a vamp, building in volume from a creepy opening to a chaotic finish. Throughout, drummer Moon, credited for contractual reasons as "You Know Who," plays resonantly miked timpani. A Hammond organ adds to the ghostly atmosphere but Stewart's vocals carry the track. Stewart works outside the tradition of "Ol' Man River" as a conventional vocal solo. He eroti-cizes the bridge to questionable effect, singing "You and me we sweat and toil. / Our bodies all naked and wracked with pain" (℗ Sound Example 8.14). As the song proceeds, the listener gets a hint of how a thoroughgoing heavy metal vocal version might go, but Stewart doesn't quite go all the way. Like Bill Medley and Cher, Stewart delivers a strangely underdone perfor-mance, perhaps reflecting the hurried nature of the project, which was recorded in four consecutive days and released in stores just two months later.[10]

Two obscure recordings mark the effective end of the high season and the farthest journey "Ol' Man River" made into the land of rock.

The progressive rock band Child placed an epic, six-minutes-plus "Ol' Man River" as the last track on side two of their eponymous 1968 LP: recorded in New York and released by Jubilee Records. Side one closes with

"You'll Never Walk Alone." Placement of these often paired songs in these positions again hints at a surprising indebtedness to Sinatra's and Charles's 1963 concept LPs. Child's version opens with swirling electric sounds—perhaps evoking the river—followed by a bit of the chorus tune played in naïve fashion on some sort of xylophone. Entrance of an organ sets up the start of the verse, spoken by the group's lead singer—listed as Teddy on the liner. Teddy whispers "Colored folks work on the Mississippi," changing the lyric a bit at "Can't look up / Don't make a sound / Don't dare make the white boss frown." A lonely harmonica plays the first measure of the chorus over and over behind Teddy's hushed recitation. The line "and pull that rope until you're dead" is spoken in a void, the instruments having fallen silent—this is "Ol' Man River" for tripped-out headphone listening. The electric guitar comes swooping in for a brief lick, again the opening measure of the chorus (◉ Sound Example 8.15). After yet another shift in texture, Teddy finally starts singing the chorus, which unfolds somewhat conventionally—the other four members singing backup to Teddy's lead or all joining in to sing harmony. Child's exploration of the verse shows a sense for the song's dramatic potential within a proto-progressive rock context. This white rock band explores the full breadth of "Ol' Man River," touching on how black vocal groups were singing it in the 1960s (see Chapter 10) but also investing the song with rock grandeur that's worlds away from the way legitimate white baritones—also hankering for some metaphorical grandeur—sang it into the 1950s. It's a weird, desperate recording.

The obscure Southern rock band Potliquor included "Ol' Man River" as the second track on their debut LP *First Taste* from 1970. The track—tellingly?—was left off a 2010 CD re-release. Formed in Baton Rouge, Potliquor recorded on the small Janus Records label: this was not a version destined for wide release. The four members of Potliquor start their "Ol' Man River" on the verse—"Let me go way from the Mississippi / Let me go way from the white man's toil"—singing in close, unaccompanied harmony and with utter commitment in a slightly country vein. Inclusion of the verse offers the first clue that Potliquor, like Child, intends to explore Hammerstein and Kern's song to the full. George Ratzlaff's vocal on the chorus sits entirely in the rock vein, with added guitar soloing behind. The bridge gets a stop time accompaniment that exposes Ratzlaff's raw sound even more starkly. He makes the listener long to hear Janis Joplin sing "Ol' Man River" and hints at just how imaginable such a performance might be. The tempo slows at "land in jail," setting up an intense and deliberate final A phrase. The flexibility of tempo across this recording demonstrates a step-by-step exploration of the lyrics: this is a closely shaped, hard rock "River" (◉ Sound

Example 8.16). At the close, the band goes into a vamp—like so many other rockers—but here the extension carries more weight because of the group's preceding, point-by-point treatment of the song.

"Ol' Man River" did not survive into the 1970s as a space for creative remaking—except for the reggae "Rivers" discussed earlier. Child's and Potliquor's obscure tracks are among the last to bring something new to the song, even if both are, in the end, metaphorical attempts to latch on to the song's big emotions that have much in common with the white trained singers discussed in Chapter 6. The rock singers, having hijacked white masculine singing for the mainstream, unsurprisingly do so in part by stealing an earlier generation's song. None of the earnest 1960s versions by white singers hint at an engagement with the racial content of Hammerstein's lyric in the changing context of American race relations. But these are anomalous recordings. One possible reason "Ol' Man River" disappeared from white singers' repertoires was the fundamental change in American society that came with the official end of segregation, marked by passage of the Voting Rights Act in 1964. Segregation, of course, continued, but the pathos of the nobly suffering black man—central to the world of "Ol' Man River"—was gone in the face of the thousands who marched and let themselves be arrested and beaten. The late 1960s saw disastrous riots in urban black neighborhoods. One likely reason Hammerstein and Kern's song disappeared around 1970 is that the lyric finally became completely anachronistic.

The recorded high season versions of "River" covered in this chapter, together with others mentioned in previous chapters, provide evidence from across the popular music marketplace that Hammerstein and Kern's song remained a viable song choice. No other Broadway show tune received this kind of varied treatment in the 1960s. But "Ol' Man River" had transcended that category long before. In a decade when show tunes were not part of rock and youth-oriented pop, unexpected artists found something in the song—or tried to—and, most important, did not treat it as a "standard" to be discarded but as a tune that still had some life in it. When these singers and musicians, and those who followed them, dropped "Ol' Man River," some forty years after its appearance in *Show Boat*, the old song's season in the popular music spotlight was finally over.

9

The High Season on Television

I n his book *Colored People*, a memoir of the transition from a racially
segregated to a more integrated nation, Henry Louis Gates Jr. describes
television as "the ritual arena for the drama of race."[1] "Ol' Man River,"
sung on television at least twelve times between 1958 to the end of the
1960s, played a part in this drama. Consistent viewers of variety television
could have seen and compared, in memory at least, an unprecedented range
of performances, several of which leveraged star personas to reinvent the
song all over again. The range of performers is, in retrospect, almost dizzying: black pop singers Sam Cooke and Cab Calloway, hailing from sharply
contrasting generations, both sang "Ol' Man River" solo; iconic white stars
Bing Crosby, Frank Sinatra, and Dean Martin shared a trio version and each
sang it solo as well; Judy Garland and Sammy Davis Jr. each sang it twice on
TV; the Temptations folded "Ol' Man River" into a medley of South songs;
and the non-singing actor Henry Fonda spoke Hammerstein's words in a
performance that reinvigorated the song's meaning yet again. Who sparked
whom to take up "Ol' Man River" is hard to know but the song was everywhere on television in these years. These versions are valuable for their live-
ness, their inclusion of an onscreen audience (always almost all whites), and
the added expressive elements of costuming, setting, staging, and framing
for the small screen.

"Ol' Man River" was on television in earlier years too, charting among
the top five standards heard on television during several weeks in 1950.[2]
Black bass Billy Eckstine sang "Ol' Man River" on *The Ed Sullivan Show* in
1953.[3] These versions are harder to view today than those from the song's
high season a decade later. Frank Davis's performances of "Ol' Man River"
on Fred Waring's television show in 1952 (discussed in Chapter 4) and

Raymond Scott's "spirited arrangement" on the popular *Your Hit Parade* in 1955 are, happily, still around to be seen. Unless noted, the high season versions discussed here are usually available somewhere on the Internet.

Sam Cooke kicked off the song's television high season in 1958 on *The Steve Allen Show*. It was an auspicious time for Cooke, who had just broken into the pop charts with "You Send Me." After attaining star status on the black gospel circuit with the Soul Stirrers, Cooke effectively crossed over to the pop market as a solo act in the early days of rock and roll. He would produce some thirty Top 40 hits and largely manage his own business and artistic affairs. Like Robeson in his early years, Cooke was restrained and dignified yet approachable, devastatingly attractive and emotionally opaque, an articulate singer whose vocal timbre alone sent a thrill through his listeners—Cooke sang sweet high notes in contrast to Robeson's rich lows. Toward the close of his prematurely shortened career—Cooke was shot dead in 1964 at age thirty-three—he began to write and record songs that directly engaged with the civil rights struggle, most memorably, the posthumously released "A Change Is Gonna Come," which begins "I was born by the river," an opening that echoes both "Ol' Man River" and Langston Hughes's "The Negro Speaks of Rivers."

In 1958, after the breakout success of "You Send Me," Cooke made a bid for adult, white audiences. He got a booking at New York's Copacabana supper club and released a self-titled LP. (The long format was generally an adult medium in these pre-Beatles years.) Cooke chose to promote his club date and LP by singing what Steve Allen called "the old standard 'Ol' Man River'" on national television.

Cooke did not sing live but instead lip-synced to his record, which contains prominent white-sounding backup singers who were not pictured onscreen. Cooke's arrangement clicks along at a swinging 176 bpm, with a vamp on the words "rolling along" that sets the entire performance in a danceable groove (⊙ Sound Example 3.45). Cooke's easy delivery of high notes, part of his pop-gospel appeal in "You Send Me," takes all the effort out of Kern's vocal. Cooke also uses the modified harmonies—making all three A phrases uniform—which narrows the song's vocal range. Consistent smiling from Cooke—he's just moving his lips; he can fake the singing—adds to the sense of mismatch between the song's heavy words and the singer's light touch. Wearing an open shirt and dark pants—his wardrobe always suggested soft, luxurious fabrics caressing his tall and trim body—Cooke is discovered on a vaguely Southern, minimalistic television set: spindly blossoming trees on square stands, picket and rail fences, a stump for Cooke to lean on, one hand in his pocket. This guy doesn't look like he's had to sweat or strain a day in his life. And that—of course—is the point. Cooke delivers an effortless rendering of a song about heavy labor. He refuses to take up the burden of the song, even to critique it. This powerful choice—Cooke suggests its meaning is nil: for him, at least—gives the lie to the lyric without changing a word. (Cootie Williams's parody from twenty years earlier made the same argument but, of course, did change the words.) Cooke tacitly argues that what white performers can do in treating "Ol' Man River" as a rhythm tune, a black man may also do, and in the process he might just challenge white pop stars' claims to being cool.

The only time Sinatra sang "Ol' Man River" as a rhythm tune was when he shared the song with Crosby. On Sinatra's 1959 special, sponsored by Timex, Crosby and Sinatra, together with Dean Martin, sang "Ol' Man River" as the climax to a medley of "Good Old Songs"—that is, songs with the world "old" in the title, among them "Old Devil Moon," "Down by the Old Mill Stream," and "My Old Flame." A specially written musical introduction claims the trio wants to revive "those songs with plenty of soul that rock and roll just won't do." "Ol' Man River" closes the medley and is the only song sung in its entirety: it's also the only song in the medley that rock and rollers regularly did. The trio sings the A phrases together in a clipped style: Crosby's characteristic approach to the tune shapes the whole. Martin, in particular, yucks it up, responding physically to hyperactive fills from the orchestra in the breaks (furious strings quote the song's ubiquitous verse). Each man takes a line of the bridge solo: Martin puts on a silly voice for "wracked with pain." Is the voice meant to sound comically black, like a moment of minstrelsy, or is this just Martin's way, his need to play comedy while Sinatra and Crosby stay classy? (Martin's solo version suggests an answer.) Sinatra shows how he might have swung the tune. Crosby, on this one occasion, doesn't sing the Crosby blue note in the bridge. Perhaps he preferred not to share his personal way with Kern's tune with colleagues who might steal it.

This is the only time Sinatra had fun with "Ol' Man River," surely a matter of deference to Crosby: it may be Sinatra's special but "Ol' Man River" remains Crosby's song. Still, it's tempting to imagine Sinatra trying to pull rank and sing it in a serious style—his way—while Crosby and Martin played backup chorus. The gravitas, even majesty "Ol' Man River" imparts to black men in *Show Boat* is not something three white pop stars could pull off. For a group of white guys—two of them Italian (Crosby calls Sinatra and Martin "pizza pushers")—"Ol' Man River" can only be a rhythm tune. Sinatra and other white singers found a way to play it serious in solo performances, but they could only do so without the social context backup singers provide. Unlike Joe in *Show Boat*, who acts as the leader of the men of the black chorus, metaphorical Joes like Sinatra must stand alone.

Frank Sinatra, Bing Crosby, and Dean Martin share a trio version of "Ol' Man River" to close out a medley of "Good Old Songs" on Sinatra's television special sponsored by Timex in 1959. (Photofest)

Crosby, Sinatra, and Martin each sang solo versions on television. Crosby tossed off his up-tempo version on a minimal set with a levee motif in the late 1950s. Martin did his up-tempo "River" on the second season of his long-running variety show. The March 23, 1967, episode of *The Dean Martin Show* opened with Martin singing "Ol' Man River" at 122 bpm. The tune was part of his current Vegas act and he had sung it as far back as 1947 in his vaudeville days with Jerry Lewis. Back then, Martin "played it straight" while Lewis "mugged it up" pretending to conduct the musicians in the orchestra pit.[4] On television twenty years later, Martin mugs his way through most of Hammerstein and Kern's song, almost breaking during the first break when the (again) hyperactive arrangement has the backup singers doing some overdone dooby-dooby-do's. This is one slick, jazzy, swinging version but Martin resists the joke just waiting to be made at the lyric "get a little drunk"—Martin's drinking was a big part of his persona. On the half chorus return to the bridge, the beat slows to a more deliberate pace, hinting at a big finish, but Martin demurs, climbing up on a padded stool, undercutting any possible drama. Even as he shouts the "tote" and "lift" lines, there's little pathos here. And while Martin takes some vocal pleasure in the high notes that end the song, he throws "Ol' Man River" away with a casualness that suggests a defining lack of seriousness. As with Cooke's similarly casual television version, persona trumps song in Martin's solo "River."

Sinatra sang the song as a dead-serious anthem on his 1967 special *A Man and His Music + Ella + Jobim*. His spoken introduction sets "Ol' Man River" where Sinatra always placed it—in a class apart.

> You know, ladies and gentlemen, in my business—[referring to the band] in our business—when a song lingers on through the years we call it a standard. But there are some songs that transcend the word standard. They kinda become classics, like this great song by Jerome Kern and Oscar Hammerstein II from *Show Boat*.

Here, for the only time captured in any medium, Sinatra sings "here we all work while the rich folk"—not the white folk—"play." He also elects to sing "boss man" rather than "white boss." Sinatra departs from his standard practice with the lyrics, eliding the racial dynamics of the original at a moment in history when race was at the top of the national agenda and Sinatra's own status as a white man, with increasingly conservative political leanings, might have come to his and his audience's mind. As shown later, Sammy Davis Jr. also departed from his standard approach to the lyric during the fraught late Sixties. Sinatra opts for his quiet, intimate manner of singing "Ol' Man River," with piano accompaniment only until the final A phrase, where the full orchestra comes in for the big finish, which has Sinatra, now standing, tapping into *The Concert Sinatra* conceit that this song is a kind of epic anthem—a choice reaching back to his MGM white tuxedo version.

Judy Garland sang "Ol' Man River" twice during the run of her short-lived television series, both times spotting the song during the so-called Trunk Sequence. "Trunk" numbers closed each episode. Setting aside guest stars, comedy, and production numbers, Garland appeared alone to sing one last time for the crowd. She put sure-fire songs in this closing segment: besides "Ol' Man River," the only other song to be performed on two occasions in the "Trunk" spot was the anthem "When the Sun Comes Out."

Garland's first "Ol' Man River" aired on December 8, 1963. There's no real evidence she sang it in concert before this. She wears a sleeveless black dress and doesn't hold a microphone. (Both versions are generally on YouTube: I distinguish them here by Garland's wardrobe.) While stepping forward to sing, Garland plays with her hair, seemingly thinking through what's to come. The musical arrangement—one she used across the 1960s—begins with an overwrought orchestral fanfare that abruptly transitions into a quiet string intro for the vocal chorus. Garland never sang the verse, sidestepping the question of lyrics singers like Sinatra had to deal with each time they sang the song. Like many Garland performances from this period, she begins very softly and ends very loudly—"Ol' Man River" is an obvious candidate for this treatment, as so many examples have shown. The end of the first A phrase features a deceptive cadence—the harmonies don't fully close but instead come to an uncertain rest. This trait of Garland's arrangement lends itself to a kind of personalizing of "Ol' Man River" not heard in the more stolid closes of more conventional arrangements. Garland extends the blue held notes on "soon" and "forgotten," leaning on the final –n of each word. On the bridge, she finds pathos in Kern's angular and repetitive vocal line rather than Hammerstein's words, emphasizing the "and"— another blue note—in the line "bodies all achin' AND wracked with pain." She nods at the line "Lif' dat bale!"—properly enunciated as "Lift that bale"—as if acknowledging the task to be done, as it if to say "yes, I will lift that bale" (◉ Sound Example 9.1). This is, perhaps, a feminine touch. Male singers—especially white ones—tend to play the boss man here, shouting "tote" and "lift." Garland plays the submissive role, internalizing the boss man's words and making them her own, inviting the informed listener to interpret this performance choice through her biography. On the final A phrase, the camera cuts to a new angle from below, suggesting the perspective of a member of the live studio audience. We look up at a performer deeply into herself. Garland is not singing to the crowd or the camera but to something bigger than any audience, something less specific and more universal. She is a figure of power and resolve looking upward at we don't know what. Voice, persona, and framing unite to take the song into deeply personal territory and very far from its origins in *Show Boat* or traditions among solo singers. After finishing her vocal, punctuated by a big, bold gesture with her arms, Garland ignores the closing fanfares of the arrangement, breaking out of her mode of intense concentration almost immediately. She smiles freely and blows a kiss to the cheering audience.

Garland's second "Ol' Man River" finds her in a sparkling white dress, initially leaning on the trunk holding a white microphone. This version aired March 22, 1964, on the series' penultimate episode. Garland is presented in a single long shot, which frames her subtly and effectively for the viewer. As before, it's never clear who she's singing to: Garland never addresses the camera and, again, seems to be in her own world. This time, at the end of the song the camera cranes up and looks down on Garland, framing her as a supplicant to some force she can't reach rather than a towering figure taking the viewer to the beyond. Garland holds the first syllable of the final "along" a very long time, reaching out with her free hand, then moving that hand to her cheek before finally finishing the tune. She bows quickly at the end, while the fanfare close to her arrangement plays on. She doesn't look quite so pleased as after her earlier try at the song, although her performance is every bit as controlled. Indeed, the two are largely the same interpretively. The primary difference comes in how the television camera frames her efforts.

Garland kept on singing "Ol' Man River," including it in her sets during a tour of the United States and London in 1967. Captured on record during her engagement at the Palace in New York, she prefaced the song with words to the audience: "I'll stay as long as you want me. As long as you want me I'll stay. Now we'll do a song, ok. Oh, I love you so much." The same arrangement follows.

There's genuine Hollywood pathos—and a bit of mystery as well—in Garland's "River." This isn't a signature Garland song from the past: unlike so much of her repertoire from these years, there's no nostalgia inherent in hearing her sing it. Garland reinvented "Ol' Man River" as an expression of her 1960s self. The song, reinterpreted as a meditation on laboring on despite physical and emotional exhaustion, fit her public image nicely. As one reviewer noted of a Christmas night performance in 1967,

> personal theatre for many, vicarious nostalgia for the rest, there is a deep, or masochistic sense of participation in almost every number: Will Our Judy Make It Over the Rainbow? At times, as in "Ol' Man River," when a long phrase of pure pre-war Garland melody flowed, the question might rise—is she putting us on the rest of the time? Is the fumbling and indecision part of the act to win sympathy, rivet attention, build suspense? As the latter-day Billie Holiday appeared to do.[5]

Was the song a display of strength and mastery or of weakness? "Ol' Man River" would seem to be an unlikely vehicle for such ambiguity. And yet, Garland can be credited with a thorough reinvention of the song as special

Judy Garland sang "Ol' Man River" on two episodes of her mid-1960s television series. (Photofest)

material for her own special talent. Perhaps Cleo Laine's "Control Yourself," performed some three or so years after Garland's death, was also a comment on Garland's way with the song.

Garland's "Ol' Man River" works as innovative in part because of her obvious distance from the song's original context. When she nods at "lift that bale," the knowledgeable listener is more likely to reflect on Garland's time at MGM—where drugs were used to keep her working at a furious pace— than to think through any possible, wholly unlikely connection between the singer and manual labor along the Mississippi. Garland's persona is so overpowering and so specific to tales of suffering and surviving that Hammerstein's lyric turns metaphorical—but, importantly, not universal. As with Cooke and Martin, Garland's persona trumps the song, turning it into a star vehicle pure and simple.

This hasn't prevented other women from including "Ol' Man River" in their acts, among them Broadway star Patti LuPone in her show *Coulda, Woulda, Shoulda... Played that Part*, during which LuPone reportedly introduced the song by saying, "There were only two things standing between me and this role." Laughs surely followed, falling silent so the audience could attend closely to a diva working unlikely alchemy on the song. A London reviewer responded with passion to an analogous club performance by Carrie Smith, an African American jazz and blues singer whose career was mainly in Europe. This review from 1979 makes one long to be in the room: "'Ol' Man River' simply exploded out of her. The treatment was dramatic, defiant, intimidating, a parade of vocal bicep which brandished her greatest gift, the iron of the blues shouter, and rammed it into the mind. It may be a one dimensional thing, but it is a rare thing, and it works."[6]

The single live performance of "Ol' Man River" seen by perhaps the largest audience dates to February 23, 1964. The Beatles were making their third appearance on *The Ed Sullivan Show*. Also on the show that night was Cab Calloway, a black bandleader and singer whose career reached back to Harlem in the 1930s, who sang a rhythm version of "Ol' Man River." The Beatles opened and closed the show; Calloway's two-song turn came near the end of the hour. Was anyone in TV land paying attention or were they just waiting for the Fab Four to come back on, as Sullivan had promised? Either way, America's televisions were on and Calloway's "Ol' Man River" simultaneously entered millions of living rooms.

On the Beatles' night, Calloway did two fast numbers in a row. His first was the jazz standard "St. James Infirmary." Alone before the camera, with an unseen band accompanying him, Calloway delivers a broad, comic, sexy, full-out performance, displaying his big voice and great range. On the applause, he sets the tempo for "Ol' Man River" by pounding furiously on the floor. It's fast: 165 bpm, enhanced further by Calloway's constant marking of the offbeats, whether by snapping, stomping with his heel, or madly waving his head in time to the music. He gives a fully engaged, physically unrestrained performance. Calloway strikes the floor for emphasis on "tote" and "lift," wiggles his hips, and moves his hands fluidly down his body on "body all weary" in a strangely sexual manner. Calloway's musical innovation is replacing Hammerstein's "rollin'" with "strollin'." The end of each A phrase features a high, held "strollin' along" that overwhelms all else and provides a manic moment of release—not unlike Screamin' Jay Hawkins's later recording but here contained by the beat, which never stops. Calloway shows how even in the 1960s there were still new ways to shape the tune (⊙ Sound Example 9.2).

On the applause, Sullivan remarks, "Brings back a lot of memories of the good old days back at the Cotton Club." The comment's an implicit nudge from the older generation—courtesy of Calloway's example—that the craziness of rock and roll might not be all that new. "Ol' Man River"—performed by the fifty-seven-year-old Calloway with all the physical vitality of Little Richard—makes the point nicely. (Calloway was still singing "Ol' Man River" at age eighty.)[7]

Crosby, Sinatra, Martin, and Calloway reprised old tropes for "Ol' Man River." Cooke, with his suave approach, distanced himself from the song's direct content, and Garland, as she did with so many songs, made "Ol' Man River" her own in a way few could copy. All these high-profile performances provide the context for several forgotten televised versions of "Ol' Man River" from the high season that speak directly to the social-political tenor of the times. For how could a lyric like Hammerstein's not resonate in the age of Martin Luther King Jr.? Two contrasting performances by Sammy Davis Jr. from the second half of the 1960s and a spoken-word version by actor Henry Fonda from 1964 suggest the larger resonance the song could have.

Sammy Davis Jr.'s first recorded "Ol' Man River" dates to 1958: the year Robeson sang it for the last time in Carnegie Hall and Sam Cooke delivered it on television. Davis did his "Ol' Man River" at Manhattan's Town Hall, an estimable venue where many baritones, black and white, including Robeson, had sung the song as an encore. Davis loved to talk before singing, a practice that proves valuable across his history with "Ol' Man River." At Town Hall, he prefaced the song with these words.

> Ladies and gentlemen, a song that has meant an awful lot to me for many, many reasons. And this has always been a song that has made me sort of realize the tremendous insight that a gentleman named Oscar Hammerstein must have into the hearts of human beings. This lyric was written many, many years ago but in analyzing the lyric it says so much that still needs to be said today. We'd like to do it for you.

Davis's approach to the song, supported only by piano until the final phrase of the chorus—likely modeled on Sinatra's intimate style—is very flexible rhythmically. He never really falls into a tempo: individual phrases and lines rush forward or hold back in direct response to the changing ideas of the lyrics, which seem to drive his choices. The effect sounds spontaneous even though this early performance sets the pattern for several decades of Davis's performances of "Ol' Man River" that are largely identical in their delivery.

Like Sinatra, Davis always sings the verse and takes what might be called the white singer's approach to key lines, singing "here we all work" and identifying only a "big boss." The first tilt toward a suppressed bitterness underlying Davis's reading comes with the line "you don't look up, you don't look down," which he fairly spits out, suddenly rushing forward rhythmically. Another enduring idiosyncratic performance choice follows with a revision of the verse's penultimate line: Davis replaces Hammerstein's "what does he care if the world's got troubles" with "what does he care if his folks ain't happy." The meaning of the new line is opaque. Is Davis suggesting that black folks are the children of the river? The revision is less generic, more personal than the original, going beyond the vague "you and me" of the chorus to come. Davis's folks are—unambiguously for the listener—black folks. The directness of Davis' racial identification is central to his personal cultivation of "Ol' Man River," even though he almost always edited out Hammerstein's racially specific descriptors.

Davis's free rhythmic treatment of Kern's tune continues in the chorus. Certain lines rush forward, bitten off with evident anger. On others, such as "soon forgotten," Davis sings with drawn out, lyrical beauty. The orchestra finally enters on the final A phrase, helping shape this last phrase into one big crescendo. Here, Davis pushes further on the angry side, with a confrontational "I'm sick. I'm sick of trying" but he tacks back to, for the time, extreme dialect with the revised line, "But I'se skeered. I'se skeered a dyin'" (⊙ Sound Example 9.3).

Like Garland, Davis chose to sing "Ol' Man River" twice on television. And also like Garland, his two versions are quite different in their visualization, even if Davis largely sticks to the vocal approach heard on his 1958 concert recording.

The March 11, 1966, telecast of *The Sammy Davis Jr. Show* (which I have viewed only in the Paley Center for Media's archival collection of vintage television) opens with a hip instrumental. Davis appears in silhouette, dancing up-to-date, hip-shaking moves in a sequence that highlights special effects, such as multiple Davis silhouettes leaping into and out of each other. It's a visually bold, totally contemporary opening. Davis establishes his physical presence, the dynamic power of his body, as well as his ability to be entirely of the moment. He appears ageless to the extent that his moves are the gestures of unselfconscious youth. The sequence ends with no titles: Davis's body alone identifies him.

Abruptly the mood changes with a cut to an almost entirely black screen. Off in the distance Davis stands in a single pool of light, silhouetted from above. He begins to sing "Ol' Man River," again starting with the verse, only piano accompanying him. The camera begins a very, very slow pull in toward Davis, who remains almost entirely immobile, only moving his arms. When we're close enough to register his face—given the low resolution of television, this doesn't really happen until the bridge—Davis is shutting us out. His eyes remain almost entirely closed throughout. When he opens them, he registers something off camera, creating the sense of an "other" implicit in Hammerstein's lyric. Indeed, Davis opens his eyes only on the "tote" and "lift" lines, both delivered as impersonations of the "big boss," accompanied by explicit gestures—a pointed, commanding hand. At the end of the bridge, on the familiar hinge moment for so many interpretations of the song—Davis copies Sinatra and drops down to a low note and draws out the moment (although he doesn't connect the vocal line across to "Ah gits weary")—the camera begins to crane upward, initially framing Davis's full body from above before pulling away to where it started out at the top of the number. As Davis's body recedes into the distance and shrinks in size, his voice grows louder. Only after his one-shot performance of "Ol' Man River" do the credits roll for the show.

Davis's physically contained delivery is the expressive opposite of Cab Calloway's manic embodiment of "Ol' Man River" as a rhythm tune. Davis hardly moves and when he does his sharp arm gestures suggest furious violence contained with great difficulty. Framed by an artsy camera strategy that at once distances the viewer—we are denied the front row seat Garland's show provided—and puts us, at times, too close for comfort, Davis's performance is almost entirely internal. The viewer witnesses a display of personal emotion that seeks no social connection.

After the credits and the first commercial break, Davis appears, cigarette in hand, as a hipster host. With all the intensity of "Ol' Man River" apparently gone, he's ready to party and welcome his first guest, Rat Pack buddy Peter Lawford, onto the show. But the radioactive half-life of the opening song lingers, for the pair quickly find themselves returning to "Ol' Man River." Lawford starts the gag, complaining about the opening number, saying "Everyone in the business knows that 'Ol' Man River' is my song." This opening gambit doesn't lead to a discussion of race—Davis doesn't, for example, say that the song was written for Robeson or sung by a black character in Show Boat—but instead dwells on the quality of "Ol' Man River" appreciated by so many singers. As Lawford says, "There aren't that many big songs around." Davis mollifies Lawford's petulance—presumably meant to be taken as charm—by sending him off with a buxom music librarian, who will help Lawford choose another "big" song.

Davis returned to "Ol' Man River" on a March 1969 episode of *The Hollywood Palace*, a vaudeville-style variety show that ran for almost a decade. As the episode's host, Davis performed several numbers while also introducing several featured performers. For his solos, Davis offered the comedy dance number "Choreography," introduced by Donald O'Connor in the 1954 film *White Christmas*, and a tap dance routine featuring four drummers from the worlds of jazz and Latin music. Davis opens the show with a stunning (and long) song-and-dance production number to the Fifth Dimension's current hit "Up, Up and Away," which has Davis and a group of leggy female dancers—black and white—doing hip gyrations, pelvic thrusts, and booty shakes in a seriously funky display of "sock it to me" Sixties attitude. Dressed in tight pants and high-heel boots, Davis anticipates the hypersexuality of the pop star Prince, who came along just a decade or so later. With barely a minute to catch his breath, Davis goes right into "I Gotta Be Me," one of his signature tunes taken as a request. He starts the song using a broad Jewish accent, in the context of this book giving just a taste of what Stan Daniels's approach to "Ol' Man River" might yield when applied to this tune. Given the tremendous variety of poses contained in just his own contribution to an episode of the *Hollywood Palace* that also featured black comic Nipsey Russell and James Brown, the "Godfather of Soul," singing "I'm Black and I'm Proud," Davis's decision to close the show with an intimate performance of "Ol' Man River" takes on even greater resonance. Having himself performed a broad range of black popular culture personas, Davis turned to Hammerstein and Kern's old song as a vehicle to usher the viewer out from the show's realm of entertainment and into the broader world beyond the television screen.

In his spoken introduction back in 1958, Davis universalized the song, drawing attention to Hammerstein's ability to see into the "hearts of human beings." Introducing the song in 1969, after eleven transformative years in race relations, Davis situates "Ol' Man River" in the history of "his folks."

> I would like to close the show tonight with a song that means an awful lot to me. I think it means a lot to my people. Though it was written many, many years ago I can think of no better testimony than right now for what it has to say in terms of man's inhumanity to man and the hope that one day we will all respect each other for the dignity of man.

Davis begins from a sitting position on the edge of the stage. He again adopts his free rhythmic approach, although the effect is less mannered than in the earlier performances. Davis again starts with the verse, only this time he sings "here we all work while the white folks play"—the only time he ever played the race card in Hammerstein's lyric. A cut to a second shot during the verse reverses the angle and looks out over the audience. Slowly, the camera begins a long semi-circular tracking shot all the way around Davis's seated position quite near the front row of the audience. The heavy television camera, positioned on the stage, is turned on the audience members, who are visible throughout as the house lights remain up for the duration of the song. The audience, virtually all white, sits very still, listening closely. The historical precedent for this unexpected shot is the similar treatment of Robeson's seated figure in the 1936 film *Show Boat*. There, using an approach defined by Hammerstein in the script, a crane-mounted movie camera could circle Robeson's form with ease, highlighting his body as a piece of sculpture. Here, in the more constrained visual context of television, the circling shot places Davis's singing figure relative to the audience and makes the song a social event.

Davis, a black star accustomed to addressing the white majority, had entertained this crowd, now he wanted to tell them something important from the depths of his soul and from his position as a voice for his "people."

Sammy Davis Jr. on television, his rapt studio audience visible to home viewers in a similar fashion to his 1969 "Ol' Man River" on *The Hollywood Palace*. (Photofest)

The change in his approach from "big boss" to "white boss" is telling, as is a revision of the bridge lyric. Davis impersonates the white boss with the words, "Hey you, boy, lift that barge." ("Boy" proves a resonant addition to Hammerstein's lyric, as several examples in the next chapter show.) As with Garland, only here more a propos to the song, Davis can easily be heard as expressing his own experiences of work, perhaps specifically during his personally disastrous period in the segregated military during World War II (described in detail by Davis in his 1965 autobiography *Yes, I Can*). Whatever it had been for Davis before this performance, in 1969 "Ol' Man River" becomes a song about his experience of being black in Jim Crow America, a song to use to get his white audience to think.

The end, as always, rises to an emotional and dynamically epic height. Further changes to the lyric suggest a direct engagement with the specifically racial potential of the song heard by earlier singers such as Robeson. Davis sets aside his customary "I'se skeered of dyin'" and instead voices a defiant "but I ain't afraid of dyin'." Rising to his feet at just this line, the camera angle again sets him in context with his listeners. The television viewer watches the audience attend to this expression of racial resistance. If anger had always lurked beneath the surface of Davis's complicated delivery of the song, in this performance resolve and defiance contained by absolute expressive control take over. Davis—like Robeson—resists the lapse into noble suffering in Hammerstein's final lines, changing the text to imply strength ready for the struggle ahead. (The change didn't stick. Davis reverted to "skeered of dyin'" in his 1985 UNICEF concert in Paris.)

At the end, Davis responds briefly and ambiguously to the applause: he kisses his fingers (as if to blow a kiss), then makes a peace sign, then closes his hand into a raised fist (giving a mini black power salute), then quickly leaves the stage without bowing. The episode is abruptly over, no "we'll see you next week" or "good night everybody."

On November 10, 1964, the Bell Telephone Hour devoted a full hour to the lyrics of Oscar Hammerstein. (Hammerstein died in 1960.) The lyricist's son William produced the show and actor Henry Fonda hosted. On hand to perform musical selections was a lush studio orchestra and the equally lush Buster Davis Singers, the kind of mixed chorus that could be heard singing transparent, wispy, whiter-than-white background vocals behind pop singers across the 1950s and 1960s. Soloists included the dashing John Raitt (a Gordon MacRae–type baritone) and the lovely Florence Henderson (a standard white ingénue)—they would do Hammerstein's conditional love duets, like "People Will Say We're in Love" and "If I Loved You"—as well as Barbara McNair, an elegant black singer often seen on such television variety shows. (This show, sadly, seems to be unavailable for viewing outside archival collections. I watched it at the Paley Center for Media, which is open to the public and has branches in Manhattan and Beverly Hills.)

The program frames Hammerstein as an optimist. Optimism, described in Fonda's introductory words as "a rare and wonderful point of view, an affirmation of life, a promise, a faith, a dream, a celebration," forms the controlling theme of the show. While the program is mostly music, Fonda appears every once in a while to speak a lyric rather than having a singer sing it, drawing attention to Hammerstein as a wordsmith in an effectively understated way.

Show Boat figures in the show quite a bit. Fonda repeats a famous Dorothy Hammerstein anecdote: she pointedly noted that *her* husband wrote "Ol' Man River" while all Kern did was write dum-dum-dee-da. Richard Rodgers, Hammerstein's partner in the 1940s and 1950s, is quoted calling *Show Boat* "a noble work of collaboration, achieved by people of deep feeling and high talent." And Fonda nicely situates Hammerstein's generational longevity, noting that the "people who sighed over *Show Boat* were bringing their children to see *Carousel*," Rodgers and Hammerstein's bittersweet musical of 1945. The expected *Show Boat* medley begins with an operetta-style rendering of "Make Believe," which segues into the perky charm solo "Life upon the Wicked Stage" done as comedy. Then it's time for "Ol' Man River." Fonda provides the introduction.

> If Oscar Hammerstein preferred to look on the bright side, he was still aware that there are clouds as well as silver linings. If he was fundamentally optimistic it was not without a very clear understanding of the human condition. He knew and understood trouble and pain. He cared deeply about people. No lyric ever written for a musical show expresses a more profound compassion than this one.

At this point the viewer might be forgiven for expecting Paul Robeson to stride onto the screen. He was, after all, still alive. But, given his persona non grata status and his post-1960 withdrawal from the public sphere, it would have been impossible to engage Robeson for a major network television show and have him sing the song Hammerstein and Kern wrote for him almost forty years earlier. John Raitt had the most powerful male voice on the telecast, but he didn't sing "Ol' Man River" either. Had Gordon MacRae been the romantic leading man on the show, he might have been the choice to sing it. (MacRae sang "Ol' Man River" on television in 1975.) Indeed, no one sings "Ol' Man River" on the Bell Telephone Hour. Instead, Fonda recites the lyric, beginning with the verse: "There's an old man called the

Mississippi." The full chorus lyric follows, with no applause at the close. The show abruptly segues into a medley of love songs around the theme of "romance," as Fonda notes, "the happiest emotion any of us can know."

Fonda's delivery of the lyric is not outwardly dramatic but instead remains in the actor's default style—a straightforward, low key, plain and simple American voice, albeit a white voice here speaking a black man's words as scripted by a Jewish American. (Could Fonda's spoken "Ol' Man River" have been the inspiration for Stan Daniels's spoken version in a Yiddish accent? Hammerstein's Jewish background goes unmentioned on the Bell Telephone Hour.) Fonda's Joe relates intertextually to the movie

Actor Henry Fonda recites the lyrics to "Ol' Man River" on a 1964 episode of the Bell Telephone Hour devoted to Oscar Hammerstein II. (Photofest)

actor's star persona as a common man of noble stature—which is, of course, exactly what Joe is. Fonda plays Joe as a Tom Joad–type figure, borrowing the cadences from his delivery of Tom's "I'll be there" speech at the conclusion of the film of John Steinbeck's *The Grapes of Wrath*. In Fonda's voice, "Ol' Man River" comes off with cinematic understatement and zero self-pity as the direct, calmly stated words of a stoic American poet of the underclass. (Fonda's persona, however plain-spoken or honest in its effect, is no less a performance than more histrionic identities.)

Fonda's ability to be intense without being overwrought and the musicality of his voice prove beautiful in their ordinariness. Able to shape the lyric out of phase with Kern's patterned melody, Fonda makes the distinction between river and singer less melodramatic, more a meditation on the indifference of nature to human toil and the trials of an unjust world, not an emotional speech but a coming to awareness of the human condition. This is only possible without Kern's melody, which prescribes certain emphases and is, in some passages, impossible to sing softly.

Fonda's approach and persona remind the listener that "Ol' Man River," while deeply invested in the African American experience, is also a song about and for working men. It's a shame Bruce Springsteen didn't follow Fonda's example and lend his plain and simple American voice to Hammerstein and Kern's tune. But the distance between Springsteen and Broadway is, perhaps, just too wide. Attending a party at Sinatra's house where guests gathered around the piano to sing Sinatra's kinds of songs, Springsteen admitted to his wife that he just didn't know this part of the American songbook.[8] Still, as the transforming triangulation of Fonda, Steinbeck, and Hammerstein suggests, "Ol' Man River" has the potential to highlight the shared experience of all those who have labored on the land and struggled to survive. Springsteen's own work—on albums like *Nebraska* and *The Ghost of Tom Joad* but also in his renderings of folk songs associated with Pete Seeger—draws on themes of working lives that tap the same vein of American life found in Steinbeck's fiction. (Seeger sang "Ol' Man River" at least once—at a 1998 tribute to Robeson.)[9] And Springsteen has never shied away from imaginatively entering the lives of others, however distant from himself—whether the Vietnam veteran in "Born in the U.S.A" or illegal immigrants from Mexico seeking a better life north of the border in "Sinaloa Cowboys." Springsteen has not, however, explicitly crossed the black-white color line in this way. Hammerstein, in writing a song for a black workingman to sing, also demonstrated his desire to imagine the lives of others whose experience was far from his own. That he did so with subtlety and complexity—and across the color line—allowed "Ol' Man River" to take on a multitude of guises. But a disruption in the song's passage from generation to generation of popular musicians, a product of the rock-era juggernaut of singer-songwriters and albums of all original material prevented post-1970 musicians from claiming the song as their own. Still, Fonda's Steinbeckian spoken version from 1964 helps us imagine a performance of the song by Springsteen, a wordsmith who, like Hammerstein, put the experience of working people into words to be sung.

It's important to remember that Robeson sang "Ol' Man River" as a workingman's song as well, often at events in support of unions. Robeson's funeral—which included the playing of a recording of him singing "Ol' Man River"—was held in the evening, according to a family friend, "so that working people can attend."[10]

10

cɜ

Sons and Daughters of Joe

"Black is coming to Broadway these days, and I mean real black, not just someone singing 'Ol' Man River'—even though that's quite a radical song if you ever listen to it." So wrote Clive Barnes in his *New York Times* review of *Ain't Supposed to Die a Natural Death*, a 1971 play that put life in America's urban ghettos on stage.[1] Barnes was right: "Ol' Man River" is quite radical—*if* you really listen to it. He was also correct that in the era of Black Power, "Ol' Man River" could never hope to be taken as "real black," even for Broadway's white middlebrow audiences. In his opinionated 1972 book *American Popular Song*, composer Alec Wilder noted of "Ol' Man River," "undoubtedly the lyric accounts for half of the song's acceptance, though it is frowned on by the society of the seventies."[2] Davis and Wilder agreed—quite soon after the high season closed—that the metaphorical power of blacks laboring on the Mississippi for King Cotton and the notion of the noble, long-suffering black man were, perhaps, finally and definitively out of date. This shift occurred rather quickly given the frequent appearances of "Ol' Man River" during the high season.

Robeson knew "Ol' Man River" could be a radical song and he used his own version to declare himself a radical back in 1949. Robeson forced his listeners to re-hear "Ol' Man River" as radical by making changes that pushed on themes Hammerstein left veiled but nonetheless there to be revealed. And although Robeson's specific changes were not adopted by others—except for frankly political musical groups like the New York City Labor Chorus—he was not alone in using "Ol' Man River" to take popular music into the realm of protest. This final chapter considers other African American performers who changed the song in ways that highlighted the serious racial issues lodged in Hammerstein's lyric. Dating from the late

1950s to the 1990s—during and beyond the high season—these performers reinterpreted Kern's music through innovative black musical styles that
arrived on the scene after "Ol' Man River" was born: rhythm and blues,
doo-wop, post-1920s blues, gospel, and soul. Kern and Hammerstein could
never have anticipated the musical resources later black performers would
have at their disposal when interpreting the song. "Ol' Man River," by
virtue of never having completely left the mainstream of popular music,
remained to be remade by these new black voices in these new black styles.

"Ol' Man River" was conceived as a kind of nineteenth-century song,
modeled on the Negro spiritual. Returning for a moment to Hammerstein
and Kern's original plans for featuring Robeson in *Show Boat*, in addition to
the role of Joe they hoped to insert into act two a short recital featuring
Robeson and his regular accompanist Lawrence Brown. Robeson would
play himself, his biography rewritten to make him the son of Joe, the stoic
stevedore who sings "Ol' Man River." In a speech leading into the scene,
Cap'n Andy laid out the rise of concert spirituals in simple terms, offering
a distorted history of Robeson's rise on the New York scene.[3]

> ANDY: Joe's son—'member him when he was a little pickaninny wouldn't study
> 'rithmetic wouldn't learn to read but he knew all the river songs, that ever was.
> Parthy used to have to keep shuttin' him up wel, [*sic*] sir—he's now singin' in
> concerts all over the country, and makin' good money, too an' you know what he
> sings? The same dem fool old songs they sung forty years ago on these levees.

Stage directions follow, describing Robeson, "in evening clothes in front of
a piano, with his accompanist, Lawrence Brown, in a velvet drop, as he
appears at his recitals." Robeson and Brown's recital in *Show Boat* would
have featured real spirituals and, one imagines, another reprise of "Ol' Man
River" (three were already written into the script). If he didn't program it
during the recital scene, audiences would likely have requested it.

This multigenerational plot had a parallel strand: Magnolia and Ravenal's
daughter Kim, played by the actress who played Magnolia, would perform
an up-to-date jazz number just after Robeson's recital. (Kim grows up to be
a Broadway musical comedy star.) Thus, Hammerstein's original plot for
Show Boat turned on a common interpretation of American popular music
history, with nineteenth-century black song types—spirituals and blues—
turning into 1920s popular music hits—Negro spirituals on the concert
stage and syncopated jazzy tunes on the Broadway stage.

Hammerstein and Kern's plan was scrapped when Robeson refused to
play Joe but the generational updating of black musical styles dramatized
in the Robeson-Kim plot continued in the real world. As previous chapters

have shown, the "same dem fool ol' songs"—"Ol' Man River" prominent among them—lived on to be transformed by each new shift in popular music history. Indeed, "Ol' Man River" provides an ideal test case of this axiom of American musical history.

Some of the singers and musicians who effected these transformations on "Ol' Man River" can, in terms of their artistic inheritance of a song written for Robeson, be understood historically as the sons and daughters of Joe. This chapter zeros in on African American performers who tried, in some measure, to use "Ol' Man River" as a tool for the expression of African American identity, history, or activism. All of these performers treated Hammerstein and Kern's song as a serious expression of the black experience, as a song about working people or the powerless, and, in some cases, as a song of protest. Several of these versions were created with a black audience in mind: live recordings reveal how those audiences responded. Others, aimed at the mass audience for pop music—majority white in a majority white nation—committed themselves to the notion that "Ol' Man River" could foster understanding between the races or articulate, in the medium of popular music, the serious side of the black experience for a national—and thus, interracial—audience.

As Robeson consistently did after World War II and as Sammy Davis Jr. did just once in his 1969 *Hollywood Palace* "Ol' Man River," black performers made small adjustments or additions to Hammerstein's lyrics that wrestled the song toward a specific meaning. Such changes take hold of "Ol' Man River" with the intent of making the audience think in new ways. Changing the lyrics assumes that audiences hear the differences and appreciate the interpretive distance traveled between "Ol' Man River" as written and as remade for a specific moment in time. Adding commentary between Hammerstein's lines serves a similar purpose, allowing the singer to step outside the song while still in the midst of performing it. Black singers' additions and changes to the lyric take on added resonance during the song's high season, chiming with earlier strategies used by black performers to gloss their performances of Hammerstein and Kern's song.

The Ink Spots, a long-lived black pop vocal quartet that splintered into many separate groups in the mid-1950s, turned in a light R&B version in 1959, complete with a honking sax solo, almost a required element for a pop-oriented Ol' Man Rhythm in these years. The bass lead shows all the inventiveness of the best such recordings. He doesn't sing the tune straight but instead finds new ways to reduce the tune to musical essentials. His innovation is to repeat "rollin', rollin', rollin', rollin'" at the end of each A phrase. Like many other versions from these years, the Ink Spots fall into a vamp at the close. But rather than sing ecstatically over this, as later singers

would, the bass starts talking, commenting on the song just sung (⏵ Sound
Example 10.1).

> Ol' Man River's floatin' sure.
> Tired a livin'.
> Oh-oh.
> I ain't tired a livin' either.
> Something wrong there.
> Hallelujah, brother.
> I wonder what his point is?

This spoken, somewhat bemused close to the record recalls a recording of
"Old Folks at Home" made by Louis Armstrong and the Mills Brothers in
the late 1930s. After turning in a swinging version of Foster's South song,
complete with mock hallelujahs, Armstrong leaves the listener with some
choice words: "We sure is a long way from home—yeah!" The distance between the sentiments of the lyric and the urbane style and success of the
singers is emphasized in both recordings.

While no black female singer recorded a slow, earnest, anthem-like "Ol'
River"—there are no African American analogues for Judy Garland on record—
several did record the number as a rhythm tune. Ruth Brown was the first, with
a rollicking version made in 1954. Lesser-known singers Hadda Brooks and
Gloria Lynne followed. None of these exercised the option of rewriting the lyric
to pointed effect. Mae Barnes and Jackie "Moms" Mabley, however, did.

Mae Barnes's career reaches all the way back to the 1920s: she was around
when "Ol' Man River" debuted. As a nightclub singer in the 1950s, Barnes
was known for altering well-known lyrics, a practice that encouraged close
listening. Her take on the Gershwins' "Summertime" has the line "Your daddy's a millionaire / And your mommy's a contest winner / So ch-do-dem-up,
skoot-em-up, baby / Don't you cry," and later "One of these mornings / You're
gonna wake up singin' / 'You ain't nothin' but a hound dog.'" Her "Ol' Man
River," from 1958, also changes the lyrics—but with added meaning. Backed
up by three "Ol' Man River" veterans—drummer Jo Jones (featured in a
drum solo between Barnes's sung choruses), Buck Clayton on trumpet, Ray
Bryant on piano—Barnes sings the tune at a blistering 179 bpm and even
fills the breaks with scat vocals. Hers is among the most virtuoso jazz takes
on the song (⏵ Sound Example 10.2). But even at this tempo Barnes was not
content to leave the words alone, especially at the bridge, which she sings as

> Tow that barge!
> Lift that bale!

Where's that mop?
Get that pail?

Deftly eliminating the lines about drunkenness and jail, Barnes extends
the voice of the boss and inserts images of stereotypically female labor into
Hammerstein's masculine text. When sung by a woman, lyrical references
to mops and pails suggest the world of domestic servants, ubiquitous on
1950s and 1960s television and recently given a new reading in Kathryn
Stockett's 2009 book *The Help* (made into a film in 2011). Barnes's "River"
highlights the work done by black women, as well as men, even as Barnes
herself enjoys the luxury of creative work as a singer.

An even more empowered revision of the lyrics was captured live at a
1964 performance by Jackie "Moms" Mabley. Mabley was an innovative
standup comic with a long career, most of it spent entertaining black audiences at venues like the Apollo Theater and all along the Chitlin' Circuit. In
the 1960s, white audiences came to know Mabley on records and television,
and even at Carnegie Hall. Her live "Ol' Man River," included on the LP *The
Funny Sides of Moms Mabley*, attacks almost every element of Hammerstein's
lyric, not in the spirit of satire but with a voice of refusal. Mabley's version
is perhaps the strongest rewriting of all. It is intensely personal in diction
but would surely resonate with any black American who fled the South and
harbored no desire to go back. From the first A phrase, Mabley makes it clear
this performance of "Ol' Man River" will be about her.

Ol' Man River
Now you've heard of Ol' Man River.
They say he don't know nothin'
But let Mom tell you something
I'm gonna let that Ol' Man River keep on rollin' along.

Now listen, I eat potatoes and I wear cotton.
But outside that, baby, it's been forgotten.
I'm gonna let that ol' Mississippi just keep right on rollin' along.

Mabley doesn't work: she consumes. And like the "smoke a little tea" version from the 1930s, she's not interested in painting a sympathetic picture
of black laborers. Mabley allows no sentiment as she spells out a statement
of personal history that rejects the South and embraces New York City—
where "Ol' Man River" was born—in no uncertain terms. On the bridge and
final A phrase, Mabley exalts in her new Northern home, with none of Lou
Rawls's ambiguity about the South she left behind (⏵ Sound Example 10.3).

I was born on the Mississippi shore,
But I ain't goin' – back down there no more.
Cause' I can't lift no barge.
And I can't tote no bale.
And getting much too old
To spend the rest of my life in jail.

I'm gonna stay right in New York City,
Where I know it's free.
Right there on that Hudson
Where I can see Miss Liberty
And let that ol' dirty river,
that ol' muddy river,
that ol' . . .
Let it roll, let it roll, let it roll along.

Like some jazz versions, Mabley uses the tune of Kern's first A phrase throughout the chorus. Her revision is as much about the groove as it is the song. Having dispatched Hammerstein's lyric point for point, Mabley and her audience are ready to roll into the future.

Many singers profiled in previous chapters invested interpretive energy in Hammerstein's quotation marks around the lines "'Tote dat barge!' / 'Lif' dat bale!'" White male singers with trained voices often shouted these lines. There is a parallel tradition among black vocal harmony groups of using the white boss's lines of dialogue in the bridge lyric to activate a full dramatic rendering of the entire song, verse and chorus. The flexible collective voice of such groups brought expressive resources solo versions couldn't tap.

As with most all approaches to "Ol' Man River," this practice has roots reaching back to 1928. At a time when few black vocal groups were being recorded, the white group the Revelers brought out the drama in the bridge by inserting, between the lines, two replies to the boss. When commanded to "Tote dat barge!" by a deep-voiced member of the group, the remaining Revelers shout "Yes, sir." in high, almost squeaky voices (⊙ Sound Example 10.4). The cartoonish—to present-day ears, offensive—effect of the Revelers' bridge points toward the importance of content and tone when "Ol' Man River" is realized as a drama. When the black men working and the "white man boss" are embodied, questions of dignity move to the center. An artifact of the later 1920s, the Revelers' "River"—as noted it starts out with the n-word—misses the mark.

Unsurprisingly, black vocal groups did not emulate the Revelers. In fact, the Mills Brothers, the best-known black pop vocal group of the 1930s, did not record "Ol' Man River." The Ink Spots (discussed earlier) did not record "Ol' Man River" until the 1950s and did so then in a rhythm version that questioned the song after it had been enjoyed. Two other established black vocal pop groups from before the high season turned in subtle versions that sensitively probed the song's dramatic potential, refusing to take the inherently light rhythm tune approach. These versions avoid any confrontational stance and can be heard as directed at a knowing black audience. They may also reflect the characteristic care taken by black pop singers during the era of Jim Crow when addressing potentially controversial racial questions. Later groups, coming of age in more assertive times for African Americans in the public sphere, would take a more combative, even angry approach.

The Golden Gate Quartet's 1938 "Ol' Man River" begins softly, with one member singing "de darkies all work on de Mississippi" in a hushed tone, as if watching others at work. On "don't look up and don't look down," the rest of the group comes in, singing quickly and quietly, as if the voices of the laborers advising each other to keep on working, to not draw the attention of the "white folks." The end of the verse has an interjection that emphasizes the goal of peace after death: "Show me that stream called the river Jordan—boy, THAT'S the old stream what I long to cross." Here, the added word *boy* reads as dramatic interplay between solo and group, as a conversation among black folks. But in the chorus, a second added *boy* comes across differently. The white boss enters the scene, saying "Tote that barge, boy." The boss speaks in a manner that expects the "boy"—an adult black male, addressed in the strategically demeaning, customary manner used by white Southerners—to deliver: it's not the histrionic threat shouted out by so many white male singers but a taunt from a boss with the power to harm and no need to yell (⊙ Sound Example 10.5 includes both phrases where the Quartet added the word "boy"). The Golden Gate Quartet presents black voices complaining in a constrained manner, recognizing that raising their voices too loud might be dangerous, seeing salvation only across the Jordan. The effect is haunting: the opposite of the self-indulgent emoting of white singers crying their suffering to the heavens. At the close, the group turns to the singing of harmony, a strategy that calls for more conventional applause from their audience and one that would be repeated in later black vocal groups' arrangements. "Ol' Man River" remained in the Golden Gate Quartet's repertoire into the mid-1950s.[4]

Skipping forward twenty years, the Delta Rhythm Boys recorded a similarly sensitive take on the song in Sweden in 1957. The Delta Rhythm Boys, like the Ink Spots and the Golden Gate Quartet, were a black pop vocal group who enjoyed a long career and success with white audiences as well as black.

They were especially active on radio and film. Their "Ol' Man River" is stark—accompanied only by sparse gospel-style piano chords and flourishes—and turned inward emotionally: like the Golden Gate Quartet, the Delta Rhythm Boys dramatize the internal lives of the workers, not their actual labors. On the bridge, they don't play the boss man but instead sing "tote" and "lift" sotto voce (℗ Sound Example 10.6). The Delta Rhythm Boys use "Ol' Man River" to display their voices in a sonic tableau of working men reflecting on their labors all while not giving in to what might be called excess showmanship. Like the Golden Gate Quartet, theirs is a modest version that, in its use of understatement, effectively remakes a song often done flippantly or with excess bombast. Neither version makes the case for injustice: both stick to noble suffering, if in a different key from Robeson's pre-1940s way.

Rhythm versions dominated in the long wake of the Ravens' 1947 hit record, which several doo-wop groups copied. But in 1963, another doo-wop group—the Flamingos—laid down a similarly influential version that, if not a hit, highlighted and expanded the drama of the song and opened the way for more aggressively political readings of "Ol' Man River" in the age of Black Power. Like the Ravens, the Flamingos were emulated by multiple other groups, including the Earls (a white group), the Drifters, the Persuasions, and the Temptations (Motown's flagship male group). The Temptations would keep the Flamingos' dramatic take in their repertory all the way into the 1990s, when they performed "Ol' Man River" on television on *The Arsenio Hall Show*.

The Flamingos were a major doo-wop group of the 1950s. Their signature hit, "I Only Have Eyes for You," dressed a pop and jazz standard from the early 1930s in the trappings of early rock and roll. The Flamingos recorded several such classic prewar pop songs, so their taking on "Ol' Man River" comes as no surprise. However, the generous proportions and dramatic consistency of their version of Hammerstein and Kern's tune makes it stand out in their entire output. When performed at the Apollo Theatre in Harlem in 1962, *Variety* described their "Ol' Man River" as "a production number with drama galore, often a bit too much."[5] The Flamingos "brought tears to the eyes of adults and teenagers when they sang their dramatically emotional arrangement" at Baltimore's Royal Theatre and earned a standing ovation from adults and teenagers at the Minneapolis Club Chalet.[6] Baltimore deejay Fat Daddy was impressed: "When a vocal group can stand up before a house full of teenagers and get them to applaud a song like 'Ol' Man River,' which certainly ain't rock and roll, then that group just has to be the King of Vocal Groups."

The Flamingos' "River," imagined with a black audience in mind, yielded a rare two-sided 45. At over five minutes in length, the Flamingos' reconceived

The Flamingos' dramatic "Ol' Man River" was widely copied by other all-male vocal groups of the 1960s. (Photofest)

"Ol' Man River" as a short play. The arrangement begins with a shimmering chord, setting the key but giving no clue as to the tune. Rippling piano gestures rise and fall above an ominously repeating pedal tone in the bass. This vaguely watery opening cuts off abruptly with the entrance of the singers on the verse, alternating solo and group lines in a kind of call and response that immediately removes any sense that this "River" will foreground the bass solo, as was the case with the Ravens and most previous doo-wop versions. Collective labor along the Mississippi is emphasized at the start and remains a theme throughout.

The Flamingos opt for the "here we all work" version of the verse. By 1962, there was really no other option left. "Colored folks" worked—and still works—in the dramatic context of *Show Boat*, where the black chorus is playing their roles within a clear historical frame, within the era of Jim Crow segregation. The Flamingos, a black group endeavoring to update the song for a pop audience in the early 1960s, relied on the listener registering without emphasis that they were "colored." It's unlikely they would have used the word "colored" to describe themselves anyway, with the transition from "colored" to "Negro" to "black" already under way, especially among young people. And as this version was copied in the years to come, few obvious options offered themselves. "Negroes all work" misses the empowered use of Negro by African Americans in the period and "black folks work" doesn't fit Kern's tune. By the time African American came into use, the sense that Hammerstein's opening lyric needed updating had passed away, along with the song's place in popular culture more generally. Equally noteworthy is the Flamingos' removal of any reference to white folks or bosses: they sing "rich folks" and "rich boss" instead.

In an arrangement filled with sudden shifts of tempo and style, at the line "you don't look up," the entire group sings in unison in a kind of forced march, which itself ends abruptly at "Bend your knees. / An' bow your head. / An' tote dat barge until you're dead." These three lines are put into quotes— just like "Tote dat barge!" from the chorus bridge—by giving them to an emphatic solo voice, who sings-shouts them in the voice of the big boss himself and without accompaniment. Forceful short rolls on the timpani musically depict the physical acts of bending the knee and bowing the head (⊚ Sound Example 10.7). The effect is shocking, blunt, even cruel in a pop music context. There's little that's entertaining about this stretch of the arrangement. Instead, the Flamingos push hard on Hammerstein's lyrics to depict coercive labor practices with a muscularity that cannot be denied— especially when heard beside generations of rhythm or easy listening versions of the song. The listener is on notice that this "Ol' Man River" will explore the lyric point by point and won't shy away from or sugarcoat the scene of human labor in the American landscape latent in the lyric. The drum rolls also suggest dramatic action performed onstage which later listeners can only imagine, part of the "production number" quality *Variety* wasn't quite sure about. (The Flamingos were influential in the addition of visual interest to doo-wop performance, pioneering the notion of the fully choreographed vocal group.) The musical accompaniment shifts quickly to tremolo strings and heavenly, high harmonies for the conclusion of the verse, the lines about leaving the Mississippi and crossing the Jordan. These conventional, quite pretty doo-wop harmonies acquire added pathos for coming only after the harsher textures that start the verse.

Only on the word "cross" does the beat finally get going, a steady, slow swing that's fortified with strings and piano. And only here does the Flamingos' bass Jake Carey step forward to provide some of the traditional pleasures of "Ol' Man River." He sings the first A phrase in straightforward fashion and the first break is filled out with harmonized oohs from the other group members and more piano noodling. But the strings stay agitated: the listener gets little chance to relax or appreciate Carey's resonant voice on its own. Indeed, Carey has no intention of showing off his vocal prowess, for with the second A phrase he starts to talk rather than sing, denying any easy enjoyment of the tune by turning the lyric into prose: "You know, he don't plant taters. / And he don't plant cotton." But the lure of those lyrical high notes on "soon forgotten"—drawn out by so many singers—are irresistible and Carey sings the phrase to the close with an ear to vocal beauty.

The texture grows in complexity on the bridge, with more prominent drums working in opposition to the vocal oohs and more dramatic violin gestures, including sigh gestures and a rapidly descending chromatic line, all competing for attention. The tension breaks at "'Tote dat barge!' / 'Lif' dat bale!'" Both lines are heard twice: first, the group chants the words in a loud, emotionally flat unison; then, a single voice shouts the lines with angry forcefulness. With all the accompanying voices falling silent—as in the parallel spot in the verse—the scene of labor abruptly returns (⊙ Sound Example 10.8).

For the final A phrase, the earlier rhythmic texture returns briefly only to fall away at "I'm tired of living," when the group unites for a strong, unison conclusion. The Flamingos draw out the penultimate note—the "a" of "along," beloved of white trained male singers—ending the record with a flourish of harmony (⊙ Sound Example 10.9).

The Flamingos' 1963 "Ol' Man River" radically rethinks "Ol' Man River" by exploiting the inherent dramatic potential of the vocal group. Girl groups divided forces like this all the time, usually to talk about boys. Here, the boys—singing as men—divide into different perspectives to dramatize their position as workers under a big boss.

Other male vocal groups quickly copied the Flamingos' "Ol' Man River." The Earls followed the Flamingos' vocal arrangement closely but with only organ, bass, and drums for accompaniment. With slightly slower tempos throughout, the Earls end up sounding less urgent and less angry. The effect of the Flamingos' abrupt changes and layered textures is lost. While bass Larry Chance does speak a fair amount—often in close imitation of the Flamingos' Carey—the slower tempo takes the bite out of the approach. Chance doesn't exhort or emote; the drama is poorly paced (⊙ Sound Example 10.10). Bill Pinkney and the Original Drifters covered the Flamingos' arrangement in 1971. Their version—like the Earls', it's slower and with a stripped-down accompaniment—nonetheless enjoys a powerful solo in Pinkney, who speaks the boss man lines in the bridge (⊙ Sound Example 10.11).

In his autobiography, Otis Williams, a member of the Temptations, acknowledged the group's debt to the Flamingos: "probably the most difficult of all the songs in our repertoire is 'Ol' Man River,' a tune we started doing in 1964 after seeing the Flamingos do it at the Uptown in Philadelphia."[7] The Temptations followed the Flamingos closely, making only one substantial addition—a repeated, unfolding chord for the final "along"—that was picked up by several subsequent groups.

The Temptations used the song often as they entered the world of supper clubs, when Motown's bid for the white audience reached for the adult market. It was part of their Copacabana debut in 1967, where they took a routine created for black audiences to a very different—older, richer, white—downtown crowd. Also on their Copa program were imitations of the Four Freshmen (a white pop vocal group), and the Ink Spots and the Mills Brothers (classic black pop groups of the Jim Crow era). *Billboard* noted, "They sing 'Ol' Man River' Motown style—and it comes off."[8] This Motown version was captured on *Temptations Live!*, a 1966 LP recorded at the Rooster Tail, a black club in Detroit, and in the studio on *The Temptations in a Mellow Mood*, a 1967 LP including several Broadway standards. One audience member remembered the group's performance of "Ol' Man River" on Motown revue shows in the 1960s as "spellbinding" some thirty years later.[9] They sang it in 1975 in the Philippines, at a party given by President and Mrs. Marcos just after Muhammad Ali knocked out George Foreman in the so-called Thrilla in Manila.[10] They kept it in their programs in Las Vegas and London in the 1980s and, in 1992, the Temptations, with their original bass Melvin Franklin still singing the lead, performed the Flamingos' arrangement—verse and all—on *The Arsenio Hall Show*, the only network late night show with a black host and a frequent television venue for the group.

But the Temptations didn't always do the full Flamingos version. On their 1969 television special, "Ol' Man River" was part of a medley, following a very fast "The Best Things in Life Are Free," a Broadway show tune, like "Ol' Man River," that dated to 1927. Franklin introduced the tune.

> The best things in life are free. Or are they? It's taken much too long for a country as great as ours, with its unlimited resources and ingenuity, to realize the importance of the togetherness of all its peoples. In spite of the hardships that seemed to be a way of life for many in the past, there was always a song to sing, a prayer to say and be heard. Whether or not it was on the banks of the Mississippi or in a little white church across the field, I do believe that then and there the true meaning of love and understanding became a reality. And yet sometimes, I'm afraid its true freedom was as costly as life itself. So they sang.

The group starts "Ol' Man River" at the chorus but they only get through the first half, breaking off before the close of the second A phrase and seguing into, of all songs, "Swanee." This Tin Pan Alley South song—introduced by Al Jolson in blackface in 1919 and George Gershwin's first hit—suggests a certain timidity on the group's part. They didn't reproduce the Flamingos' confrontational "Ol' Man River" on television in 1969. Instead, and not-withstanding the veiled critique of the spoken introduction, they located the song within what looks like a Hollywood minstrel medley lacking only tambourines. In bright red outfits—sequined vests with long fringe—the Temptations wouldn't look out of place in the "Swanee" production number from Judy Garland's 1954 *A Star Is Born*, one of the last such Hollywood brownface routines. Motown's goal of reaching a middlebrow Broadway and Hollywood white audience is never clearer than here and it's telling that the Temptations—and not the super-sophisticated Supremes—are the Motown performers required to make this backward turn. Depending on the viewer's perspective, the line between high-energy minstrelsy and the embodiment of black hipness is hard to find in this routine. After a dance chorus of "Swanee," the beat stops as the group looks offstage. They sing, "Steamboat's a comin' just for me." Suddenly very serious, they offer Foster's "Old Folks at Home." Finally—it's not over yet—the medley ends with more of the up-tempo "Swanee." In this case, "Ol' Man River" is slipped in as a vocal feature among dated South songs—despite the Temptations' experience with Hammerstein and Kern's song in the Flamingos' dramatic version.

The Persuasions, a black vocal harmony group formed in the mid-1960s, offer proof that the Flamingos' version works without instrumental support. The group's live version from 1969 uses only voices and can sound a bit spare at times. But it's the connection with their audience that counts. The Persuasions included "Ol' Man River" on their debut LP *Acappella*, a live re-cording that captures the hi-wire act that is vocal a cappella. (The record was made with the help of Frank Zappa.) The Persuasions offer a chance to hear "Ol' Man River" as a street corner symphony—or, perhaps, given their use of the Flamingos' arrangement, street corner opera. The "classic" stature of "Ol' Man River" in the traditions of doo-wop are in evidence here—black vocal groups had been singing it for over two decades. But when performed in 1969, the Persuasions' changes to the lyrics speak to the audience with a directness that clearly calls for a political understanding of what "Ol' Man River" can do.

The Persuasions' "River" slightly adjusts the much-used "here we all work" opener to the verse for a more direct address to the listener that evokes the "you and me" of the chorus. There is no presentation of labor here, no audience watching: "we" are all workers.

> We all work on the Mississippi.
> We all work on the rich man's land.

Most of us work from dawn 'til sunset.
Waiting for judgment day to come.

We don't look up.
We don't look down.
We don't dare make the rich man frown.

In this stripped down version, the "rich man's" cries of "Bend your knees an' bow your head" are punctuated not by drum rolls but by vocal reactions from the audience. The angelic harmonies of "Let me go way" also receive praise from the crowd (⊕ example 10.12).

Only at the start of the chorus does the audience register that they are in for the bass voice treat that is "Ol' Man River." And bass singer Jimmie "Bro" Hayes does not disappoint. With little need to preach to the choir, he can relax and just sing. The Persuasions keep it pretty quiet. This is a sung version to lean toward and listen to closely. Further changes to the lyrics follow.

He don't plant cotton.
He don't lift bales.
He's soon forgetting.
He don't even care.

Hayes speaks some lines at the bridge, a common enough approach in doo-wop. Added collective pronouns and repetitions of phrases—"'Til our poor bodies, our poor bodies are wrecked with pain."—continue the theme of this as "Ol' Man River" sung by and for an assembly of working folks. The inevitable shouted "tote" and "lift" lines go by very quickly. At the unfolding chord close—they follow the Temptations here—the Persuasions emphasize the beauty of their harmonizing.

The Persuasions' "River" turns up on a 2002 double-CD anthology titled *Soul and Inspiration* and co-produced by Rhino Entertainment and WQED, Pittsburgh's public radio and television station. The liner notes begin:

In these challenging times, we require all the heavenly inspiration we can get just to navigate another day. This extraordinarily varied anthology expertly weaves together seminal gospel, soul, jubilee, pop, and doo-wop recordings to make one uniformly uplifting statement. These songs have remained relevant to the human condition no matter what the musical fashion. . . . And each and every song harks back to the church, central to the African American musical heritage.

Packaging secular and sacred black musics—doo-wop and gospel—is an ongoing strategy for the Pittsburgh station, surely, in part, as a strategy for community engagement across racial lines and effective fundraising for public media. And once again, "Ol' Man River" proves its expressive flexibility. On the *Soul and Inspiration* compilation, it shares space with Sunday school songs like "Jesus Loves Me," Sam Cooke's anthem "A Change Is Gonna Come" sung by Aaron Neville, and "We Shall Overcome" sung by gospel singer Mahalia Jackson, who sang just before Martin Luther King Jr. delivered his "I Have a Dream" speech.

Soul and Inspiration is best understood in historical terms as an answer record of sorts to the Americana LPs discussed in earlier chapters. "Ol' Man River" fits in both worlds but only as different performers and musical traditions inflect the song with different meanings. Grand orchestral visions of "Ol' Man River" minimize the black experience Hammerstein embedded in the lyric. The Persuasions' live a cappella performance, reliant entirely on the group's unsupported voices that are completed by the responding crowd, claims the song as part of the black experience and offers an inspirational vision of the American landscape grounded in black musical traditions and black economic history.

A final legacy of the Flamingos' "River" was a radical parody called "Ol' Pig Nixon," created and performed in the early 1970s by the Lumpen, a singing group cum "educational cadre" delivering the message of the Black Panther Party (BPP). The Lumpen formed spontaneously among four young men working in the Oakland, California, headquarters of the Black Panthers. With the addition of an all-volunteer interracial funk band drawn from sympathetic Bay Area musicians, the Lumpen briefly toured the nation, playing colleges and community centers and cutting at least one single: "Free Bobby Now," part of the campaign to get BPP co-founder Bobby Seale out of jail. A planned LP didn't materialize and the group's radical lyrics eliminated any prospect of radio play.

The Lumpen offered music with a message, entertainment intended to educate. As Lumpen member Michael Torrance remembered, "We had a lot of choreography. We wanted to take the model that was popular and recognizable to the people in the community, particularly the black community. And this is along the model of, say, the Temptations but also with the strong rhythm of James Brown, but with moves.... The choreography was part of the story. So that with our steps you would see us throw grenades, you would see us pump shotguns." They also acted out street scenarios, such as police harassment of black men being answered by direct resistance. The group sometimes encountered resistance while performing. Torrance remembered being chased from the stage mid-performance on several occasions, including an event in New Jersey where their parody of "Ol' Man River" raised the ire of the Citizens' Council, a group of white vigilantes.[11]

The goal of educating their listeners relied for the most part on lyrics. The group's theme song featured the repeated line "We want freedom. We're determined. It's the destiny of our community" over a funk groove similar to the "Theme from *Shaft*." The Lumpen also changed the lyrics to familiar songs in an effort to articulate BPP tenets or build support for specific political positions. For example, their version of Curtis Mayfield's "People Get Ready" turned this generalized civil rights anthem into a specific demand, vamping on the line "Bobby and the people must all be free." "Ol' Pig Nixon" took a similar tack.

The Lumpen built their version on the Flamingos' dramatic arrangement—which they knew by way of the Temptations—but changed virtually all the words, creating an almost complete parody text of verse and chorus. (The text given below combines two sources: Rickey Vincent's *Party Music: The Inside Story of the Black Panthers' Band and How Black Power Transformed Soul Music* and a fragmentary recording of the Lumpen in performance posted on the website itsabouttimebpp.com.)[12]

verse
Here we all suffer in the hands of fascists.
Here we are pained while the rich pig plays.
Getting no rest from the dawn til the sunset.
Getting no rest until freedom day.

They chained us up!
They shot us down!
They spread our blood all through the ground!
Well lift that gun.
And show no fear.
We'll shoot those pigs until they're dead.

chorus
Never be free
While Agnew breathes.
Lift up our guns
To end this madness.
Lift up our guns
And run the pigs along.

Ol' Pig Nixon,
That Ol' Pig Nixon,

> He don't know nothing
> We all should do something
> For Ol' Pig Nixon
> He just keeps oinking along.
>
> [...]
> Never give up till the pigs are gone.
>
> We get weary,
> And we're so tired of suffering.
> We're tired of suffering
> But not afraid of dying.
> But Ol' Pig Nixon
> He just keeps oinking along.

While the Lumpen's text doesn't exactly fit Kern's tune, it does effectively build on the dramatic trajectory of the Flamingos' original, always with the intent to turn "Ol' Man River" into an expression of militant, explicitly violent resistance—something it had never been before. In the verse, where the Flamingos, Temptations, and Persuasions all dramatized physical oppression—"Bend your knees"—the Lumpen called for violent action— "Well lift that gun." The corresponding differences in staging and the combined effect of words and action on the Lumpen's audiences can be imagined. Pervasive references to guns and the direct threat to Vice President Spiro Agnew (and implicitly to President Nixon) carry this theme into the chorus. The implicit critique of the Flamingos' dramatic musical arrangement—which had kept Hammerstein's words—is brought forcefully to the front by the Lumpen's explicit language. For the group, songs such as "Ol' Pig Nixon" carried significant costs: FBI harassment and no possibility of radio play or a performance career unconnected to activist contexts. In that sense, the Lumpen used "Ol' Man River" much like Robeson did in his postwar years, as part of a musical career where activism came first, where performance served political struggle. Notably, both Robeson and the Lumpen kept "Ol' Man River" but felt it necessary to significantly change the words. It's curious that on the final A phrase, the Lumpen did not incorporate Robeson's revisions: "laughing...instead of crying...keep fighting until I'm dying." Perhaps neither the Lumpen nor anyone around them in the BPP knew Robeson's better words for this spot, one measure of how forgotten the still-living Robeson was by the early 1970s. Or perhaps they did know Robeson's revisions and rejected his idea of laughing instead of crying in the face of injustice as too tame for the purposes of revolutionary action.

The climax of "Ol' Pig Nixon" returns to the hated figure of Nixon. The Lumpen apply the Temptations' unfolding harmony approach to Nixon's "oinking," giving the musical arrangement a slightly comic slant. Repeating the crowd-pleasing gesture three times, the final time the group changes the words to "But Ol' Pig Nixon. / He won't keep oinking too long," a revision promising revolutionary change in politics and society. The Flamingos' theatrical arrangement—with its own 1960s lineage among black vocal groups—and the activist tradition of making Hammerstein and Kern's song a vehicle for political resistance come together in this final, defiant version from the high season of "Ol' Man River."

On Christmas Eve 1931, the strains of "Ol' Man River" rose up from a shantytown in the yard of the New York Central Railroad in lower Manhattan.[13] A "sentimental negro" at a "decrepit piano" was singing the blues by way of a show tune that all the jazz bands were playing. "Ol' Man River" was, by the pop music standards of 1931, a blues song. As the meaning of the word *blues* changed, "Ol' Man River" moved in and out of the category. Rhythm and blues musicians, always keyed to popular success, embraced it: hard-core blues stylists generally let it alone. But the blues is a capacious category and at least one outsider musician remade "Ol' Man River" into a singular blues creation.

Abner Jay (1921–1993), singer and one-man band, recorded for his own small label and sold his discs at his impromptu live shows, leaving what one writer aptly called "a bread crumb trail of albums" that, as Jay predicted, became expensive collector's items.[14] From the 1950s to his death, Jay traveled the country, mostly the South, in a converted mobile home, offering shows on his own portable stage. He described himself, in the title of one of his hand-lettered album jackets, as the "last ole minstrel man" and reportedly said of his music, "Forget about your Tchaikovsky. He Russian. I'm your classical American music. Like it or not—I'm IT."[15] Jay claimed to know more than six hundred songs: "Ol' Man River" was among those he chose to record. Jay's "River" as it appears on his 1974 LP *Swaunee Water and Cocaine Blues* is most readily available on YouTube. Like so many makers of concept albums, Jay positioned "Ol' Man River" at the end of a side: side two. The cover image, repeated on several of his LPs, shows Jay lying stomach-down on the bank of a river, drinking directly from the source. His connection with Hammerstein's lyric could hardly be more direct.

Jay begins his "Ol' Man River" by reversing the parody approach: he keeps Hammerstein's words and remakes Kern's tune. Jay's new melody opens with a chant-like phrase that takes all the melodrama out of the verse, replacing it with a resigned but clear-eyed statement of the situation.

At "let me go way from the Mississippi," Jay finds some inspiration in Kern's falling melodic line, but again arrives at a thoroughly personal revision of the original (☉ Sound Example 10.13). At the chorus, Jay sticks to Kern's melody about half the time, somewhat undoing the rising trajectory of the song's range, creating a kind of stasis across the tune. He consistently draws out the length of the phrases, letting the meaning of the text rather than the set eight-bar phrases of popular song set the pace. Jay shouts passionately but not dramatically at the bridge and at the conclusion of the final A phrase, where he does take advantage of Kern's rising line (☉ Sound Example 10.14). Like some of the cubist jazz arrangements discussed in earlier chapters, Jay selects out the bits of Hammerstein and Kern's song that allow him to tell the story he wants to tell. The themes of hardship and endurance—central to the blues—are solidly there in "Ol' Man River" the show tune. Jay shows how these themes might be pulled apart and restitched together in a blues idiom, taking the song into a new realm but, as with so many such remakings, remaining strongly connected to the original.

If forced to put Abner Jay's "Ol' Man River" into a tidy generic box, blues is the best choice. And if "Ol' Man River" can be made to fit this secular realm of existential meditation on the trials of human existence, can it also be turned toward the blues' sacred counterpart, toward thoughts of a transfigured life to come? Can Hammerstein's invocation of "the River Jordan" guide "Ol' Man River" across yet another generic divide into the world of gospel? Two recorded performances provide the answer: an undeniable yes. And here, at last, in the realm of gospel, "Ol' Man River" as a woman's song can be heard live on record and video.

Committed gospel singers avoid secular music. That the Caravans—a group that never sought to cross over into popular music—included "Ol' Man River" in their concerts marks the song as, potentially, a sacred hymn. The Caravans were an all-female singing group accompanied by organist James Herndon. Soloist Cassietta George competes on even ground with Herndon's organ throughout an "Ol' Man River" recorded live in concert in 1965. George and Herndon share an adaptation credit for the performance as included on the 1969 LP *The Caravans in Concert*, on which—once again—"Ol' Man River" closes a side: side one. Like so many black singers, George changed Hammerstein's lyrics: preferring "potatoes" to "taters," for example. The bridge lyric is entirely rewritten and, given George's ecstatic vocal style, at times it's difficult to decipher. The new bridge removes the boss man in favor of an entirely original metaphor for life's troubles drawn from nature. The singer offers counsel that God is the only real friend in such circumstances (☉ Sound Example 10.15).

> Look up! Love waits!
> Through storms and rain
> With a heavy burden
> Any one full of pain
> The fact, my friend,
> You're not good to the end.
> Without my God
> You don't have no friend.

This change, which works wonderfully with Kern's laboring melodic line, suggests a partner song for "Ol' Man River," another inspirational show tune with a Hammerstein lyric that has transcended its original context: "You'll Never Walk Alone" from *Carousel*. "You'll Never Walk Alone" is the *other* show tune often anointed by gospel singers as carrying a religious message. Elvis recorded it with gospel tunes in 1968, as mentioned earlier. The last two singers of "Ol' Man River" discussed in this book—Aretha Franklin and Ray Charles—both recorded both songs.

Aretha Franklin recorded "Ol' Man River" in 1966, just before transitioning from Columbia Records to Atlantic Records. While at Columbia, Franklin recorded many Broadway and Tin Pan Alley tunes, without much success on the charts. On "Ol' Man River," Franklin changed the verse lyric in a unique way.

> Here we all work at one job or another.
> Why should I work while he rolls and plays.
> I get tired. So tired and weary.
> Got to keep toiling day by day.

Franklin eliminates the regionally grounding word *Mississippi*, instead pulling in close to the workers at the heart of Hammerstein's lyric, a group with whom she directly identifies. Her verse revisions also remove all mention of the boss overseeing the laboring souls. An up-tempo rhythm treatment of the tune follows in a familiar 1960s vein.

After moving to Atlantic Records, Franklin stopped recording standards and switched to soul songs. Her signature hits arrived immediately and, for a season, she was at the center of popular music as the Queen of Soul. But Franklin never lost her connection to the black church. In 1972 she reaffirmed the gospel roots of soul singing on the live double-LP *Amazing Grace*. The last track on the final side is Hammerstein's "You'll Never Walk Alone," which Franklin draws out to expansive proportions—a single pass through the chorus takes her almost five minutes—using a slow, gospel approach designed to build and build in intensity. With chorus and responding audience, Franklin utterly transforms Rodgers and Hammerstein's anthem, doing exactly what great American singers so often do: take a song and make it not only completely their own but also an occasion for passionate communion with their audience at a specific time and place.

When Franklin reached for "Ol' Man River" two decades later, she gave it the same full-on gospel treatment "You'll Never Walk Alone" received in 1972. Only this time, given the context and a very different audience, she didn't get the same response to her gospel remaking of Hammerstein and Kern's anthem. In 1994, President Bill Clinton invited Franklin to revisit her career and personal journey in a special concert at the White House. The event was videotaped and aired on the PBS series *In Performance at the White House*. "Ol' Man River" had been heard on the series seven years earlier during the administration of Ronald Reagan. For that event—a salute to Jerome Kern—no one sang Kern's most famous song. Instead, composer and show host Marvin Hamlisch played it on the piano.

Franklin preceded her "Ol' Man River" with a spoken introduction, a common practice as we have seen which, once again, revealed much about the meaning of the song for this singer on this occasion. Franklin speaks these words, with many pauses in between phrases, while playing a free introduction on the piano that gives no hint of the song to come.

Aretha Franklin performing at the Clinton White House, in a concert tracing her personal journey that included an impassioned gospel-style "Ol' Man River." (Photofest)

I'd like to do the next selection in honor of and in memory of our foremothers
and fathers, who so courageously graced the cotton fields from sun up to sun
down, and whose descendants became the sharecroppers of the time, of which
my grandmother's family was one of the many thousands.

Franklin begins singing at the chorus using the slowest tempo in the
song's recorded history. Lining out "Ol' Man River" phrase by phrase, she
embellishes on almost a word-by-word level—adding, for example, a slide
down then back up on the word "Ol'." The first A phrase alone takes a
minute and twenty seconds. Franklin takes an assertive, even accusatory
approach to the "he don't plant" phrases, punctuating her strong delivery
of the word "don't" with strong piano chords, re-routing the harmonic
path of the song in the process (⊚ Sound Example 10.16). Her singing
only intensifies on the bridge. And Franklin, like Robeson, removes
Hammerstein's reference to drink. In her version, blacks who "get uppity"
find themselves "in jail." Just after Franklin sings "get uppity," the image
cuts to President and Mrs. Clinton where it stays to the end of the bridge.
The First Lady sways unsurely to the very slow beat while President Clinton
leans forward.

Franklin's original revision "get uppity" puts the bridge lyric into a new,
historical light which, together with her spoken dedication to "our foremothers and fathers," provides the key to her entire rendition. Franklin
sings "Ol' Man River" as a song about the past: a past where getting uppity—
stepping beyond their prescribed subservient station as defined and en-
forced by whites—could land an African American in jail, a dangerous place
where black citizens frequently remained at the mercy of lynch mobs. Born
and raised in Detroit, where her father was a pillar of a prosperous black
community, and singing as an invited guest in the seat of national power,
Franklin is not offering personal experience here. Rather, she uses an
altogether unique tool of Jim Crow popular culture—the song "Ol' Man
River"—to deliver a gospel memorial to the black generations who came
before her. Franklin's use of the verb *graced* to describe these figures in the
landscape gives her portrait of the river a majesty that puts slaves and
sharecroppers at the center of American history. It's not an activist performance per se—but in context, of course, it is. Franklin—invited to tell her
own story in song at the White House; the ultimate "boss man's" mansion
and a house built by slaves—took the opportunity to tell a much broader
story than that of her own success in popular music, her own achievement
in helping transform the black gospel voice into the sound of soulful popular music. And Hammerstein and Kern's song for Paul Robeson was there
to help Franklin in doing so.

Franklin's 1990s "River" is a rarity. The work of Hammerstein and Kern's song as an active presence in American culture has been largely over since the start of the 1970s. If almost everything that could be done to the song was already discovered in 1928, since about 1970 there have been few inventive variations on the set patterns. Disco and hip-hop—alike driven by urban contexts and electronic sounds, similarly unconnected to rural labor and the acoustic musical past of horns or guitars—cut off "Ol' Man River" from the mainstream. The song's thorny examination of Jim Crow America from a black perspective also lost its sharpness after the laws upholding segregation were struck down and after black Americans began insisting on full equality. As a 1972 article about advertising targeted at black consumers put it, "The stereotype of the black man—a stereotype that comes right out of 'Ol' Man River'—must be abandoned. . . . the myth of the black male being inferior is passé."[16] The pose of noble suffering with which the song most naturally aligns has ceased to carry much meaning—except within *Show Boat*, where "Ol' Man River" continues to this day to do its magic with white audiences for Broadway musicals, whether on Broadway or in the opera house, or whenever sung in concert style by a black baritone or bass. In or out of *Show Boat*, this approach—the way Robeson sang it in the 1930s—still works mightily, and not just with white-haired folks, as Lawrence Beamen's performance on *America's Got Talent* reveals.

I have saved for last my favorite version of "Ol' Man River," a recording by Ray Charles on his 1963 LP *Ingredients in a Recipe for Soul*. This take on "Ol' Man River" sits squarely in the middle of the song's high season and is meaningfully positioned on a concept album as well. Charles's singing, set like a jewel in an expensive pop arrangement utilizing strings and mixed chorus, layers the history of the work in black and white popular music so audibly that it serves as a fitting metaphor for the entire history of the song and as a conclusion for this book.

Ray Charles was a major figure on the popular music scene in 1963: he had already earned the soubriquet *genius*. And with the success of his 1962 album *Modern Sounds in Country and Western Music*, he was—like Sinatra—a maker of concept LPs and in a position to sing with violins, something Charles loved to do. *Ingredients in a Recipe for Soul* combines Charles with a studio orchestra of Hollywood professionals and the Jack Halloran Singers, a group of white singers more frequently heard backing up Pat Boone or Bing Crosby. They are, in effect, descendants of Fred Waring's Glee Club. Charles's "Ol' Man River" uses the same forces as the Waring/Frank Davis version from ten years earlier to very different effects. The most musically significant difference is the setting aside of Davis's serious, trained, Robeson-esque vocal delivery in favor of Charles's soulful, gospel, bluesy approach. The contrast between these two black singers—both accompanied by white instrumentalists and chorus—speaks to the profound musical transformations going on in the years when these records were made.

As on *The Concert Sinatra*, released the same year as *Ingredients in a Recipe for Soul*, "Ol' Man River" serves as the final track on Charles's side one. A careful progression of musical and lyrical ideas leads the listener to Hammerstein and Kern's song, which works as a well-prepared culmination of the side. The first track, a spirited lament called "Busted," sets the tone and topic: making no appeal for pity, Charles states that he's broke—in the literal sense of having nothing. The lyric even speaks of rural labor: "Cotton is down to a quarter a pound / And I'm busted." The album's exploration of physical exhaustion and poverty despite heavy labor is there from the start. Horns and rhythm section accompany "Busted," with not a violin to be heard. Track two, "Where Can I Go?," ratchets down the energy a notch, and at track three, "Born to Be Blue," the tempo slows further and, for the first time, the violins enter.

The next track—which precedes "Ol' Man River"—is "That Lucky Old Sun." A chord from the strings sets the key for Charles's immediate entry on the lyric. He sings the first phrase in a free, almost declamatory manner, contrasting his labors, begun at break of day, with the sun above him, which is free to lazily "roll around heaven all day." Charles's statement of the lyric is haloed by wordless support from the Halloran singers. This track continues the pattern of the side: slowing down the tempo and deepening the mood with each subsequent selection. Charles's vocal delivery is explicitly emotional. If "Busted" was a public complaint, "That Lucky Old Sun," especially in the bridge that references "the Lord above," comes across as a private prayer.

"That Lucky Old Sun"—an AABA popular song composed in 1949—owes an obvious debt to "Ol' Man River." Both songs set the singer's hard labor on the land against an indifferent, easily personified force of nature that "rolls around heaven" or "jes' keeps rollin' along." Both include a vision of a river, the crossing of which will relieve the singer's pain. The difference—of course—is the absence of a racial dimension in "That Lucky Old Sun." It's just about the toil of physical work: "Ol' Man River" is about more. In Hammerstein and Kern's theater song, both the original context and the verse lyric explicitly identify the singer as black, his boss as white. This difference in specificity between the songs is reflected in the lists of singers who sang both or only one.

"That Lucky Old Sun" was a number one hit for singer Frankie Laine in 1949. Laine's recording, at a moderate tempo, features anodyne backing vocals and strings much like those on Charles's. Louis Armstrong recorded the tune with a Laine-like pop arrangement in 1949 as well. Charles could be riffing on either or both discs. A hit as big as "That Lucky Old Sun" was sure to produce multiple covers. Many singers who recorded "Ol' Man River" also recorded "That Lucky Old Sun" in the 1950s: Frank Sinatra, Bing Crosby, Dean Martin (with a light rhythm version), and Sam Cooke (on his 1957 LP, which also included "Ol' Man River" although the two songs appear on different sides). Aretha Franklin recorded a passionate version shortly after Charles's more introverted take came out. Like "Ol' Man River," "That Lucky Old Sun" welcomed a variety of approaches: black vocal harmony (the Deep River Boys), doo-wop (the Velvets), fast rhythm tune (the Isley Brothers did the tune like their big hit "Shout"), swinging big band (Louis Prima and Keely Smith in a Las Vegas mood), soul jazz with a Latin beat (Grant Green), as well as varied emotional versions (white pop singer Bobby Darin in a classic pop style; black R&B singer LaVern Baker in a female take on the song; black soul singer Solomon Burke in a funky soulful track). Even Pat Boone, icon of white teenagers, tried out "That Lucky Old Sun" on his 1956 LP *Howdy!* All of these singers—except, perhaps, Boone—could reasonably have also recorded "Ol' Man River." The recording histories of these two work-centered songs parallel each other in these cases.

But "That Lucky Old Sun" attracted another group of white artists unlikely to have taken up Hammerstein and Kern's song. Johnny Cash sang "That Lucky Old Sun" on a television special in 1976, then recorded it on his 2000 album *American III: Solitary Man.* The television version, with Cash lip-syncing in front of a roaring campfire, has Nashville Sound strings and vocals; the album version, from a quarter century later, uses only guitar and harmonium, for a spare effect. Country singer Willie Nelson recorded "That Lucky Old Sun" twice: in 1976, and then in 2008 with country singer Kenny Chesney, on Chesney's album *Lucky Old Sun.* For Cash, Nelson, and Chesney—three white men—"That Lucky Old Sun" delivers the core country music theme of hard work in a suitably masculine tone. "Ol' Man River" does this too but with the added caveat of a clear-eyed description of how racial discrimination has made a substantive difference for black and white Americans' experience with both hard work and the land, specifically in the South. "That Lucky Old Sun" lived on beyond 1970, in part because it carries no political content, forges no specific connection to social history, balances no conflicting stereotypes, welcomes no easy parodies. By comparison, Hammerstein and Kern's "Ol' Man River" is richer in its themes, more open to interpretive possibilities, demands greater attention to the meaning found in the details, digs deeper into American life and history.

Only Ray Charles made the imaginative leap to use the rather generic lament "That Lucky Old Sun" as preparation for the highly specific "Ol' Man River." The transition between the two songs slows the tempo of side one of

Ingredients in a Recipe for Soul yet again. The listener is led into a quieter and quieter, more and more contemplative place. (On side two, a similar progression leads in an uplifting direction, culminating with Hammerstein's "You'll Never Walk Alone," another example of this anthem's connection to "Ol' Man River" in the realm of soul and gospel music.)

Charles's "Ol' Man River" begins with a raft of violins playing Kern's verse: this could be a Gordon MacRae or Frank Sinatra arrangement. The Jack Halloran singers come in on the verse, singing "Here we all work on the Mississippi. / Here we all work while the white folks play" (◉ Sound Example 10.17). They sound like Fred Waring's similarly all-white chorus but the choice of lyrics doesn't dodge the racial issue. The Halloran Singers—white folks playing black folks commenting about white folks at play—sing without irony or false emotion. Will Friedwald comments on veteran pop arranger Marty Paich's string-heavy arrangement for Charles as being "so plain vanilla, I can't imagine any self-respecting Caucasian ever wanting to sing in front of it."[17]

The arrangement shifts a bit on Charles's entrance on the chorus. A bump in the sound indicates there may have been some last-minute splicing here: perhaps the opening pass through the verse was added later. In any event, like all performers who take on the racial questions at the heart of "Ol' Man River," Charles's version includes the verse. The tempo is extremely slow: an almost glacial 32 bpm. Charles sings the tune in fragments, breaking it into short phrases, clusters of words separated by long stretches of piano commentary far in the background (suggesting it's not Charles at the keyboard). The extra time created by the slow tempo makes room for Charles to add to the text. In the first A phrase, he injects a phrase that will recur: "I want you to know he just keeps rollin' along." At the second A phrase, the Halloran singers come in, singing the tune at the very slow tempo in a sustained style in some passages and acting as response to Charles's call in others. When Charles sings the lyric "he don't plant taters" at a conversational pace, the singers respond with the single word *taters*, sung in sustained style at 32 bpm. This moment sorely tests the contemporary listener: I have witnessed individuals laugh aloud with embarrassment and shake their heads in silent disbelief (◉ Sound Example 10.18). But the uncomfortable contrast between the "chalky white background" and Charles's vulnerable, soulful delivery is all to the point. The racially inflected popular music ingredients don't mix so much as coexist in the same unlikely soundscape, a textural motif developed across side one and brought to a hushed climax here. And Charles keeps on adding to the lyric. The second A phrase lyric is amplified this way: "I want you to know they're soon forgotten."

At the bridge, the back and forth between Charles and the singers continues, the latter responding with "you and me," "sweat and strain," "'achin','" "'achin' with pain," and "tote that barge"—all sung as if sleepwalking. Charles, by contrast, heats up his delivery, especially on the line "wracked with pain." The key "tote" and "lift" lines get an original addition. Choosing not to imitate the white man boss, he sings, "Somebody said lift that bale." And Charles adds in that same phrase once again at the close of the bridge: "And if you drink a little Scotch, I want you to know you're gonna land in jail." An R&B singer like Charles doesn't worry about black stereotypes of drunkenness: intoxication is what the music is there to assist, one reason for its success. He seems more insistent on reaching his listener. Charles's thrice repeated insertion—"I want you to know"—begs the question, who is "you"?

Which returns this book to a question posed in Chapter 1. Who are "you and me" in the world of "Ol' Man River"?

Every performance of "Ol' Man River" outside the context of *Show Boat* answers this question in one way or another. How these lines should be sung, who they address, what they capture about the American experience of race cuts close to the limits of the sayable in American popular music. This book has discussed many, many examples of performers using "Ol' Man River" to various ends. But since Hammerstein and Kern wrote the song for a black man to sing while playing a black character, the voices of African American performers stand out in the performance history of "Ol' Man River" as a space where popular music and musicians have addressed the realities of American life.

Popular music was the first place where black individuals were permitted to address the nation on something close to their own terms. Written by two Jewish New Yorkers for the most famous black star of the time, "Ol' Man River" has been an important part of this history of black addressing white on issues that matter. Ray Charles's impassioned, even tearful performance sounds out from the blandest of classic pop settings, creating a contrast that was no accident. As the liner notes for *Ingredients in a Recipe for Soul* state, "Nothing in the arrangements was calculated to diffuse commercialism throughout the Charles interpretations. For this, to his way of thinking, would have defeated the genuineness and the legitimacy of the whole." The note begins, "There is much, much more than music contained in the grooves of the record herein," a sentence that resonates across the entire history of "Ol' Man River" and its multitude of performers. This song served many purposes. In Charles's case, Hammerstein and Kern's tune helped a black American "genius" take his listeners deep into a painful place where the emotional nakedness of his vocal performance could be heard in dialogue with white choral singers who perform as if they have no clue of the meanings of the words they sing. "I want you to know," Charles repeats, as if speaking both to the listener and his uncomprehending musical collaborators. Here—in a rare and beautiful and wrenching moment—"Ol' Man River" is given voice by a powerful black man using the powerful expressive tools of soul music while the song's white audience not only listens but responds—as it turns out, uncomprehendingly. Uniquely among all versions of "Ol' Man River," Charles puts the interracial dynamic of "colored folks work while the white folks play" into a performance of the song itself. This—Charles proclaims—is how "Ol' Man River" should be sung and heard. In his remaking of Hammerstein and Kern's song for Paul Robeson, Ray Charles delivers a potent message about how black and white have lived side by side in the soundscapes of popular music history and the landscape of the nation. Charles's decision that he should sing "Ol' Man River" affords but one example—the last in this book—of the role this particular and peculiar song has played in the singing of the American experience of race.

A SELECT LIST OF RECORDED VERSIONS
OF "OL' MAN RIVER" (1928–2011)

Includes commercially released piano rolls, 78s, 45s, LPs, CDs, and mp3s only. Most all were made for the Anglo-American market. All the versions mentioned in the book are listed, as well as others that did not make the story told in these pages. Televised versions and live performances captured on bootlegs or video—mostly accessed on the Internet—and live radio, nightclub, and stage performances reviewed or mentioned in newspapers and magazines are omitted.

1928

- Victor Arden (piano roll)
- Ben Bernie and His Hotel Roosevelt Orchestra
- Bix Beiderbecke and His Gang
- Castle Farms Serenaders
- Ciro's Club Dance Band
- Deep River Orchestra, with Joe Wilbur, vocal
- Fred Elizalde
- B.F. Goodrich Silvertone Quartet
- Jack Hamilton and His Entertainers
- Jack Hylton and His Orchestra
- Al Jolson, with Bill Wirges Orchestra
- Layton and Johnstone
- Phil Ohman (piano roll)
- Lou Raderman and His Pelham Heath Inn Orchestra
- The Revelers
- Willard Robison and His Orchestra
- Paul Robeson, with orchestra of the London *Show Boat*
- Allen Selby and His Frascatians
- Noble Sissle and His Sizzling Syncopators
- "Kenn" Sisson and His Orchestra (rec. 12/27/27)

– Sammy Stewart and His Orchestra
– Don Vorhees and His Orchestra
– Paul Whiteman and His Orchestra, with Bing Crosby, vocal
– Paul Whiteman and His Concert Orchestra, with Paul Robeson, vocal

1929

– Buddy Blue and His Texans
– Comedian Harmonists

1930

– Paul Robeson, with Ray Noble and His Orchestra

1931

– Jules Bledsoe
– John Charles Thomas

1932

– Paul Robeson (Album of 78s: *Here Comes the Show Boat*)
– Lawrence Tibbett

1933

– Horace Henderson and His Orchestra

1934

– Tiny Bradshaw and His Orchestra
– Casa Loma Orchestra
– Luis Russell and His Orchestra, with Sonny Woods, vocal

1936

– Putney Dandridge and His Orchestra
– Nat Gonella and His Georgians
– Henry King and His Orchestra
– Paul Robeson

1937

– Willie Lewis and His Entertainers

1938

- Golden Crown Quartet
- Golden Gate Quartet
- Clyde McCoy and His Orchestra
- Cootie Williams and His Rug Cutters, with Jerry Kruger, vocal

1939

- Martha Raye, with Dave Rose and His Orchestra

1940

- Al Goodman and His Orchestra
- Snub Mosley and His Band
- Les Paul Trio

1941

- Henry "Red" Allen and His Orchestra
- Bing Crosby, with Victor Young Orchestra
- Harry James and His Orchestra, with Dick Haymes
- Willie Lewis and His Negro Band
- Robert Weede

1942

- Benny Carter and His Orchestra

1944

- Cozy Cole's All Stars, with Coleman Hawkins
- Stan Kenton and His Orchestra
- Frank Sinatra (V-Disc)

1945

- Bing Crosby, with Camarata Orchestra
- Alex Kostelanetz and His Orchestra (Album of 45s: *Music by Jerome Kern*)
- Phil Moore Four
- Frank Sinatra (Columbia)
- United States Air Force, The Singing Sergeants
- Jerry Thomas and His Hawaiian Orchestra, with Marcel Bianchi, Hawaiian guitar

1946

- Loumell Morgan Trio
- Caleb Peterson (Album of 45s: *Till the Clouds Roll By*, original sound-track recording)
- The Pied Pipers, with Paul Weston Orchestra
- Boyd Raeburn and His Musicians, with Mel Tormé and the Mel-Tones
- Fred Waring and His Pennsylvanians, with Walter Scheff, vocal (Album of 45s: *Program Time*, released as LP in 1950)

1947

- Jan August
- Tommy Dorsey and His Orchestra, with Stuart Foster, vocal (Album of 78s: *Show Boat*)
- Todd Duncan
- Harry Horlick and the Decca Salon Orchestra
- Quintet of the Hot Club of France, with Django Reinhart and Stephane Grappelli
- The Ravens

1948

- Tommy Dix
- Paul Robeson, with Columbia Concert Orchestra (Album of 45s: *A Robeson Recital of Popular Favorites*)

1949

- Jazz at the Philharmonic, with Hank Jones, Ray Brown, Buddy Rich
- Robert Merrill, with Russ Case Orchestra
- Robert Merrill (LP: *Show Boat*)

1950

- Dusty Brooks and the Four Tones
- Robert Maxwell (LP: *Harpist's Holiday*)
- Roy Milton and His Solid Senders

1951

- Joe Bushkin
- Tony Fontane (LP: *The Immortal Music from Show Boat*)
- Al Hibbler, with the Ellingtonians

– Gordon MacRae, with Carmen Dragon and His Orchestra
– Kasagi Shizuko
– Charlie Ventura's Big Four (with Buddy Rich, Chubby Jackson, Marty
   Napoleon)
– William Warfield (LP: *Show Boat*, original soundtrack recording)
– Leonard Warren (LP: *Songs for Everyone*)

1952

– Sidney Bechet
– The Teddy Cohen Trio (LP: *Teddy Charles and His Trio*)
– Joe Bushkin (LP: *After Hours*)

1953

– Louis Hawkins (LP: *Goldie Plays by the Sea*)

1954

– The Ames Brothers, with Hugo Winterhalter and His Orchestra
– Chet Atkins
– Ruth Brown and the Drifters (released in 1956 as Ruth Brown and Her
   Rhythmakers)
– Salvatore Baccaloni
– Erroll Garner (released on the 1992 CD *Solo Time! The Erroll Garner
   Collection, Vols. 4 & 5*)
– The Gems
– Art Van Damme Quintet

1955

– Sidney Bechet, with Claude Leuter and His Orchestra
– Eddie Condon and ensemble (LP: *Bixieland*)
– Tito Rodriguez y su Orquesta

1956

– Rolf Billberg Quintet
– Hadda Brooks
– Bing Crosby, with Buddy Cole Trio
– Ted Heath and His Music (LP: *Kern for Moderns*)
– Howard Keel (LP: *Show Boat*)
– Robert Merrill (LP: *Show Boat*)

– Fred Waring and His Pennsylvanians, with Frank Davis, vocal (LP: *In Hi Fi*)

1957

– Joe Bushkin (LP: *Piano after Midnight*)
– Delta Rhythm Boys (LP: *Delta Rhythm Boys in Sweden*)
– Erroll Garner Trio (LP: *The Most Happy Piano*)
– Earl Grant
– Neal Hefti and His Orchestra (LP: *Concert Miniatures*)
– Lester Lanin and His Orchestra (LP: *Lester Lanin at the Tiffany Ball*)
– George London (LP: *George London on Broadway*)
– The Skylarks, with Buddy Bregman, conductor (LP: *Ridin' on the Moon*)
– The Sparks
– The Tune Weavers

1958

– Mae Barnes, with Jo Jones, Buck Clayton, and Ray Bryant
– Count Basie and His Orchestra (LP: *Not Now, I'll Tell You When*)
– Frankie Carle (LP: *Show Stoppers in Dance Time*)
– Sam Cooke (LP: *Sam Cooke*)
– Sammy Davis Jr. (Live LP: *At Town Hall*)
– Fairweather-Brown All Stars
– Screamin' Jay Hawkins (LP: *At Home with Screamin' Jay Hawkins*)
– Gordon MacRae (LP: *Gordon MacRae in Concert*)
– Mitchell-Ruff Duo (LP: *Plus Strings and Brass*)
– Ralph Sharon Quartet and Friend [Candido] (LP: *2:38 AM*)
– The Smart Set
– Ann Weldon

1959

– Jesse Belvin (LP: *Just Jesse Belvin*)
– Tony Bennett, with Count Basie and His Orchestra (LP: *In Person!*)
– Dave Brubeck Quartet (LP: *Gone with the Wind*)
– Sam Butera and the Witnesses
– John Cali (LP: *Banjo on My Knee*)
– The Dukes of Dixieland (LP: *Up the Mississippi*)
– Pete Fountain (LP: *Pete Fountain's New Orleans*)
– Bob Grant and His Orchestra (LP: *Song Hits of 1927*)
– The Ink Spots

- Jo Jones, with Ray Bryant, piano, and Tommy Bryant, bass (LP: *Jo Jones Plus Two*)
- Stanley Melba (LP: *An Evening with Jerome Kern*)
- Oscar Peterson, with Ray Brown and Ed Thigpen (LP: *Plays the Jerome Kern Songbook*)
- André Previn (LP: *Plays Songs by Jerome Kern*)
- Earl Wrightson, with Percy Faith and His Orchestra (LP: *An Evening with Jerome Kern*)

1960

- The Australian All-Stars (LP: *Jazz for Surf-Niks, vol. 2*)
- Count Basie and His Orchestra (LP: *Live!*)
- The Cues
- Kenny Dorham (LP: *Plays Show Boat*)
- Maynard Ferguson (LP: *Newport Suite*)
- The Guitar Choir, with Bob Brookmeyer and Phil Woods, arranged and conducted by John Carisi (LP: *The New Jazz Sounds of Show Boat*)
- Bill Holman's Great Big Band (LP: *Thrilling Modern Arrangements of Great Standards*)
- Ricky Lane and Willie (LP: *Original Amateur Hour 25th Anniversary Album*)
- Wingy Manone
- Santo and Johnny (LP: *Encore*)
- Joe Venuti
- Bob Wallis' Storyville Jazzmen (LP: *Ole Man River*)
- Nat Wright

1961

- Gene Ammons (LP: *Jug*)
- Gloria Lynne, with the Earl May Trio (LP: *I'm Glad There Is You*)
- Bobby Rydell (LP: *Rydell at the Copa*)
- Sam Sacks
- The Salems

1962

- Van Alexander and His Orchestra (LP: *Swing! Staged for Sound*)
- Tony Bennett, with Ralph Sharon and His Orchestra (LP: *Live at Carnegie Hall*)
- Ronnie Cates and the Travelers
- Martin Denny (LP: *Martin Denny in Person*)

- Bob Havens (LP: *New Orleans Dixieland*)
- Johnny Nash
- Ike Quebec (LP: *It Might as Well Be Spring*)
- Della Reese (LP: *Della on Stage*)
- Frank Sinatra (Live: *Sinatra and Sextet* released 1994)
- Jimmy Smith (LP: *Bashin': The Unpredictable Jimmy Smith*; also released in 45 single version)
- The Spotnicks (LP: *The Spotnicks in London: Out-A Space*)

1963

- Ray Charles (LP: *Ingredients in a Recipe for Soul*)
- Floyd Cramer (LP: *Comin' On*)
- Bo Diddley (LP: *Surfin' with Bo Diddley*)
- Ray Ellington, with the Mike Sammes Singers and the New World Show Orchestra (LP: *Jerome Kern Spectacular*)
- The Flamingos
- John Gary, with the Marty Gold Orchestra (LP: *Encore*)
- Marty Gold Orchestra (LP: *Sounds Unlimited*)
- "Big" Tiny Little (LP: *Movin' On*)
- Grady Martin and His Slew Foot Five
- Lou Rawls (LP: *Tobacco Road*)
- Charlie Rich
- Frank Sinatra (LP: *The Concert Sinatra*)

1964

- 101 Strings (LP: *Jerome Kern and Vincent Youmans*)
- Albert Ayler (LP: *Goin' Home*)
- Sam Butera and the Witnesses (LP: *King of Clubs*, live in Las Vegas, rec. 1963)
- The Earls
- Byron Lee and the Dragonaires
- The Lettermen; solo by Jim Pike (LP: *You'll Never Walk Alone*)
- Don Shirley

1965

- Mr. Acker Bilk and His Paramount Jazz Band
- Cilla Black (LP: *Cilla*)
- Don Gardner and Dee Dee Ford
- Jimmy Holiday

– Fausto Papetti (LP: *I Remember. N. 2* [Italy])
– The Righteous Brothers (LP: *You've Lost That Lovin' Feelin'*)
– Joe Williams (LP: *The Exciting Joe Williams*)

1966

– Willie Bobo (LP: *Uno Dos Tres 1-2-3*)
– Clea Bradford (LP: *Now*)
– Cher (LP: *The Sonny Side of Cher*)
– Aretha Franklin (LP: *Soul Sister*)

1967

– Judy Garland (LP: *At Home at the Palace*)
– The Pineapple Heard
– Billy Stewart (LP: *Teaches Old Standards New Tricks*)
– The Temptations (LP: *The Temptations in a Mellow Mood Sing a Taste of Honey and Other Favorites*)
– The Temptations (LP: *Temptations Live!*)

1968

– The Beach Boys (unreleased)
– The Jeff Beck Group, with Rod Stewart, vocal (LP: *Truth*)
– Jimmy Castor (LP: *Hey, Leroy*)
– Child (LP: *Child*)
– Earl Hines Septet (LP: *Plays Evergreens*)
– Patty Pravo (LP: *Patty Pravo*)
– The Silvertones, with Tommy McCook and the Supersonics

1969

– The Caravans (LP: *The Caravans in Concert*)
– Jack Jones (LP: *Where Is Love?*)
– The Persuasions (LP: *Accapella*)
– Les Tres Guitars (LP: *Yestergroovin'*)

1970

– Ivory Joe Hunter (LP: *The Return of Ivory Joe Hunter*)
– Potliquor (LP: *First Taste*)
– Freddy Quinn (LP: *Wo Meine Sonne Scheint*)
– The Satisfactions

– The Upsetters (LP: *Eastwood Rides Again*, track titled "Django [Ol' Man River]")

1971

– Bill Pinkney and the Original Drifters
– Dorothy Squires (LP: *Live at the London Palladium*)

1972

– John Fahey (LP: *Of Rivers and Religions*)

1973

– Wolfman Jack (LP: *Through the Ages*)
– Cleo Laine (quoted inside the song "Control Yourself" on the LP *Live at Carnegie Hall*)
– The Platters (LP: *The Platters Live*)

1974

– Frank Chackfield and His Orchestra (LP: *The Incomparable Jerome Kern*)
– Abner Jay (LP: *Swaunee Water and Cocaine Blues*)

1975

– Jim Croce
– Henry Cuesta (LP: *Lawrence Welk Presents the Clarinet of Henry Cuesta*)
– Vlady & Mary

1976

– Bing Crosby, with the Joe Bushkin Quartet (LP: *Live at the London Palladium*)
– Erroll Garner (LP: *Gershwin and Kern*)
– Jo Jones, with Harry "Sweets" Edison, Tommy Flanagan, and Roy Eldridge among others (LP: *The Main Man*)
– Sherrill Milnes (LP: *The Songs America Loves*)

1977

– Wild Bill Davison, with the Dutch Swing College Band (LP: *Featuring Famous American Jazz Giants*)

– Lionel Hampton and His Jazz Giants
– Al Hirt (LP: *Our Man in New Orleans*)

1978

– Ran Blake (LP: *Take One*)

1980

– Derek Smith Trio (LP: *Plays Jerome Kern*)

1981

– Eddie "Tan Tan" Thornton (LP: *Musical Nostalgia for Today*)

1982

– Prince Alla (LP: *King of the Road*)
– Stephane Grappelli and Martin Taylor (LP: *We've Got the World on a String*)

1983

– Ran Blake (LP: *Suffield Gothic*)

1985

– Dennis Brown (also included on 1988 LP: *Good Vibrations*)
– The Phabulous Pheromones (LP: *A Taste of the Phabulous Pheromones*)
– Elizabeth Welch, Liz Robertson, and Elaine Delmar (LP: *Kern Goes to Hollywood*, original cast album)

1986

– Bum Steer

1987

– Stephane Grappelli (LP: *Plays Jerome Kern*)

1988

– Ruby Braff (LP: *Bravura Eloquence*)
– Simon Estes (LP: *Ol' Man River: Broadway's Greatest Hits*)

1989

– George Adams (LP: *Nightingale*)

1990

– Stephane Grappelli (LP: *Live in Tokyo*, released 2005)

1991

– Screamin' Jay Hawkins (LP: *Black Music for White People*)
– Art Pepper (CD reissue: *Winter Moon*, recorded 1980)
– Lenny Solomon, with Peter Appleyard, vibes (CD: *After You've Gone: The Classic Jazz Violin of Lenny Solomon*)

1992

– Adam Makowicz Trio (CD: *The Music of Jerome Kern*)

1993

– George Feyer (CD: *Plays the Essential Jerome Kern*)
– Dick Hyman and Ralph Sutton (CD: *Concord Duo Volume 6*)
– Malachi Thompson and Africa Brass (CD: *Lift Every Voice*)

1994

– Hadda Brooks (CD: *Anytime Anyplace Anywhere*)
– Rosemary Clooney (LP: *Still on the Road*)
– Die Mainzer Hofsänger (CD: *Ein musikalischer Bilderbogen*)
– Samuel Ramey (CD: *So in Love: Sam Ramey on Broadway*)

1995

– André Previn and Friends (LP: *Play Show Boat*)
– Roger Whittaker (LP: *On Broadway*)

1996

– Giora Feidman Trio (LP: *To You!*)
– Davis Gaines (LP: *Against the Tide*)

1997

– The All-American Boys Chorus (CD: *by Request*)
– Göteborgs Musiken (LP: *At Work*)

- Hans Knudsen Jump Band (CD: *Jump in Focus*)
- Milton Nascimento (LP: *Nascimento*)
- Michael Strassen (CD: *Loving You*)
- Voices of Ascension

1999

- Ib Glindemann and the Danish Radio Big Band

2001

- New York City Labor Chorus (CD: *Workers Rise: Labor in the Spotlight*)

2002

- Chet Atkins (CD: *Solo Sessions*, posthumous release of home recordings)
- Rosemary Clooney (CD: *The Last Concert*)
- Nueva Manteca (CD: *Congo Square: Tribute to New Orleans*)

2004

- Denyce Graves (CD: *Kaleidoscope*)
- Ricardo's Jazzmen (CD: *Live Pa Long John*)

2007

- Oral Moses (CD: *Sings Songs of America*)
- Saint Michael's Singers of Coventry Cathedral (CD: *Swingin' with the Saints*)
- Syd Lawrence Orchestra (CD: *Re:Generation*)
- United States Marine Drum and Bugle Corps (CD: *Chimes of Liberty*)

2008

- 103rd Street Gospel Choir, Pat Lewis (CD: *Gospel Favourites*)
- Markus Burger / Jan von Klewitz: Quarta (CD: *Spiritual Standards from the New World*)
- Henry Butler (CD: *Pia NOLA Live*)
- John Miller (CD: *John Miller Takes on Broadway*)
- Philharmonic Wind Orchestra (CD: *The Power of Love*)

2009

- The City Champs (CD: *The Safecracker*)
- The London Double Bass Sound (CD: *The London Double Bass Sound*)

2010

- Art Lande (CD: *While She Sleeps: Piano Lullabies*)
- Les Doigts de l'Homme (CD: *1910*)

2011

- Berlin Philharmonic Horn Quartet (CD: *Four Corners*)

2012

- Danny Wright

2013

- The Silvertones (Digital album: *Keep on Rolling*)

Baritones from around the world, sometimes singing in translation...

Kees Pruis (Dutch), Muslim Magomaev (Azerbaijani-born "Soviet Sinatra"), Peter Dawson (Australia), Ivor Emmanuel (Welsh), Heinz Woezel (German, 1950s), Bruce Low (German), Karl Ridderbusch (German), Wei Qixian (China, 1950s and 1960s)

ACKNOWLEDGMENTS

My thanks to

- Carol Oja, who suggested that "Ol' Man River" was a book-worthy topic.
- Timothy Babcock at Pennsylvania State University Special Collections, for television clips of Frank Davis on *The Fred Waring Show*.
- Jerome Camal, for the link to the Lumpen.
- Kelsey Kline, for help with Brubeck.
- Katie Kinney, Ashley Pribyl, and Jennifer Psujek, for research assistance, fact-checking, and proofing.
- Dan Viggers, for the musical example.
- Joellyn Ausanka, for moving this book through production at Oxford University Press, and Patterson Lamb, for copyediting the text.
- Barbara Shaal, Dean of the College of Arts and Sciences, Washington University in St. Louis, for generous support of the images in this book.
- Nathan Platte (University of Iowa), Andrew Weaver (Catholic University of America), the Society of Professors Emeriti of Washington University, and my colleagues in the Department of Music at Washington University, for chances to present this project as a work in progress.
- Brad Short, Washington University music librarian, for purchasing many, many versions of "Ol' Man River."
- the many students in my popular music courses at Washington University, especially those who read the manuscript during the fall 2013 semester, among them Billy Biegler, Daniel Hodges, Katie Kinney, Darren LaCour, Sarah Luehrs, Ashley Pribyl, Milena Schaller, and Dan Viggers.
- my teachers, colleagues, friends, and neighbors, old and new: among them Albin, Alex, Angie, Angie & John, Ben, Bill, Bill, Brad, Bruce, Chris, Colin, Craig, Dafydd & Renaud, Denise, Dolores, Erin, Gaylyn, Geoffrey, Gerald, Heather & Carlos, Heidi, Hugh, Iver, Jeffrey, Jennifer, Jim,

Joe, John, Julia, Louise, Mary, Mitchell, Nate, Nick & Maura, Nicole, Paige & Pannill, Pat, Paul, Peter & Julian, Philip, Ray, Rich, Rob, Robert, Seth, Sterling, Steven, Susan, Tabea, Tili & Lionel, Tom, and William.

– my parents, Ron and Linda Decker.
– my invaluable editor, Norm Hirschy, for encouragement and good advice all along the way on this our second project together.
– my sons, David and James, who always showed some interest when I played them *yet another* recording of "Ol' Man River."
– and finally, my wife, Kelly—my first and best reader and friend for more than twenty-five years. In this case, she urged me on to the finish at just the right moment.

NOTES

ABBREVIATIONS

BAA   *Baltimore Afro-American*
LAS   *Los Angeles Sentinel*
NYT   *New York Times*
PT   *Philadelphia Tribune*
PC   *Pittsburgh Courier*

CHAPTER 1

1. Charles Bernstein, *Attack of the Difficult Poems: Essays and Inventions* (Chicago: University of Chicago Press, 2011), 143.
2. "Mississippi," *American Heritage Dictionary of the English Language*, 4th ed. (New York: Houghton Mifflin, 2009); Keith A. Baca, *Native American Place Names in Mississippi* (Jackson: University of Mississippi Press, 2007), 58.
3. *Variety*, 1 August 1956, "It Figures."
4. Jerome Kern to Vaughn DeLeath, 3 May 1938, Gershwin Fund Collection-Correspondence, Library of Congress, Music Division.
5. *PT*, 1 October 1966, Julia Jordan, "Germantown Gems."
6. *NYT*, 6 December 1928, "Topics of the Times."
7. *NYT*, 23 April 1932, "Radio Round-up."
8. *NYT*, 8 October 1933, Orrin E. Dunlap Jr., "Harmonies Galore."
9. *Billboard*, 21 December 1940, "Operators Can Service Public in ASCAP Situation."
10. *BAA*, 28 December 1940, "Opinion: The Radio War."
11. *Billboard*, 2 August 1952, and *Variety*, 22 April 1953.
12. *Broadcasting*, 21 September 1959, "Mr. K Gets 'Top 25'."
13. *NYT*, 20 May 1929, "John Charles Thomas a Hit at the Palace."
14. *PC*, 21 April 1928, "A Footnote to *Show Boat*."
15. Richman, *The Stage* (UK), 10 June 1937, "The Variety Stage"; Eckstine, *BAA*, 24 September 1949, "Mr. B Goes to Town," and *BAA*, 24 November 1951, "Ballads and Bop Score with Columbus Audience"; Eddy, *BAA*, 9 October 1937, "The Sec'y Comes to Bat Again," and *Variety*, 15 February 1961, "Night Club Reviews: Eddys', K.C."; Laurence, *Variety*, 3 March 1943, "Night Club Reviews: La Vie Parisienne (New York)"; Jeffries, *Billboard*, 10 December 1949, "Night Clubs – Vaudeville: Follow-Up Reviews – Bop City, New York" and *Variety*, 14 April 1953, "Night Club Reviews: Mapes Skyroom, Reno"; Avalon, *Variety*, 30 August 1961, "Night Club Reviews: Salisbury Beach Frolics"; Cohen, *Variety*, 22 August 1943, "Night Club Reviews: Esquire, Montreal"; Reeves, *Variety*, 20 February 1952, "House Review: Capitol, Wash."; Smith, *PC*, 20 November 1937, "Rollin Smith Gets Big Break in London."

16. Will Friedwald, *Stardust Memories: The Biography of Twelve of America's Most Popular Songs* (New York: Pantheon Books, 2002), 116.

17. *BAA*, 29 December 1928, Maurice Dancer, "Harlem Show Talk."

18. Todd Decker, *Show Boat: Performing Race in an American Musical* (New York: Oxford University Press, 2013), 101–103.

19. *BAA*, 23 November 1935, "Radio Insults Will Be Tuned Out by Juniors."

20. *BAA*, 7 November 1942, "Corporal Sings 'Ol' Man River' but 'Cuts' Offensive Epithet."

21. *PC*, 30 April 1941, "Paige to Face Top Chicago Hitters."

22. John Colville, *The Fringes of Power: Downing Street Diaries 1939–1955* (London: Weidenfeld & Nicholson, 2004), 190.

23. *PM*, 10 December 1945.

24. Sherrill Milnes, with Dennis McGovern, *American Aria* (New York: Schirmer Books, 1998), 173.

25. Albert Murray, quoted in Henry Louis Gates Jr., *Thirteen Ways of Looking at a Black Man* (New York: Random House, 1997), 28.

26. *PC*, 14 March 1942, "Bland's Songs Found 'Offensive' to Pupils."

CHAPTER 2

1. *BAA*, 29 May 1943, "Anne Brown Heard at Ship Launching."

2. *Radio Times*, 28 June 1929, Countee Cullen, "All God's Chillun Got a Song."

3. *Billboard*, 22 September 1945, "Robeson's Ad-Lib."

4. Raymond Knapp, *The American Musical and the Formation of National Identity* (Princeton: Princeton University Press, 2005), 188.

5. Charles Bernstein, *Attack of the Difficult Poems: Essays and Inventions* (Chicago: University of Chicago Press, 2011), 146.

6. Eslanda Robeson to Lawrence Brown, 20 March 1928, Lawrence Brown Papers, Schomburg Center for Research in Black Culture, New York Public Library, New York (hereafter Brown Papers) 3/8.

7. Eslanda Robeson to Lawrence Brown, 15 February 1929, Brown Papers 3/8.

8. Edna Ferber, *A Peculiar Treasure* (New York: Doubleday, 1939), 306.

9. Todd Decker, *Show Boat: Performing Race in an American Musical* (New York: Oxford University Press, 2013), 36–37.

10. Robeson-Brown recital programs, Brown Papers 5/1. Decker, *Show Boat*, 139 erroneously gives the date Robeson first listed "Ol' Man River" on the program as January 1931.

11. *BAA*, 24 January 1931, Carl Diton, "Robeson Mixes Classics and Comedy."

12. *NYT*, 23 March 1931, "Paul Robeson Sings 'Spirituals.'"

13. *NYT*, 11 April 1931, "Bledsoe Gives Farewell Recital."

14. Decker, *Show Boat*, 48.

15. *NYT*, 20 November 1932, "Recorded Music: British Sets."

16. *BAA*, 12 October 1935, "'An Actor Cannott Eat His Ideals.'"

17. *BAA*, 12 March 1938, Lillian Johnson, "A Woman Talks."

18. *Answers* (London), 8 April 1939, Elliseva Sayer, "I Meet Paul Robeson."

19. *NYT*, 20 December 1937, "9,000 in London Ask Help for Loyalists."

20. *BAA*, 5 February 1938, "Paul Robeson Sings in Madrid."

21. *NYT*, 26 June 1940, Howard Taubman, "American Music Heard in Stadium."

22. *NYT*, 18 July 1947, "Robeson Cheered by Stadium Crowd."

23. *BAA*, 11 May 1946, Margaret T. Goss, "Robeson's Season's Finale Shows He's Still Tops."

24. *NYT*, 21 April 1949, "Paris 'Peace Congress' Assails U.S. and Atlantic Pact, Upholds Soviet."
25. *BAA*, Chatwood Hall, 16 January 1937, "Robeson Acclaimed in Soviet Recital"; *BAA*, 13 September 1955, Chatwood Hall, "Why I Went to Russia…And Why I Left."
26. *NYT*, 9 June 1949, "Paul Robeson Stirs a Moscow Audience."
27. *BAA*, 25 June 1949, E. B. Rea, "Encores and Echoes."
28. *NYT*, 13 June 1949, "'Ol' Man River' Retained."
29. Decker, *Show Boat*, 147.
30. Jordan Goodman, *Paul Robeson: A Watched Man* (London: Verso, 2013), 118, 172.
31. Goodman, *Paul Robeson*, 25.
32. Shana L. Redmond, *Anthem: Social Movements and the Sound of Solidarity in the African Diaspora* (New York: New York University Press, 2014), 120.
33. *NYT*, 21 July 1949, "Newark Pickets Robeson."
34. *NYT*, 16 April 1973, "Robeson, at 75, Is Feted in Absentia."
35. Goodman, *Paul Robeson*, 188.
36. Goodman, *Paul Robeson*, xi.
37. Redmond, *Anthem*, 136.
38. Unattributed 1955 clipping in London Metropolitan Archives 4231/B/02-004, John L. Watson, "Robeson's Songs and Propaganda Not Effective."
39. *BAA*, 17 June 1950, "Paul Robeson in London."
40. *Daily Worker*, 15 April 1951, John Pittman, "Mister Freedom, Himself."
41. *NYT*, 1 May 2002, "Soulful Songs of Sorrow in America and Abroad."
42. *NYT*, 1 May 2002, James R. Oestreich, "Soulful Songs of Sorrow in America and Abroad."

CHAPTER 3

1. Gary Giddins, *Bing Crosby: A Pocketful of Dreams, the Early Years, 1903–1940* (New York: Little, Brown, 2001), 170.
2. Don Rayno, *Paul Whiteman: Pioneer in American Music Volume I: 1890–1930* (Lanham, MD: Scarecrow Press, 2003), 603.
3. Rayno, *Paul Whiteman*, 184.
4. Tim Brooks, *Lost Sounds: Blacks and the Birth of the Recording Industry, 1890–1919* (Urbana: University of Illinois Press, 2004), 384.
5. *PC*, 22 January 1938, Porter Roberts, "Praise and Criticism."
6. *NYT*, 8 October 1933, Orrin E. Dunlap Jr., "Harmonies Galore."
7. Richard Crawford and Jeffrey Magee, *Jazz Standards on Record, 1900–1942: A Core Repertory* (Chicago: Center for Black Music Research, 1992).
8. *PC*, 27 October 1934, "After Yawning."
9. Todd Decker, *Show Boat: Performing Race in an American Musical* (New York: Oxford University Press, 2013), 44–47.
10. *Billboard*, 26 July 1941, "Amusement Machines Music: On the Records."
11. *Variety*, 14 February 1945, "House Review: Earle, Philly."
12. *Variety*, 29 October 1943, "House Review: Orpheum, L.A."
13. Louis Armstrong, *Swing that Music* [1936] (New York: Da Capo Press, 1993), 19.
14. *Variety*, 20 August 1958, "Night Club Reviews: Fairmont Hotel, S.F."
15. *Billboard*, 12 June 1943, "Night Club Reviews: Casa Manana, Culver City, California."
16. *Billboard*, 26 February 1949, "Vaudeville Reviews: Paramount Theater, New York."
17. *Billboard*, 15 July 1957, "Reviews of New R&B Records."

18. *Variety*, 3 July 1957, "The Sparks to Decca."
19. John Storm Roberts, *Latin Jazz: The First of the Fusions, 1880's to Today* (New York: Schirmer Books, 1999), 102–3.
20. Will Friedwald, *Stardust Memories: The Biography of Twelve of America's Most Popular Songs* (New York: Pantheon Books, 2002), 139.
21. *Billboard*, 23 April 1955, "Review Digest: The Skylarks, Statler Hotel, Los Angeles."
22. *Billboard*, 16 December 1944, advertisement.
23. Billboard, 12 April 1947, "National, in Folk Music Expansion, Inks Hillbillies."
24. *Billboard*, 24 April 1948, "The Ravens."
25. *PC*, 28 June 1947, "Ravens' New Wax Hit Rated Show Stopper."
26. *Variety*, 29 February 1956, Herm Schoenfeld, "Jocks, Jukes, and Discs."
27. *Variety*, 5 October 1977, "Unit Review: Bing Crosby Show."
28. *Variety*, 28 March 1956, "Reviews: Palace, N.Y."
29. *Billboard*, 20 July (Ted Leslie) and 14 September (Taber and Greene) 1929; 15 February 1930 (Eddie Leonard).
30. Michael K. Bourdaghs, *Sayonara Amerika, Sayonara Nippon: A Geopolitical Prehistory of J-Pop* (New York: Columbia University Press, 2012), 14.

CHAPTER 4

1. Will Friedwald, *Stardust Memories: The Biography of Twelve of America's Most Popular Songs* (New York: Pantheon Books, 2002), 108.
2. *NYT*, 22 February 1942, "Over Radio to Bataan Traveled a Song of "Old Doug MacArthur Just Fightin' Along."
3. *NYT*, 17 January 1948, "Campaigning Song Extolls Eisenhower."
4. Gerald Nachman, *Seriously Funny: The Rebel Comedians of the 1950s and 1960s* (New York: Pantheon Books, 2003), 181.
5. Phil Silvers, with Robert Saffron, *The Laugh Is on Me: The Phil Silvers Story* (Engelwood Cliffs, NJ: Prentice-Hall, 1973), 87.
6. Gerald Bordman, *Jerome Kern: His Life and Music* (New York: Oxford University Press, 1980), 400.
7. *Variety*, 14 November 1956, "Television Reviews: Television Followup [*sic*] Comment."
8. *Broadcasting*, 19 May 1958, "In Review: Phil Silvers on Broadway."
9. *BAA*, 11 April 1964, "TV Flubs Effort to Prove Mistake on 'Ol' Man River.'"
10. *Jet*, 20 January 1992, "Black Attorneys' Ire Remains Despite Apology by Lawyers' Assn. for Blackface Skit."
11. *PC*, 30 April 1932, Floyd Snelson, "Seasoned *Rhapsody* Is Tremendous Success."

CHAPTER 5

1. www.giorafeidman-online.com/en/biography.
2. Peter T. Kiefer, *The Fred Waring Discography* (Westport, CT: Greenwood Press, 1996), vii.
3. Virginia Waring, *Fred Waring and the Pennsylvanians* (Urbana: University of Illinois Press, 2007), 297–98.
4. *PC*, 31 January 1953, "Izzy Rowe's Notebook."

CHAPTER 6

1. Todd Decker, *Show Boat: Performing Race in an American Musical* (New York: Oxford University Press, 2013), chapter 4.
2. *NYT*, 19 October 1931, "James Barton Sings and Dances at the Palace."

3. *LAS*, 14 March 1957, Stanley Robertson, "LA Confidential."
4. *Variety*, 10 February 1943, "New Acts: Ann Robinson."
5. *Variety*, 18 July 1945, "House Review: New Acts, Annabelle Hill."
6. *Variety*, 27 November 1946, "Vaudeville: Zanzibar, N.Y."
7. *Variety*, 3 November 1954, "Reviews: House Reviews, Apollo, N.Y."
8. *Variety*, 7 October 1959, "Night Club Reviews: Safari, Scottsdale."
9. *Variety*, 11 February 1948, "House Reviews: Oriental, Chi."
10. *NYT*, 23 July 1947, "Templeton Again Soloist."
11. Susan Manning, *Modern Dance, Negro Dance: Race in Motion* (Minneapolis: University of Minnesota Press, 2004), 10.
12. *NYT*, 1 December 1930, "John Charles Thomas Sings Cowboy Songs."
13. *NYT*, 19 October 1942, "A Recital by List Delights Audience."
14. Will Friedwald, *Stardust Memories: The Biography of Twelve of America's Most Popular Songs* (New York: Pantheon Books, 2002), 123.
15. *NYT*, 28 March 1932, "Sing 'Old Favorites' at Opera Concert."
16. *NYT*, 26 February 1934, "Concert Is Given in Minstrel Style."
17. *NYT*, 3 May 1935, "Opera Ball Gayety Recalls Old South."
18. *NYT*, 23 February 1930, "The Microphone Will Present."
19. *Billboard*, 7 July 1951, "Music: Album and LP Reviews."
20. *Billboard*, 3 April 1954, "Night Clubs – Vaude: Hotel Sands, Las Vegas Nev."
21. William A. Everett and Lee Snook, "MacRae, Gordon" in *Grove Music Online* (www .oxfordmusiconline.com).
22. *BAA*, 4 October 1947, "RCA Refuses to Race Ban Race Slur."
23. *BAA*, 13 December 1947, "*Afro* Protest Brings Change in Lyrics of 'Ol' Man River.'"
24. *PC*, 6 March 1948, "Dorothy Maynor Teams with Robert Merrill."
25. *BAA*, 9 October 1937, Malcolm Fulcher, "Believe Me."
26. *BAA*, 25 June 1949, "Words of 'Ol' Man River.'"
27. Weede and Godfrey audio accessed at the Paley Center for Media.
28. Non-commercial discs of Eubie Blake and others, New York Public Library for the Performing Arts, New York.
29. Decker, *Show Boat*, 209–11.
30. This rare recording can be heard at the Recorded Sound Research Center at the Library of Congress.
31. *Spin*, April 1990, "Living Poets Society."

CHAPTER 7

1. Alec Wilder, *American Popular Song: The Great Innovators, 1900–1950* (New York: Oxford University Press, 1972), 56.
2. *NYT*, 4 August 1943, "Frank Sinatra Sings to 7,000 at Stadium."
3. Pete Hamill, *Why Sinatra Matters* (Boston: Little, Brown, 1998), 127.
4. *BAA*, 30 October 1943, "The Week."
5. *BAA*, 19 February 1944, "Orchids."
6. Will Friedwald, *Sinatra! The Song Is You: A Singer's Art* (New York: Scribner, 1995), 318, 320.
7. Todd Decker, *Show Boat: Performing Race in an American Musical* (New York: Oxford University Press, 2013), 180–83.
8. Tom Santopietro, *Sinatra in Hollywood* (New York: St Martin's Press, 2008), 82.
9. *Variety*, 13 November 1946, "Film Review: *Till the Clouds Roll By*."
10. *Variety*, quoted in Gene Ringgold and Clifford McCarty, *The Films of Frank Sinatra* (New York: Citadel Press, 1971), 50.

11. *NYT*, 6 December 1946, "The Screen in Review."
12. *Life*, 8 March 1948, "Last Year's Movies."
13. Will Friedwald, *Stardust Memories: The Biography of Twelve of America's Most Popular Songs* (New York: Pantheon Books, 2002), 129.
14. Nancy Kovaleff Baker, "Abel Meeropol (a.k.a. Lewis Allan): Political Commentator and Social Conscience," *American Music* 20/1 (Spring 2002), 55–56.
15. Friedwald, *Sinatra!*, 320.
16. Harry Connick Jr., "A Perfect Singer," in *The Frank Sinatra Reader*, edited by Stephen Petkov and Leonard Mustazza (New York: Oxford University Press, 1995), 253.
17. Friedwald, *Sinatra!*, 54.
18. Friedwald, *Stardust Memories*, 128.
19. *NYT*, 18 April 1973, "Sinatra at White House Gets a Standing Ovation."

CHAPTER 8

1. *NYT*, 25 September 1957, "Home Is Guarded in Levittown, PA"; *BAA*, 21 December 1957, "Pa. Court Asked to Curb Anti-Myers Harassment."
2. *NYT*, 31 May 1949, "Bunche Says Negro Will Win Equality."
3. Jordan Goodman, *Paul Robeson: A Watched Man* (London: Verso, 2013), 239.
4. *BAA*, 17 November 1951, "Along Pennsylvania Avenue."
5. Todd Decker, "Fancy Meeting You Here: Pioneers of the Concept Album," *Daedalus* 142/4 (fall 2013), 98–108.
6. *Billboard*, 26 October 1959, "Reviews of This Week's LPs: Very Strong Sales Potential."
7. Fred M. Hall, *It's About Time: The Dave Brubeck Story* (Fayetteville: University of Arkansas Press, 1996), 63.
8. *Down Beat*, 1 October 1959, "Review: *Gone with the Wind*."
9. Rod Stewart, *Rod: The Autobiography* (New York: Crown Archetype, 2012), 95.
10. Martin Power, *Hot Wired Guitar: The Life of Jeff Beck* (London: Omnibus Press, 2011), 152.

CHAPTER 9

1. Henry Louis Gates Jr., *Colored People: A Memoir* (New York: Knopf, 1994), 27.
2. *Variety*, 26 July and 9 September 1950.
3. *PT*, 24 January 1953.
4. *Variety*, 25 January 1947; *Billboard*, 1 April 1967.
5. *Variety*, 27 December 1967.
6. *Melody Maker*, 15 December 1979.
7. *BAA*, 26 December 1987, "Cab Calloway at 80."
8. Marc Dolan, *Bruce Springsteen and the Promise of Rock 'n' Roll* (New York: Norton, 2012), 325.
9. *PT*, 10 April 1998.
10. *NYT*, 27 January 1976, Charlayne Hunter, "Mourners, at the Chapel, 'Go Tell It' to Robeson."

CHAPTER 10

1. *NYT*, 21 October 1971, Clive Barnes, "Stage: Ghetto Life of 'Ain't Supposed.'"
2. Alec Wilder, *American Popular Song: The Great Innovators, 1900–1950* (New York: Oxford University Press, 1972), 56.

3. Todd Decker, *Show Boat: Performing Race in an American Musical* (New York: Oxford University Press, 2013), 48–53.

4. *BAA*, 19 November 1955, "Golden Gate Quartet Acclaimed in Paris."

5. *Variety*, 14 February 1962, "House Reviews: Apollo, N.Y."

6. *PT*, 12 November 1963, "Masco's Notebook" and 16 January 1965, untitled photo caption.

7. Otis Williams, with Patricia Romanowski, *Temptations* (New York: G. P. Putnam's Sons, 1988), 119.

8. *Billboard*, 19 August 1967, "The Temptations Kick Up, Sing Up a Musical Storm."

9. *PC*, 23 May 1992, Steve Holsey, "The Motortown Revue."

10. *NYT*, 2 October 1975.

11. http://www.itsabouttimebpp.com/Our_Stories/The_Lumpen/the_lumpen.html; Kevin J. Mumford, *Newark: A History of Race, Rights, and Riots in America* (New York: NYU Press, 2008) discusses the Citizen's Council.

12. Rickey Vincent, *Party Music: The Inside Story of the Black Panthers' Band and How Black Power Transformed Soul Music* (Chicago: Lawrence Hill Books, 2013), 264–65.

13. *NYT*, 26 December 1931, "Christmas Comes to the 'Jungle' Too."

14. John Dale, http://www.dustedmagazine.com/reviews/1165.

15. *The Guardian* Music Blog, 29 August 2007, Chris Campion, "Unsung Heroes No. 1—Abner Jay."

16. *LAS*, 2 March 1972, "Advertising Campaign Glorifys [sic] the Black Male."

17. Will Friedwald, *Stardust Memories: The Biography of Twelve of America's Most Popular Songs* (New York: Pantheon Books, 2002), 135.

INDEX

Page numbers in **bold** indicate illustrations.